EXTRADITED

EXTRADITED

THE EUROPEAN ARREST WARRANT AND MY FIGHT FOR JUSTICE FROM A GREEK PRISON CELL

ANDREW SYMEOU

\Bb\
Biteback Publishing

First published in Great Britain in 2015 by
Biteback Publishing Ltd
Westminster Tower
3 Albert Embankment
London SE1 7SP
Copyright © Andrew Symeou 2015

ISBN: 978-1-84954-845-8

10 9 8 7 6 5 4 3 2 1

A CIP catalogue record for this book is available from the British Library.

Set in Adobe Caslon Pro and Trade Gothic

Printed and bound in Great Britain by
CPI Group (UK) Ltd, Croydon CR0 4YY

CONTENTS

NOTE FROM THE AUTHOR

I wrote *Extradited* because it's a story that needs to be heard. This isn't just another 'bleeding heart' sob story of an innocent person behind bars (we've all heard that story before). One of my key motivations behind writing this book was to show by example how vulnerable British citizens currently are – it highlights why our government must make *further* changes to the controversial European Arrest Warrant (EAW). To those unaware of what the EAW is, it is a fast-track extradition system, which was enforced in the wake of 9/11 in an attempt to fight terrorism. It means that if authorities in other European countries are to issue a warrant for a British person's arrest, Britain must send them to that country without considering any evidence at all. It is a clever idea in theory, as it is cheaper and quicker to extradite criminals – but there are barely any safeguards to protect innocent people from severe abuse (such as sloppy investigations, mistaken identity and pre-trial detention abroad). What happened to me could happen to absolutely anyone, and it's difficult for people (especially those in government) to truly understand *how* flawed the EAW is without having been an innocent person caught in its trap. I also appreciate that an innocent young man lost his life in the summer of 2007. I have absolutely no connection to the events that led to his death, and I am completely sympathetic to his family, who experienced a grave tragedy. Our campaign was a fight for justice – and this is a fight for change.

To avoid confusion, I was charged with 'fatal bodily harm' (according to Greek law). In Britain the charge would have been manslaughter, but it was translated as either 'murder' or 'manslaughter' in different cases.

For Andreas Theodoros Pericleous
27 January 1932 – 5 October 2014
A Great Uncle

PART I

Violence is the last refuge of the incompetent.
– Isaac Asimov

1

SORRY FOR MY LANGUAGE

4 April 2013, the Coroner's Court, Cardiff

I was sitting in a courtroom again, only this time it was on British soil. After spending two years of my life trapped in Greece and a further two years picking up the pieces, it was exhausting to be sucked back into the case again. My heart would have been palpitating at an extremely fast rate, but I was pumped up with prescription beta-blockers – a fantastic chemical invention.

Six years earlier, in 2007, I had gone on a two-week summer holiday to Laganas in Zante – the Greek island also known as Zakynthos. I was with seven of my best friends – 'the boys' – and the holiday was the usual mixture of sun, sea and nightlife. It was quite good fun, but nothing remarkable happened. We were just a group of normal eighteen-year-olds, and we were there to have a great time after completing our A levels. Thinking about it with hindsight, we were young and it was all very innocent.

While we were holidaying in Zante, a Welshman called Jonathan Hiles had tragically passed away after allegedly being attacked in a nightclub called Rescue. I didn't know Jonathan and had never met him. An unknown male was said to have been urinating on a raised stage where Jonathan and his friends were dancing. Some time later, after an exchange of a few words, a punch was thrown. Jonathan fell from the stage head-first and died two days later in a Greek hospital from a brain haemorrhage – it was the day before his nineteenth birthday. I can't even begin to imagine how devastating it must have been for his family.

The coroner for Cardiff, where Jonathan lived, was obliged to conduct an inquest into his death (even though six years had gone by and he had passed away abroad). I'd been summoned to appear as a witness, but I knew nothing of what had happened to Jonathan – we'd never crossed paths. During my time in Zante there had been no arguments, no fights – I didn't see any violence at all. I wasn't in the same building as Jonathan when he was struck. A full criminal trial had already taken place in Greece two years earlier and I'd been found innocent of his murder (fatal bodily harm according to Greek law). It unfolded that I was merely a random person from a photograph, which was taken on a different night from the attack.

It was Day 2 of the inquest and I sat on the second row of the public benches. My parents were sitting to my right, but we didn't feel the need to speak. The three of us were far too involved in our own thoughts. The entire left wall of the courtroom was filled with journalists and reporters, sitting wide-eyed and ready to jot down as much information as possible.

Chris Kyriacou and Charlie Klitou had been summoned as witnesses too – they were schoolfriends of mine who were in Zante at the same time as my group. In the periphery of my vision I caught sight of them entering the courtroom, but I didn't want to make eye contact. I hadn't spoken to either of them since early 2009, the year that I was extradited to Greece. The victim's dad sat to the right of the bench in front of us, the same row as the barrister we'd appointed. The room began to fill with the victim's family and friends. It was silent but filled with tension; not even a whisper went unheard before the coroner entered. I'm sure that she was eager to discover how I had become the key suspect in the first place.

Chris was called to the witness box. He was still as skinny as ever, but he'd definitely grown since the last time I'd seen him. When he began to speak I noticed that his voice was deeper than I'd remembered. It was always slightly high-pitched and a bit yappy, but what I was hearing now was the voice of a man. It was a harsh reminder of how many years had passed since I'd been wrongfully accused of this crime.

He explained to the coroner that he and Charlie Klitou were on a different holiday package from my group. The two of them had decided to book the holiday later than us, and the only available dates for the same package fell four days after we would arrive, leaving four days after we would return to London. Overall, the two of them overlapped with us in Zante for ten days.

He continued his testimony by explaining that our group of friends had gone to a series of different bars and nightclubs on the night when Jonathan was allegedly attacked. According to witnesses, the event had taken place between 1 a.m. and 1.30 a.m. on 20 July 2007. At that time, we were in another bar, which was over 200 metres from the Rescue nightclub, where we stayed until around 4 a.m.

'For the avoidance of doubt, did you at any stage that night, the 19th/20th, see Mr Symeou hit another person?' asked the coroner.

'No! And I've never seen him hit another person in my life,' Chris exclaimed.

'How long have you known him for?'

'Since Year Seven, so since we were probably about twelve years old.'

Chris told the coroner that he and Charlie had stayed in Zante for four days after my group had left the island. On the second of those days, when I was back in London, Zante police officers had unexpectedly turned up at the hotel. The police were showing photographs taken by a professional photographer in the Rescue nightclub from a special event night (the night before the incident) and one of the photographs happened to be of my face on a crowded dance floor. Chris continued to explain that the hotel manager had recognised me from the photograph as a previous guest. Knowing that we were friends, the manager had sent one of the holiday reps to Chris and Charlie's hotel room to inform them that the police wanted to see them for questioning. The officers seized both his and Charlie's passports, took them to the police station and then sat them in separate rooms.

'They asked me where my family was from; I said they're Greek Cypriot. Instantly one of them turned to me and said, "You're lucky your family are from Cyprus, or this would be a lot worse."'

The coroner asked him if he could speak Greek, to which he replied that he could understand only key words or phrases.

'They sat me down on a chair in the middle of that room, then turned all the lights off, then…'

The coroner interrupted, 'So you were in darkness?'

'Basically darkness, if you imagine a square room – there was some light coming through a glass window into the hallway every time someone opened the front door of the police station – otherwise it was basically darkness,' he answered.

Slowly more and more policemen enter this room; in total there were probably six or seven of them. One of them was the chief police officer; another one did most of the hits and beatings. There were about four others, who I think were there just to intimidate me – just holding their batons like this.

He mimicked how the officers had stood on guard with their batons in two hands, ready to use them at any moment.

I was left to sit there for a while, which obviously made me quite scared. I had no clue what was going on or what was about to happen to me. This large police officer comes in; he was about 6ft 3in. or 6ft 4in. He was big, bald, shaved head … looked like he went to the gym all the time. He walks past the room, motioning as though he was washing his hands and was like, 'I'm getting ready for you.' That intimidated me completely. I was thinking, *what* is gonna happen to me here!? They said constantly, 'You know what's happened!?' I told them, 'I don't know what happened!' And I asked them, 'What has happened!?' But they wouldn't tell me.

'So at this stage do you know what this is about? Had Jonathan's name been mentioned?' asked the coroner.

'No, I found out at about half ten that night, after about five hours!'

'So you didn't know it was about a boy who had died?'

'No.' He shook his head.

This large guy comes in the room, he did the majority of the questioning. I asked him, 'What's happened? Has there been an argument? Has someone stolen something? Has there been a fight?' As soon as I said that word [fight], he just went ballistic! He grabbed me from my neck. At this time I was eighteen, I was even smaller than I am now. I think his hand fitted around my neck. He held me there and said, 'You know what's happened, tell us now!' I'm in tears at this moment. They left me in the dark room for hours with no water. I could hear Charlie next door being hit. I could hear loud bangs and a lot of shouting. I could vaguely hear what they forced Charlie to say, which was that Andrew Symeou hit Jonathan Hiles. I glanced at the clock, it was about 12.30 a.m. when they let Charlie go. When they came back they kept on saying, 'You know that your friend's done it.'

'Was there any doubt in your mind that Mr Symeou hadn't done this?' asked the coroner.

'No doubt, no.'

'You were absolutely sure that he hadn't?'

'100 per cent sure, yes, and every time I said the words "I don't know what happened", they would hit me.'

'Where?' the coroner asked softly.

Either a back hand round the face, or they would punch me in the side of the head. At one point they grabbed my head and smashed it against the wall. He told me that if I kept on saying that I didn't know they would keep on hitting me. But I didn't know – there was no answer that I could give! It got to the point where I thought, I know that Charlie had already said it was Andrew, even though he hadn't committed the crime. My thinking was, I just have to do what they want me to do. My assumption was that I could instantly speak to someone at the embassy to sort this out.

Chris told the coroner that the officers slapped and punched him over a period of eight hours – they even threw a full bottle of water at his head. He was allowed to leave only once he'd signed a handwritten document, which was in Greek. He couldn't understand what it said and a translator was present only at the start of the interrogation. The police officers sent her out of the room so that she wouldn't bear witness to any more violence.

The document was written up already. It seemed like they had added *one sentence* on a piece of paper, [but] suddenly a whole document of writing came to me! They made me sign it. Now I know it said something about Jonathan and Andrew having an argument in a club over a girl, and then Andrew punched him. Once it was signed they told me I could leave. The young officer tried to shake my hand and said, 'Sorry that we had to beat you.' Who makes a comment like that after they have just beaten someone? Every time we go to court it seems like no one is listening, but this is what happened. Unfortunately, some-times, it looks like this is what the police there do!

'How old were you at the time?' asked the coroner.

'Erm … eighteen,' he answered.

Charlie's name was called and I heard him shuffling behind me before walking to the witness box. I noticed that he'd also grown since I'd seen him last. He was quite a good-looking guy with the same freshly cut hair that he'd always tried to maintain.

He told the coroner that when he and Chris were taken to the police station in July 2007, he was made to sit in another dark room for eight hours. The officers didn't hesitate to slap and back-slap him in the face; it seemed that his treatment was even worse than Chris's. One of the officers threatened to strike him with an ashtray and a large officer entered the room with a police baton.

> When he came in with that … sorry for my language … but I was *crapping* myself. As he came in he threw the interpreter out the room, then he came towards me and he was by my right side – but I couldn't look at him. I wanted to look at him, but the other guy said, 'You look at me in the eye!' So I was looking at the guy in front of me.

Charlie received a powerful right-hook punch to the chin, which he later went to hospital for. The officers violently interrogated him about an event of which he knew nothing. 'Whenever I would disagree or say no … they didn't like that. They didn't want me to say no,' he said. 'It came to the point when I cracked, they kept hitting me. I feared for my wellbeing and I didn't know what was going to happen next.'

2

MAXIMUM TWENTY YEARS

I was born in 1988 and raised in Enfield, north London. Life began in Palmers Green – a leafy, suburban area, home to one of the largest populations of Cypriots outside of Cyprus itself. For that reason, I'd never really felt like part of an ethnic minority growing up. I'm of Greek Cypriot origin but both of my parents were born and bred in London, so we're as anglicised as you can get.

Greek was hardly ever spoken in my household either. It's unfortunate because I've always considered it to be such a great language – soft enough to sound pleasant to the ear, but abrupt enough to give emphasis to well-timed punchlines and sarcasm. Although Greek wasn't spoken in my house, my grandparents would speak it all the time. The language would fly out of their mouths without them having to put in any effort. I definitely envied them it, even though they spoke it in its colloquial 'Cypriot-village' dialect. I attempted to learn modern Greek, but found the grammar to be complicated and difficult to grasp. At least I'd picked up the important key words and phrases, so I was fluent in what I'd call 'Greenglish' – English with the odd bit of Greek thrown in!

When I was a teenager I would make up excuses for my struggle to learn, 'Why do I need to learn Greek? Everyone speaks

English!' In fairness, it was true. Even my relatives in Cyprus could speak English. One day I asked my granddad if he was bothered by the fact that I couldn't speak Greek very well. His answer was, 'As long as you're happy, it doesn't bother me at all!'

We didn't know it at the time, but being fluent in Greek would have served me very, very well.

━━━━

26 June 2008, Enfield, north London

It's strange how fragile normal, everyday life can be. You could be spending a perfect, sunny afternoon in blissful ignorance – completely unaware of the life-changing event that'll happen in just a moment's time.

A year had passed since our holiday in Zante, and although I'd started university in Bournemouth, it had been an awful year. I'd been torturing myself with thoughts about my friend Michael; eight months had passed since we'd lost him to leukaemia. He was only twenty years old at the time and I hadn't yet come to terms with it. We'd grown up together; he was like family and his death devastated me. I'd acquired a pessimistic, 'what's the point any more' kind of attitude. My mind was flooded with negative thoughts and anger. I'd started to focus only on the bad things in my life and disregarded the good. Nothing could have measured up to what we'd lost.

I remember driving home from Chris's house and thinking, *it's only a matter of time before something else shit happens.* Little did I know that it would be in less than an hour's time.

I walked into the house. Nobody was home. I glanced at my watch – 6 p.m. My sister Sophie and my mum, Helen, would be home at any minute. I didn't have long to get ready – I was meeting the boys that evening to see the new James Bond film at the cinema. I quickly boiled up some ravioli for dinner – 'Cypriot style', with a chicken stock cube and grated halloumi.

The doorbell rang. We had a video entry system, allowing us to see who was standing at the door before opening it and on the screen I could see a group of tall, suited men who I spoke with via the intercom system.

'Is this no. 41?' one of the men asked.

'Yes, it is…'

'We're officers from Scotland Yard. And who may I be speaking to?'

I was startled by one of the officers who I caught staring at me through the window at the front of the house. I didn't say anything for a short moment, lost for words. 'Andrew,' I said.

'Well, it's actually you who we need to speak to.'

I had a feeling that I knew what it was about. Chris and Charlie had told us about the incident with the police in Greece, and I was aware that they'd been forced to sign something with my name in it. I wasn't worried though. I was happy to answer any of their questions. I hadn't witnessed any violence on my holiday in Zante – I'd only been told of Chris and Charlie's experience in the police station.

I asked the gentleman on the intercom to show me his badge and he held something up to the camera. I couldn't really make out what it was – it could have been a library card for all I knew! I opened the front door and saw my mum and Sophie walking up the driveway behind them. My mum looked at the officers, her jaw dropped and her eyes squinted in confusion. Before she had the chance to question what was happening, one of the officers said, 'We'd better go inside.' They made their way into the house and I sat down on the sofa in our living room.

'We have a European Arrest Warrant here. You're under arrest for the murder of Jonathan Hiles; you have the right to remain silent; anything you do say can be used as evidence in a court of law. You have the right to a lawyer…'

It's very difficult to describe exactly how I felt in that moment. It was too much information to take in at once, and I couldn't even begin to comprehend how much my life was about to change. It was a numbing sensation. I found it far easier to ignore my surroundings, so I stared at the television screen and watched blurred coloured images move around while the officer continued to read me my rights. I felt like a frozen statue, and as soon as I moved a muscle I'd have to accept it as true – that I was being arrested for murder.

I was snapped out of my frozen state by the sound of my frantic mum attempting to talk the officers out of it. 'Let's all sit down, I'll make everyone a cup of tea and we can talk about this! Who would like a tea?' She ran into the kitchen to put the kettle on, as though the officers would have a cup of tea then leave us alone. I picked up the bowl of pasta, continuing to eat it as though they weren't really there.

'You have to put the bowl down, Andrew,' an officer said to me. He took the pasta out of my hands and placed it on the table.

My mum then realised that the officers had no interest in de-laying their job for a cup of tea. She picked up her mobile phone and called the solicitor we'd spoken to almost a year before. When Chris and Charlie had told us about their terrible experi-ence at the hands of the Greek police, we'd eventually decided to speak to a solicitor and ask for his opinion. After all, I may have been implicated as being involved in a serious crime! The solicitor advised us that we (myself and the people I had been with on the night in question) should make statements of our whereabouts that night. We'd also collected photographs of the night – just in case anything were to happen.

Floods of tears ran down Sophie's face as they forced my wrists into handcuffs. Our eyes met for a moment and hers reflected the desperation in mine. I flicked my attention to one of the officers. 'Do you know what's disgusting about this!?' I managed to blurt out. The reality of the situation had started to kick in, as did the trembling nerves and tears.

'That someone's dead?' replied one of the officers.

'That someone's dead, the killer is out there walking the streets and you're here arresting the wrong person!' I cried.

'Andrew, we need to take you down to the station,' he said calmly, ignoring my assertion.

'How long will I be there for?' I asked, wiping my eyes with both of my handcuffed hands. I hoped the answer would be 'not very long', naively believing that they would take me in for a few questions and release me. I had nothing to do with the crime – to take it any further would be ridiculous.

'You'll be there all night.'

It felt as though my heart was drooping lower and lower into my body. I could hear my mum on the phone to the solicitor. She passed the handset to me and I held it with my cuffed hands against the side of my head. 'Remember, Andrew, don't say anything!' he said.

Not saying anything made no sense to me. I had nothing to hide and desperately wanted to tell them exactly what had happened to Chris and Charlie at the police station in Zante. I couldn't see what would be so wrong with telling them what had happened.

I asked Sophie to take my mobile phone out of my pocket. 'When Riya calls, explain what's happened – OK?' My then girl-friend had no idea what was going on.

The officers escorted me to the Ford Mondeo that was parked on our driveway. They allowed me to put a jumper over the handcuffs so the neighbours wouldn't know what was going on. All five of us squeezed in, and I was put in the middle seat in the back. I didn't say a word. I blanked out all of my surroundings. I was numb, my mind was empty and my heart continued to sink deeper into my stomach.

'You know, the father of the boy who died has really been pushing for this,' the officer driving said.

'I would do exactly the same thing,' I managed to say without choking up.

'They gave your friends a hard time over in Greece, didn't they … the police?' another officer asked.

'Yep.'

Following that comment, we sat in silence as we made our way to Edmonton Police Station.

It was my first time in a police station. I stood intimidated as they took mug shots, scanned my fingerprints and sampled my DNA before putting me in a holding cell. 'You'll go to Westminster Magistrates' Court tomorrow morning, we'll wake you up at 7 a.m.,' said a female officer before the heavy metal door thudded on impact. She turned the key and forced the lock into place – I instantly buried my face in my hands and filled them with warm tears. I held a copy of the European Arrest Warrant in my hands that the officer had given to me. '*Murder, maximum twenty years.*' Those were the only words I could see out of the whole document. I repeatedly read them and tormented myself, unable to prevent the streams of tears running down my cheeks. I just had to be patient, calm down, think as positively as possible and attempt to rest.

I lay down on the blue gym mat. My eyes flickered between the light brown painted ceiling and dark brown tiled walls. It felt like hours had passed. I closed my eyes, allowing my exhausted mind to run free. Somehow I managed to drift off to sleep. That night, for the first time, I dreamed of my friend Michael.

3

SQUASH AND ROLL

The heavy metal door swung open. I opened my eyes, disorientated and in a state of confusion. Still wearing the same clothes as the day before, I looked into the eyes of the female police officer. My mouth was dry and I could taste that my breath may have had an unhygienic whiff.

'It's 7 a.m. Come on, you're leaving for court now.'

The reality came flooding back and I was struck with overwhelming nerves. She escorted me to the front of the police station in handcuffs.

'So, are they sending you back to Greece?' she asked.

'I hope not,' I replied as she guided me into the Serco police van. They sat me down at the end of the vehicle and removed my handcuffs. I was locked in an isolated box, enclosed within white plastic walls and with little space to move. They shut the door behind them, leaving me with a small window and tiny holes to look through. I peered outside and watched the streets of London pass me by. I saw people living out their typical weekday mornings – some waiting at bus stops, others pacing to the nearest train station while jabbering on their mobile phones. I felt peculiar and insignificant; my life was falling apart but the rest of the world was carrying on as normal.

The journey seemed to take hours. I was sitting just above the rear wheel of the van on a hard, plastic seat. The vibrations of every bump trembled up my spine – and the poor maintenance of some of London's roads didn't help. The officers were listening to Johnny Vaughan's Capital FM breakfast show on the radio, chuckling as they had heard him say something funny. I tried to listen, desperately needing something to focus on so I could forget about where I was – but I failed in the attempt.

We progressed further into central London and I watched the neighbourhoods change: suburban family homes became office towers and greenery became concrete. We stopped off at one point and I assumed that we'd arrived, but they were just picking up another person for court. He was placed in his own box on the left-hand side of the van. It's funny how you take one look at someone walking into a police van and automatically assume that they've done something wrong. It turns out you think just the same, even if you're sitting in the van yourself!

It was around 9.30 a.m. when we arrived at Westminster Magistrates' Court. The Friday-morning traffic and the off-route pick-up made the trip from Edmonton seem like a day's travelling. On arrival I was put into a cell again, and I could hear people in other cells angrily banging their fists on the walls and shouting. The door slowly opened. I stood up ready to be taken to court, but another young man was put into the cell with me. There was a sudden stench of body odour. He wore blue overalls that were covered in paint and black elasticated plimsolls – the kind that primary school children wear for PE.

'You fucking wankers! Give me back my money! Give me back my money!'

He clenched his fists and pounded on the door. He forcefully ripped the plimsolls off his feet and threw them against the wall.

Time passed slowly and we sat in silence. I tried my hardest not to watch him force his finger into his nose and dig for buried treasure. When finding a bogey, he would pull it out of his nostril to examine the result. It took about five picks before seizing a big, fat one that he was satisfied with. He repeatedly rolled it in between his thumb and index finger until it was a little ball.

Squash and roll. Squash and roll. The guy was so engrossed in what he was doing that he completely disregarded the fact that someone else was sitting there watching. I couldn't help but stare, even though I didn't want to. He constantly made tutting and moaning noises. *Squash and roll. Squash and roll.* 'Fucking tossers,' I heard him mumble to himself.

There must have been at least an hour of awkward silence. Within this time a woman had opened the cell door and handed us some food that I'd started to eat.

'So why are you going to court?' I asked him.

He cleared all of the mucus from his sinuses, bringing it all into his mouth and spitting it on the floor. I looked at my microwave meal and put it to the side. He responded:

> Um … well, I was standing in the alleyway yeah, and some policeman come up to me, and he was like, 'Did you steal his wallet?' And I was like, 'Nah, man, I didn't steal no wallet.' Then he was like, 'Yes, you did.' Then he jacked my wallet, punched me round the face and now man's been in a cell for two days.

On the cell door there was a slit that could open up like a letterbox to communicate with the detainees. The slit opened and I could see a man in his thirties with a side parting and suit standing behind it. It was a lawyer that my family had hired. 'The judge is going to ask you if you'll allow them to extradite you to Greece; you have the opportunity to appeal and therefore you say *no*,' he said. 'You got that? Say *no*. Whatever you do, do *not* say yes!'

'OK, got it.'

Another hour seemed to have passed. The boy finally flicked his bogey, which landed on the floor next to him.

'So, what's your name?' I asked. Why did I ask? I didn't care what his flipping name was. I needed to prevent my mind from jabbering its way into insanity.

'Um ... Tom,' he said after a delayed moment.

My new pal Tom and I sat there in silence until he was finally summoned to face his fate. Tom was a strange boy and I'll never know what happened to him.

The cell door opened. 'Come with me,' said the woman behind it. I followed her up a steep staircase and through a narrow corridor.

Just say no, I repeated to myself.

She led me through a door and before I knew it, I was sitting in the defendants' dock overlooking a courtroom. My entire body trembled. I looked to my left and could see my family with my godfather Lef and auntie Teresa in the public gallery. My dad, Frank, gave me the thumbs up and smiled, attempting to raise my spirits and say, 'It's all going to be fine.' I remember the judge being old and wrinkly with grey hair and thick glasses. We were all asked to rise – I wanted to cry. All I wanted to do was tell the court that I was innocent so I could be left alone!

'May you please state your name.'

'Andrew Christopher Symeou,' I answered.

The judge asked me if I would allow the state to extradite me to Greece.

'No.'

The hearing lasted around half an hour. I remember the judge insinuating that I'd left my holiday earlier than the others in my group, which wasn't the case at all. I told the court that my friends

Chris and Charlie were on a different package holiday from us. I could prove that my tickets were booked from the 8th to 22 July, which was a Sunday.

'But these package holidays are Saturday to Saturday!' the judge responded.

'No,' I replied.

After putting my mum on the stand to find out about our family's finances, I was released on a promissory bail for £20,000. A bulky security guard escorted me to the court's main foyer where I was able to hug my family. We couldn't say anything for a few moments; there were no words to describe our feelings. We just cried in each other's arms. I remember my godfather Lef grabbing me with his huge hands and pulling me towards him. It was the first time that I'd ever seen him get emotional.

'When will this be over?' I remember stuttering to my dad.

'A few months,' he answered. I could sense uncertainty – there was no way he could have known.

We flagged down a black cab on Horseferry Road, still in the state of a dominating silence. My mum had a run-down, pale and emotionless face. Sophie was still in tears, her dark mascara running down her cheeks. I hadn't spoken to my girlfriend Riya since this had happened. Sophie told me that she had explained everything to her and handed my mobile back to me. I was comforted by the texts that Riya had sent. Unable to muster the ability to speak at the time, I replied saying that everything would be OK.

I couldn't process any logical thought; only images of what could happen were running through my mind. For a few moments I closed my eyes and lost myself in the sound of the taxi's engine. Pressing the side of my face against the cool glass window, the vibrations were soothing like the feeling of a pulse – a reminder that I was still alive.

27 June 2008, BBC News

REMAND OVER HOLIDAY ISLAND DEATH

A student faces an extradition hearing over the death of an eighteen-year-old roller-hockey player on holiday in Greece.

Andrew Symeou, 19, was arrested over the death of Jonathan Hiles from Cardiff, who died after an incident at a nightclub on Zakynthos in July 2007.

The Bournemouth University student, of Enfield, north London, was remanded on bail by Westminster magistrates.

He was bailed to return to the same court on 7 July, when a decision will be taken on extraditing him to Greece.

The student was arrested by the Metropolitan Police extradition unit on suspicion of manslaughter at his family home on Thursday night after a European arrest warrant was issued by Greek authorities.

His passport was also seized by police.

Mr Hiles, from Llandaff North, Cardiff, was with friends on Zakynthos when he was injured.

He was taken to hospital in Athens where he died on 22 July 2007.

Mr Symeou was given bail after his mother, Helen, pledged surety of £20,000 for him.

Under the bail conditions he must reside at the family home until he next appears in court.

++++

I wasn't in a good way when I arrived home; I was hysterical – and I'd made it even worse by searching for the case online. The first thing I found was the BBC News article. It felt like my heart had stopped as soon as I saw my name written in the piece.

I could hardly breathe. I'd always read articles about deaths or murders in the news, but the people involved in those cases were just random names and a story that I couldn't relate to. Suddenly I'd become one of the people that others would read about, and I had absolutely no clue about what had happened to Jonathan Hiles. I'd never even met him! I couldn't process any of it as reality. This was the first moment since my arrest that the thought had dawned on me: *people would think I was a murderer.* I took a deep breath in a fluster of panic, then closed my laptop and lay on my bed for a few moments. My mind was cluttered with one prevailing thought: *my life is ruined.* Burying my face into my hands, I felt like I was about to have a breakdown.

It seemed as though my mobile phone was ringing and vibrating non-stop, but I couldn't bring myself to talk to anyone. The person I needed to talk to was Riya – I finally calmed myself down and called her. I'd put it off because I knew how emotional it would be, but I had delayed for long enough. She was away on a field trip for university at the time, and was in her hotel room when I called. When she answered the phone she cried bitterly. Neither of us could have imagined that we'd ever have such a conversation.

She wasn't coming back to London until the evening, so I had to wait to see her. I missed the comforting way she'd always look up at me with sparkling eyes because she was almost a foot shorter – petite.

It wasn't long before my house was jam-packed with family and friends. In times of crisis, Cypriot people tend to eat! Several had brought huge plates of food, as though they'd pre-empted the mass of loved ones that would come to support us. The doorbell kept on ringing and I was showered with emotional hugs and kisses from friends and relatives. I had no idea how incredibly caring and helpful everyone would be. It was overwhelming and gave my family great strength.

After a couple of hours my godfather Lef called for a meeting in the conservatory. Everyone crowded around. There weren't enough chairs for everyone to sit down, so most people were standing and waiting to find out what he had to say. He took it upon himself to hang a large whiteboard on the wall. With a marker he wrote '*JUSTICE FOR SYMEOU: BRAINSTORM*' in big letters.

'Guys and girls, we're starting a campaign and this is what it's gonna be called. We need everybody's help, even the young ones,' he bellowed.

He started to list objectives, like '*create a website*', '*start a petition*' and '*find the best legal team*'. Those in the room began to throw around ideas of how to fight against my extradition to Greece. I wasn't aware of it yet, but if extradited, I could have been facing up to eighteen months in prison on remand before a trial! We needed to prove my innocence in the UK.

I sat in silence as everyone around me started to brainstorm. It was proposed that we would create awareness on social media and bombard politicians with letters. Someone had the idea that we should upload a skeleton letter on the internet for anyone to access and send to their local MPs and MEPs.

Lef's deep voice continued to resonate in the room.

The seventh of July is Andrew's extradition hearing. We want publicity! People need to know that what is happening is wrong and that we have support – so, we're organising a protest. We need as many people as possible to come. Tell your brothers and sisters, your mums and dads and all their brothers and sisters … and their nieces and nephews! I'm not talking about hundreds. I want thousands! We're gonna fill up every corridor in the courts – we'll protest in the lifts!

Some of my friends chuckled at Lef's exaggerated demand for thousands of protesters in the hallways and lifts of Westminster Magistrates' Court. I couldn't find it remotely funny; I was devastated and still couldn't begin to accept it all as reality. It sounded like we would be making such a fuss and I had no say in the decision as to whether we should campaign and protest. At only nineteen years old, I was vulnerable and everyone around me told me that it was the best thing to do. It's an awful feeling when you have absolutely no control over your own destiny.

++++

A couple of days later, my mum had a long telephone conversation with our then Labour MP, Joan Ryan, looking for some advice – but Joan was of the opinion that my extradition was inevitable. I'd been issued with a European Arrest Warrant and, apparently, they were extremely difficult for a British court to refute. My mum attempted to convince her why we should fight against it and why an investigation in the UK was necessary. Greek courts are notorious for their delays and I was facing up to a year and a half behind bars before even seeing a courtroom. We weren't attempting to prevent justice by fighting the extradition – we were trying to prevent a huge injustice! Of course I wouldn't hand myself over and serve an unnecessary prison sentence! I couldn't even bear to hear the word 'prison' – it was a chilling thought. I could prove my innocence and that the evidence against me was borne out of police brutality. A competent investigation would have exonerated me, placing me in another nightclub at the time of the alleged attack. We had nothing to hide at all – we desperately needed the British authorities to look into the case.

My mum also spoke to the detective sergeant of Scotland Yard's extradition unit. He said that legally they were unable to investigate unless the Greek authorities applied for Mutual Legal Assistance (MLA), which is an official submission to the requesting state in order to help in the investigation. We later lobbied the Greek authorities through our MP, MEPs and the charity Fair Trials International, asking that MLA be applied for. My mum asked the detective sergeant if there was any more advice that he could give us in regard to moving forward. He told her that barristers with no extradition experience aren't taken seriously. Taking his advice, my parents set up a meeting with barrister John Jones of Doughty Street Chambers.

Prior to the dreaded court hearing on 7 July, our dining room looked like a solicitor's office. My cousin Andrew, friend Sophia and my godsister Maria were all either in-between jobs or had just graduated from university and the three of them had given up hours of their time to help. They had jokingly nicknamed themselves the 'Bum Squad', but they weren't 'bums' at all – they worked long and hard to help my family. I remember them on their laptops sending emails and on the phone pushing for support from various organisations. They hunted for the best legal representation and tried to gain as much publicity as possible.

Thanks to their help and my parent's efforts, the campaign was gaining more awareness than we'd pre-empted. Sophia made a Facebook group, which invited all members to the protest on 7 July. Group numbers were growing by the hour, with over 1,000 people having joined in the first few days alone. It gave the links to the website and to an online petition that our friend Nick had set up. Hundreds of people began to sign it, most of whom I didn't even know.

I wrote a statement for the website, whereby I sent my deepest sympathies to the family of the victim. I felt sick knowing that a family could believe that I had killed their son. I couldn't even begin to put myself in their shoes, but I had no choice but to defend my innocence against the injustice. Pre-trial detention in a foreign land wasn't an option.

Other than the website statement, I had no other input towards the campaign. I was emotionally exhausted, really depressed about it and finding it difficult to cope. The campaign was being built around me and I was rarely told what was going on. I just sat on my backside in my own little depressed world at the top of the garden, smoking and eating my worries away. It seemed to be the only way for me to escape.

I was easily distracted too, because my house was usually packed with family and friends, many of whom brought food. Sometimes there would be so much food in my house that we could have set up a restaurant. Every day our kitchen island unit was covered with a variety of different dishes, like Cypriot oven-baked macaroni, meaty casseroles and soul-warming homemade soups. Italian friends of ours would bring cheesy pizzas and mouth-watering pasta bakes. I must have put on at least 10lbs within the first week, but I really didn't care!

On the day of the meeting with barrister John Jones, it felt almost surreal as I stepped out of my front door – it was the first time that I'd left the house in eight days. On the way to Russell Square in town, I remember sitting on the London Underground with an unsettled, queasy feeling in the pit of my stomach. I was overwhelmed with anxiety just being out in public.

Doughty Street consisted of rows of tall and narrow Georgian terraced houses – most of which had probably been converted into offices. As I entered the chambers I noticed that the building's depth gave the illusion that it never ended. I felt out of my comfort zone as I sat at the oval wooden table in one of the boardrooms. Pouring myself a glass of water, I explained to John

Jones what I knew about the case against me in Greece. We hardly knew anything at the time; we were aware only of the two false statements that were beaten out of Chris and Charlie.

John insisted that we hire a Greek lawyer and retrieve the investigating case file from Zante. My dad told John that someone had recommended George Pyromallis – a Greek lawyer based in Athens who John also happened to know.

I explained to John that we had photographs from several different sources, all showing me in a different place on the night of the attack. There were also several witnesses who had been with me, a few of whom were girls that weren't part of my immediate circle of friends. It was at this point that we learned that *no evidence* was to be considered in the extradition appeal! When issued with a European Arrest Warrant, a British court has no power to prevent an extradition based on evidence of innocence.

My entire body froze as soon as I heard about what we were up against. I didn't want it to be true. If it went to Greece I'd be facing prison on remand, but I wasn't allowed to prove my innocence first. I wasn't even a witness to the attack, for God's sake! It felt like I was being gagged and suffocated.

There had to be something that we could do to stop it from happening. John explained that we were limited to only a few articles of law upon which we could base our case. The truth was on our side – but the law upon which we could base our case. The European Arrest Warrant meant that the battle was going to be almost impossible to win.

4

THE INVESTIGATION

Ever since I'd discovered what the European Arrest Warrant was, there was an anxiety in my chest that wouldn't go away. I had absolutely no control! The only thing that comforted me was the knowledge that my family and friends were doing absolutely everything in their power to prevent the injustice.

The online petition was growing by the hour. We had far more support than I ever thought we would – and for that I was grateful beyond words. People I knew showed their support in different ways, and even a text message or an email was appreciated greatly. Some people who I hadn't spoken to in a long time had called me to ask how my family and I were doing. Some friends would text me, not even mention what was happening and just ask how I was. It was a delicate subject to broach; I guess it isn't every day that somebody you know stands accused of killing someone. The one thing I didn't appreciate was the very few people I'd had no contact with for many years who called, not to ask how we were, but to find out if the rumour was true. Some even wanted to know if I 'did it', almost as though they needed confirmation so they could then gossip with their friends about me, not knowing all the facts.

A week had passed and arguments began to form over the internet. Friends of the victim began to post obnoxious messages on our

Facebook group for the campaign. I'd read things like '*Andrew is a scumbag who deserves to go to prison*', '*He's going to go to Greece kicking and screaming*' and '*Anyone in this group is a scum-supporting idiot!*' One person even wrote that I had a 'sickening face'. My friend Sophia disabled the facility to post messages on the Facebook group before it got too out of hand. I don't know why I even bothered to read them, because being aware that there were a group of people who hated me in Wales added to the depression that I was already trying to deal with. It wasn't me they really hated – it was the thug who'd taken their friend away from them forever. It was clear that many of them wanted me to go to prison before even being tried! The possibility of me being innocent was something that they'd failed to consider, regardless of the lack of information that they had. Friends of mine would reply in an attempt to defend me – but there was no point in arguing with those who could never be reasoned with. Thanks to a group of corrupt Greek officers and two scared eighteen-year-old boys, my face represented their friend's alleged killer.

As usual, my house was full of people. My cousin Andreas brought his Nintendo Wii video-game console round for everyone to play. As I walked into the conservatory he was teaching our gran, Yiayia Nitsa, how to play a virtual tennis game. I remember us all being completely shocked at how good she was at it – she was a natural. I drew strength from seeing her smile; it was unlike the emotional greeting we'd had the previous day when she'd arrived from Cyprus.

I turned to my left and saw my dad speaking on the telephone. His face looked pale and drained.

'Who's Dad on the phone to?' I asked my mum.

Her eyes looked absolutely exhausted as she sat on the sofa holding a cup of tea. 'George Pyromallis, the Greek lawyer.'

I waited in anticipation for the phone call to end so I could hear what George had said about the case file.

My dad eventually put the telephone down. 'It took George

a while, but he finally met with the investigating magistrate in Zante. He has the file now.'

'And…' I needed him to elaborate.

'And, at a glance, he can already see huge anomalies.'

━━━

Two days before the hearing and protest, George Pyromallis had flown to London to meet us in John Jones's office. When we walked into the boardroom, a tall, dark-complexioned man in his early forties stood up to shake my hand. He was suited with neat, short hair and spoke in perfect English with a slight Greek accent. We all shook hands with John Jones and our solicitor before sitting down and discussing the case file.

Before Chris Kyriacou and Charlie Klitou were forced to sign statements implicating me in the crime, five friends of Jonathan Hiles had also signed statements with the Zante police. Three of them, Mark O'Gorman, Christopher Paglionico and Lee Burgess had all signed statements that were word-for-word identical, describing the events that led up to the attack. These statements describe the assailant as having a muscular build with short, dark brown hair.

Although I have always had short, brown hair, I wasn't muscular at all – I was very chubby. The statements did not describe my appearance. Secondly, these statements claimed to be taken by different officers, on different days, at completely different times. The statements were *word-for-word* identical, so it would be highly improbable for that to be true.

Another of Hiles's friends, Robert Hares, admitted that he did not see the punch. Yet another, Jason Mordecai, signed a statement describing the perpetrator as a tall, blond male with a heavy northern English accent who had many spots on his face.

As soon as my friends Chris and Charlie were forced to sign

statements implicating me as the assailant, *all five* of Jonathan Hiles's friends signed additional statements for the Zante police investigation. These five statements were, again, word-for-word identical, also claiming to be taken by different police officers at different times. George translated this statement for us. It said:

> I identified with complete certainty and I am absolutely sure that the individual shown in about the middle of the photograph, who has a slightly artistic-looking goatee, is the perpetrator who caused the fatal bodily injury to my friend. At this point I wish to point out that the perpetrator had shaved off his goatee on the day of the incident and had left only slightly long sideburns.

My facial hair was extremely distinctive and I could prove that I'd never shaved it off. There were pictures from my sister's graduation, which had been taken two days after I'd returned from Zante, and my facial hair was far too thick to have grown back after being shaved on the day of the alleged attack.

George told us that the police mentioned there being CCTV footage showing me as the attacker – but there was no sign of it in the case file. This would have been amazing, as CCTV data would have shown a different person throwing the punch. But George feared that it didn't even exist.

The investigation was a mishmash of unreliable information and it was clear that not all of the content had come out of the individuals' mouths. The family of the victim had lost their son in a violent attack and were entitled to a competent investigation, but this wasn't an investigation at all, it was a witch-hunt. The officers had beaten two eighteen-year-old boys, forced them to sign something that was untrue and then fabricated statements to implicate a random man from a photograph – one that wasn't even taken on the same night.

5

THE ARGUMENT

We were silent the whole journey home; no one spoke. My angry thoughts drowned out the odd hiss of the train's breaks and the rumbling sound of the Piccadilly line's track. I was trying to make sense of what I'd just discovered, but couldn't help repeating the word 'bastards' in my mind. Sotiris Siatis, Angelos Polizos and Dimitris Angeloudis, those were the police officers' names. *Farmers with police badges*, I thought. I pictured stereotypical fat, hairy Greek men wearing police uniforms with their shirts unbuttoned, revealing full chests of hair and gold crucifixes – sitting at their desks with a cigarette in one hand, pen in the other, writing statements that didn't come out of the mouths of the people who signed them. How could they not think about the life they were affecting? The *lives* they were affecting? Did they think they could get away with concocting these statements? Or did they believe that they beat the truth out of Chris and Charlie, so fabricating the evidence made everything easier? I don't think so. I think they knew exactly what they were doing. They're a police force in a small community that between the months of September and May is probably a ghost town. For the entire summer it's transformed into a 24-hour party, taken over by British tourists, many of who binge drink and cause trouble. To the

Zante police, Jonathan Hiles was just another one of 'them', and so was I. The entire investigation was disgraceful.

Our solicitors contacted Georgina Clay – the travel rep from our holiday in Zante. I didn't know her very well, but I remembered that she was a lovely girl who'd worked in our hotel the year that we were there. We wanted her to testify in the extradition appeal because she'd arranged for British consular staff to visit Chris and Charlie once they had been released from the police station in Zante.

To our surprise, she told us that the South Wales Police had contacted her in 2007 and that she had made a statement to them regarding the case. At the time we couldn't understand why the South Wales Police had started an investigation and not finished it, but it turned out to be for the coroner. When we heard that statements had been made to the British police, we realised that the five friends of Jonathan Hiles must have made statements too. We needed to see these statements – if they existed. I had no doubt that they would be real accounts of what happened on the night their friend was attacked, unlike the word-for-word identical statements they'd signed in Greece.

We had two days to go. There were over 3,000 members on the Facebook page, over 4,000 signatures on our petition and we had the potential for over 100 protesters outside Westminster Magistrates' Court. Most importantly, we had the statement from the Greek investigation, and it was clearly flawed. All that we needed was the South Wales Police file to compare it to. At the time, my case depended on it. For this reason, it was decided that we would ask for an adjournment.

John Jones had already written up his skeleton argument because our request for an adjournment could have been refused. No evidence would be considered in our appeal, so our plan was to expose the evidence in the media as absolute bullshit, to protest, to fight the extradition based on the following four technicalities, and then to demand an investigation to clear my name.

The first argument was that the proceedings on behalf of the Greek authorities constituted an abuse of process – John cited several cases whereby judges felt they had the jurisdiction to consider comparable allegations.

The second argument was that the European Arrest Warrant was not valid due to a lack of summons on behalf of the Greek authorities. George Pyromallis had advised John Jones that in Greek law, the authorities must summon the accused before formal charges are made. This is something that the Greek authorities didn't do. John Jones outlined the fact that the Greek authorities had my address from the beginning of the investigation. Thus, they were able to summon me to appear before a Greek judicial authority to present evidence of my defence at any time. John believed that the Greek authorities failing to do this beforehand and using the EAW as a summons was 'a clear breach of Greek criminal procedure and a serious violation of a fundamental safeguard of the rights of the accused'. He also cited the case of Malcolm George Hay in which a British judge had disallowed his extradition to Greece on the basis that 'he was not legally summoned'. In my case, the Greek authorities skipped the vital stage of a legal summons. For this reason, both George Pyromallis and John Jones believed the EAW to be invalid.

The third argument was that the extradition was incompatible with my human rights under Articles 3, 6 and 8. John stated that the mistreatment of Chris and Charlie suggested a risk of the same mistreatment on my return. He also cited the case of Matthew Cryer – a seventeen-year-old boy who was killed in Zante in 2008. Many witnesses had seen a nightclub security guard kick him down a flight of stairs and beat him to death, leaving him in the street in a pool of blood. The family of Matthew Cryer have accused the Zante police of covering up the killing after refusing to open a murder inquiry. The police officers had stated that he had been drinking and choked on his own vomit, but a British pathologist had later reported that he had bruises on his body that were fatal. These police officers were from the same police station where Chris and Charlie were beaten and a case was manufactured to implicate me as a killer. John Jones argued that extraditing me based on evidence obtained by torture meant that I could not be guaranteed a fair trial, which was a breach of my human rights.

The final argument was probably our weakest. John felt that we should also argue my discharge on the grounds of 'passage of time'. I was a suspect from 24 July 2007 and was arrested almost a year later, on 26 June 2008 (which wasn't really a substantial amount of time, but why not?).

Due to the EAW we were forced to fight on these technicalities. Even though I could prove my innocence, a British court had no power to consider any of it. We were pleased with the skeleton argument, but were praying that the court would allow the adjournment. We needed to find out if the South Wales Police statements would strengthen our argument.

┼┼┼┼

Later that day, my mum, sister and my auntie Teresa took me to buy a new suit. I remember picking one out and having to get a far bigger size because I'd been eating so much. As we were about to pay, the woman behind the till said, 'Aren't you lucky, they're spoiling you today! What's the occasion? A wedding? A prom?' It was quite an awkward moment, and we looked at each other, not really knowing how to answer her question.

'Not a wedding, unfortunately,' my mum said. I remember

leaving the shop and a girl I knew from school happened to approach me. The first thing she said was, 'You know, everything will be OK.' I don't think she realised how much I appreciated her saying that – and I hoped that she was right.

There was a nervous tension in my house the night before the hearing. I wasn't nervous about appearing in court, as John Jones was confident that the hearing would be adjourned. What I was more nervous about was the protest and the fact that there was a chance it might be televised on BBC News. I received several text messages from school and university friends, all wishing me the best of luck – many of whom told me that they would be coming to the protest. Every time I read the texts, I felt my heart flutter. Of course I appreciated the support greatly, but I wished that it wasn't happening in the first place.

I sat down on one of the sofas in the living room with a group of my best friends playing on my PlayStation. Tony patted me on the shoulder. 'You feeling all right? You feeling ready, yeah?'

'Course I'm ready, no problem,' I lied.

We all ended up talking about funny memories from school and from when we were young. We'd all grown up together; some of us had even known each other from the age of four. In that moment I had a warm sense of contentment. The 'adults' sat on the stools that surround the kitchen island unit, having a chat. My sister and all of my cousins were watching *EastEnders* in the conservatory. I had my friends, my family, my girlfriend, my cousins, grandparents, aunties and uncles – I had everyone around who meant the most to me. With them I felt as though I could endure anything.

6

THE PROTEST

The day we had been waiting for had finally arrived. After hearing the dreaded date spoken about over and over again for the past twelve days, I couldn't believe that the screen on my mobile phone said '*Monday 7 July*'. I woke up naturally at 6 a.m. after a night of medicated, restless sleep. My eyes opened and I remembered what the day ahead would entail. After having a warm shower, brushing my teeth and giving myself a close shave, I walked downstairs into the kitchen where the rest of my family was eating breakfast. I couldn't eat anything; I felt sick and on edge. My stomach was churning.

'You need to eat something, Sim is picking us up in twenty minutes,' said my dad. 'Come on, twenty minutes, guys!'

I forced down a buttered slice of toast, trying hard not to bring up every mouthful. My mind was at a standstill. I just remember staring into space while chewing my toast, dreading the next sickening feeling I would get once I swallowed it.

For the majority of the journey to Horseferry Road I gazed out of the window of the cab and watched a grassy suburb change into a built-up, cosmopolitan city. I frequently sipped from a bottle of water in a failed attempt to calm the burning acid in my stomach.

When we arrived I could see Teresa, Lef and my uncle George with their families standing outside a café. Sim parked the cab and I stepped out to greet them all.

'It's all gonna be fine, just relax and go with the flow,' said Lef.

While we were in the café, Denzil Hiles walked in. This was the first time that I had come face to face with a member of the victim's family. I recognised Jonathan's father from a picture in an article that I'd read online. He walked in and we made eye contact for a brief moment before he casually turned around and walked out. *He thinks I might have killed his son.* The thought passed through my mind and I felt an emotion-fuelled headache about to start. I managed to compose myself – I had to be strong because the truth was on my side.

We walked towards the Magistrates' Court and saw what looked like hundreds of people standing in the road opposite the courts. Many were holding the placards that had been made for the protest: 'GAGGING BRITISH JUSTICE'; 'BRITISH ACCUSED, BRITISH VICTIM, BRITISH WITNESSES, BRITISH JUSTICE'; 'NO TO EU EXTRADITION'; and 'JUSTICE FOR ANDREW AND JONATHAN'.

I have had doubts as to whether putting Jonathan's name on the placard was the right decision, as it was on my insistence at the time. But the statement was true – if the extradition was to be prevented and a real investigation was to be conducted instead, then his family would have had a chance to get justice for their son. My extradition to Greece would have brought justice for no one at all.

The nerves began to increase when I saw how many people had turned up. I genuinely thought that we would have been lucky if only half the number had come to support us! I couldn't believe my eyes when I saw old friends from childhood, a huge group of university friends who had travelled miles and people I'd not seen in years all there to support me. I began to feel myself burst with emotion – I can't use any other words to describe the moment other than 'surreal' and 'overwhelming'.

I saw Mr Hiles again walking to the court's entrance. In the brief moment we made eye contact, I gave him a kind nod. I don't really know why, but in that moment I felt I had to acknowledge the fact that he was living this too. As difficult as it had been for us, I knew that the situation was even more tragic and traumatic for him and his family. No matter what happened, they would never get their son back, and I sympathised greatly. There had been countless times since my arrest when I'd lain in bed for hours attempting to put myself in their position. I'd witnessed what losing Michael had done to *his* family, so being the person wrongly accused of taking Mr Hiles's son from him devastated me. I had to do everything I could to prove my innocence, without having to suffer behind bars.

I looked up and saw that my best friends had arrived. They all wore suits and looked smart – I remember my friend Anthony had even decided to wear his glasses, which he never does.

In the hallway of the Magistrates' Court, we were left in enormous suspense. I think my body language said it all, which was noticed by my lawyer John Jones. 'Andrew, try not to worry, I'm sure it will be adjourned today,' he said.

We were called into court three – the same courtroom that I'd seen eleven days previously. I walked past the public gallery on my right, where my family – Lef, Teresa, my gran, Auntie Mary, Uncle Theo – Riya and some friends were sitting down behind a sheet of glass. I was then escorted to the same defendants' dock that I'd been in the morning after I was arrested, also behind a sheet of glass, like a criminal. I felt like I had to go through it on my own and wished that I could be sitting with my family.

I could see Mr Hiles on the other side of the court; his body language was calm, he made no eye contact. I looked down in front of me where John Jones and my solicitor John Tipple were sitting confidently. We all stood as the judge walked in. It was the same old judge from before who had insinuated that I had fled Greece before my scheduled flight in July 2007.

After confirming my name, John Jones proceeded to explain our concerns. He informed the judge that we would be gaining access to the South Wales Police statements in the very near future, and believed that an adjournment would be in the interest of justice. John briefly raised the points of law of our argument and stated that there was a huge chance the South Wales Police statements would greatly strengthen our defence. The hearing was adjourned until 12 August. I was asked to stand and confirm that I understood the bail conditions the judge read to me.

I was escorted out of the defendants' dock and into the hallway of the courts where I was reunited with my friends and family. I sat down on one of the benches, not saying a word. Even though I knew that there were around 150 people outside supporting me, I was dreading walking out. I didn't want to face the BBC News cameras. The protest gave us a great amount of publicity to help the campaign, but I started to feel like I was forced into it. Everything seemed to happen suddenly – decisions made, legal strategy determined, all while I was sat at the back of my garden smoking every day, cocooned in my own little world.

My friend Kyri handed me a cup of tea that he'd bought. 'Nice and milky,' I remember him saying.

Riya sat beside me, and I was comforted as her hand met mine.

'When will this nightmare end?' I asked her, as though she could possibly answer the question.

My mum and Mr Hiles approached each other on the stairwell of the court. In an emotional embrace, she gave him our family's deepest sympathies and attempted to explain to him our situation. My dad walked towards them and pressed Mr Hiles to look at the Greek investigation. Mr Hiles needed to see how deeply flawed it was! But he refused to look at it. All he wanted was for me to be extradited to Greece.

After a few minutes, I saw Mr Hiles through a glass vision panel in the door of the meeting room. He was screaming, shouting and pointing his finger at someone in a burst of anger. Seeing over 100 people with placards outside the court protesting, as well as an adjournment in our favour, probably wasn't what he was expecting. Reading his son's name on one of the placards must have been terribly difficult, but a real investigation was needed if they wanted the chance for justice.

I put off walking outside for a few more minutes. 'Come on, Andrew, it's time to leave,' someone said to me. I stood up and my legs trembled like they weren't even my own. Approaching the exit of the courts I took a deep breath. Lef grabbed my arm as we all walked outside; he's a big guy and was like my bodyguard that day. The cold, fresh air hit my face and I heard someone say, 'Here he is!' I could see a camera pointing at me to my left and press photographers started to take photos, following me as we crossed the road. I walked towards the huge crowd of people and I received many hugs. As I looked around, I saw people crying and hugging each other. I noticed people who I never thought would have turned up to support us, which overwhelmed me to the point where I couldn't hold back my emotions. I could see my mum hiding away at the back of the protest. The media attention had left her feeling far too much out of her comfort zone and she couldn't cope with the exposure. I was a bit like her in that respect; I was grateful for the support but uncomfortable with standing in the spotlight.

My solicitor John Tipple also made a statement to the BBC and ended it with something I wasn't expecting – screaming

'JUSTICE FOR ANDREW!' at the top of his voice continuously as the supporters responded. As much as I didn't like the attention, it was made clear how serious and wrong the situation that I had been put in was.

After around half an hour of hugging and thanking everyone who came to support me, I got back into our friend Sim's cab. 'That was the craziest thing I've ever experienced,' I said to Riya and my family as the cab drove away. I turned my head and looked out of the rear window, watching the horde of supporters become smaller as we drove down Horseferry Road. I looked at my mum, whose face was pale and exhausted. Sophie and Riya were still wiping away the tears that were running down their cheeks. 'I think after today's dramas, we deserve pizza!' I said.

As we pulled up outside our house, I noticed my auntie Teresa and uncle Les had beaten us home. I walked up the driveway, comforted by the knowledge that it was over. *For now*, I thought.

We watched the BBC News piece at 6 p.m.; about thirty of us crowded around the television in my house. I thought the piece was well-rounded and successfully highlighted my plight. Mr Hiles made a statement, telling the press that he wouldn't like to be in our family's situation and expressed that it must be difficult. I appreciated him saying that greatly.

He also said, 'I don't know if Andrew killed my son … I expected to hate him, but all I saw was a frightened boy … If he did do it, then I want him to stand trial for it. If he's found guilty, fine … and if he's innocent, that's OK.'

The fact that I would be held in a foreign prison pre-trial wasn't a concern of his.

7

THE SOUTH WALES POLICE STATEMENTS

The five weeks between the hearings were exhausting, stressful and monotonous. My family and the 'Bum Squad' had become additional lawyers, working towards building the best case and campaign possible. The online petition had grown to over 4,000 signatures and another protest was being arranged for 12 August.

We'd received the South Wales Police statements a couple of days after the adjournment. I remember feeling uneasy as my dad opened the large brown envelope. What we were about to read had the potential to determine my destiny. He pulled out a hefty wad of documents and I sighed with relief when I saw the first page; it was a list of the people who'd made statements and every one of Jonathan's friends was there. My dad and I spent an entire day reading them.

Unlike the word-for-word identical statements the Zante police had written, the statements that the five had given to the British police each gave detailed, subjective accounts of the events that surrounded the attack. The statements presented an accurate description of the first day of their holiday.

They had landed in Zante on the morning of 19 July 2007 then made their way to their hotel. Taking a little while for the staff to prepare their rooms, they waited at the hotel bar area and had a beer or two. After dropping off their bags and walking into town for some food and drinks, they showered and met up again in the hotel bar. Following a few more drinks and after playing some cards, Mark O'Gorman, Christopher Paglionico, Jason Mordecai and Robert Hares headed to 'the strip', which is where the nightclubs and bars are located. They left Lee Burgess and Jonathan Hiles in the hotel bar, as they were talking to some girls.

The four boys who had gone to the strip sat in the outdoor bar area of the Rescue nightclub, where they had a drink before Jonathan and Lee caught up with them. Once they were all together, they went into the dance area of the nightclub. Their statements gave a detailed description of the layout – the raised platform dance area was 5 or 6 feet high and next to the DJ. After buying a drink at the bar, they made their way onto the raised podium to dance. All of the boys admitted to being tipsy, apart from Lee who was noticeably drunk.

They were dancing with a group of six British girls on the raised stage when a man who they didn't know barged through them and began to urinate. One of the boys describes this male as having 'hair which was cut short in a mullet style, spikey on the top. He was a big build, not fat, not all muscle.' From detailed head-to-toe descriptions, not one of Jonathan's friends had said that this male had a moustache and goatee like mine. I considered myself to be quite fat – their descriptions did not portray how I looked. Christopher Paglionico, who gave a very detailed description, admitted to seeing the male for a maximum of five seconds only, after several drinks and with flashing disco lights.

It was mentioned that the urinating male was in the company of two other males, one of whom was described by Jason Mordecai as 'a white male, early twenties … over six foot tall and of an average type build. He had shortish blond hair and he appeared to have a badly pock-marked complexion.'

Christopher Paglionico, Lee Burgess, Robert Hares and Jason Mordecai jumped off the stage because they had been urinated on and wanted to clean up in the toilet.

Mark O'Gorman and Jonathan Hiles remained on the raised platform. Mark O'Gorman stated:

We headed towards the far right hand corner of the dance stage to get off. I was walking alongside maybe slightly behind Jonny [Jonathan] and I saw the male who had been urinating in the area of the corner of the stage. He was with the same two males and he appeared to be stumbling around as if he was drunk. Jonny had to walk past him and as he did Jonny said, 'What are you doing?' I heard this as I was right alongside Jonny. This question was not asked in any way an aggressive manner or confrontationally, Jonny was not that sort of person. The male then stood face to face with Jonny who was stood about two foot from the edge of the right hand side of the stage with his back to the edge of the stage. This face to face was literally for a second or two, the other male seemed to be frowning or scowling at Jonny and almost immediately he punched Jonny with his right hand in a clenched fist to the left side of his face. This happened right in front of me and I saw Jonny stumble backwards and one of his legs stepped over the edge causing him to fall backwards off the stage. I saw him land on his head on the floor I mentioned earlier some 5 feet below the stage. As he hit the floor he appeared to immediately become unconscious, his eyes closed and he was not moving. I pushed this male and was expecting to have a fight with him. As I was preparing myself for a fight I looked over and saw that Jonny obviously needed my help.

The first thing that I thought when reading the statements was that I would never, ever commit such an offence. In no situation would I ever decide to urinate in a nightclub and then punch someone for no reason! The second thing that struck me was that Mark O'Gorman was the only eyewitness to the alleged attack. This was a complete contradiction to what was written in the Greek statements, which claimed that all five of the victim's friends were 100 per cent certain that I was the attacker.

According to the South Wales Police statements, Jonathan was taken to hospital in an ambulance. Lee was drunk and returned to the apartments while Mark and Jason went to the police station to report the attack. They stated that the police didn't allow them to make a complaint and said that Jonathan would have to do so himself.

Christopher and Robert followed the ambulance to the hospital in a taxi, where Jonathan was left on a stretcher in the recovery position. According to Christopher Paglionico, the doctors told him that Jonathan was OK and was just asleep. Tragically, Jonathan died two days later after being transferred by plane to a hospital in Athens.

The victim's friends then described how the Zante police sat them in a room together and showed them CCTV footage around the time of the incident. The CCTV mainly covered the tills behind the bars and did not show the attack. They noticed three men leaving the nightclub quickly, who could have been the perpetrator and his friends. They were also shown photographs as a group, all of which were taken by a professional photographer the night *before* the incident had occurred. I was wrongly identified as the urinating man – another blond male who I didn't know was identified as his friend. The picture of me was of my face (with my eyes closed) in the middle of a crowded dancefloor. It certainly wasn't strong enough to make an accurate identification.

Mark O'Gorman, the only eyewitness to the attack, stated:

We all made written statements to a police officer, which was translated to us by a female who I think was called Electra. I did think that when we were doing the statements everything seemed a bit disorganised. The other boys were more concerned than I was about the person urinating. Although I'm quite sure it was this male I can't be 100 per cent sure.

As mentioned previously, the Zante police had shown the photographs around a few of the hotels. At the hotel where we had been staying, the manager told the police that Chris and Charlie were my friends. After they beat them into signing statements that claimed I was the attacker, the five friends of Jonathan Hiles signed the Greek word-for-word identical statements:

I identified with complete certainty and I am absolutely sure that the individual shown in about the middle of the photograph, who has a slightly artistic-looking goatee, is the perpetrator who caused the fatal bodily injury to my friend. At this point I wish to point out that the perpetrator had shaved off his goatee on the day of the incident and had left only slightly long sideburns.

The Greek and South Wales Police statements were completely different. Surely this parody of an investigation was ridiculous enough for the British authorities to intervene?

8

JACQUI SMITH

Going to the cemetery and sitting on the bench next to Michael's grave was something that I'd do regularly. It had been almost a year since we'd lost him to leukaemia, and he was still in my thoughts every day. He was like a cousin to me and I missed him so much. Soon his bench became somewhere I would go to escape, think things through and be alone. Sometimes I felt like I had nowhere else to go. I would go every few days just to sit and watch the tall evergreen trees dance with the wind in the distance. There was something tranquil about it – and I would stay there for hours because I didn't want to return to the chaos at home. There was one particular day when I sat on Michael's bench from the early afternoon and didn't leave until sunset. When I eventually brought myself to make my way home, and I walked through the front door, I was told that the court hearing on 12 August would be adjourned too. Since the South Wales Police statements had been thrown into the mix, the Crown prosecution needed more time to build an argument.

The day of 12 August 2008 began in a similar way to the first adjourned hearing on 7 July. Actually, the morning was pretty much exactly the same. The same emotions, the same sickening feeling of not being able to eat, the same nerves and the same route in our friend Sim's cab to Horseferry Road in Westminster. As we arrived I noticed another huge group of supporters outside with the same placards. The hearing was quick, and adjourned until 30 September – another seven weeks.

The next day I remember overhearing my mum making a desperate phone call. 'Hello, I know this might sound ridiculous, but would it be possible to speak with the Prime Minister, Gordon Brown?' She hung up the phone and noticed that I was listening and chuckling.

'They put me through to a recording,' she said.

'You know you can't just call the Prime Minister. He doesn't work for T-Mobile, you can't just call him up to complain when you're not satisfied with the service!'

'But why not try?' she said.

I guess you don't get anywhere without trying, even if the odds are, well … impossible.

Although we never managed to catch Gordon on the phone, we'd written letters to him, as well as to the Home Secretary Jacqui Smith, the Greek ambassador, Jack Straw and many others. My uncle Les was listening to the radio station talkSPORT and told us that Jacqui Smith would be on the show that week. The host of the show was a presenter called Jon Gaunt, nicknamed 'Gaunty' by his fans. His style was confrontational and he had a reputation for giving both callers and his guests a hard time. At this time, we had no direct communication with anyone in the government apart from our local MP, Joan Ryan, who felt that my extradition was inevitable. Les attempted to call the show and raise my case with Jacqui to see what her public reaction would be. He managed to get put through to an assistant who asked him the nature of the question that he wanted to ask the Home Secretary. He told her that he was interested in her opinion as to whether the government thought it was justifiable to extradite British citizens without first determining if there was an actual case to answer. He purposely didn't mention my name before being put on the air:

Jon Gaunt: 'Now we have Leslie from Enfield who wants to talk about the European Arrest Warrant. Good morning, Leslie.'

Jacqui Smith: 'Good morning, Leslie.'

Les: 'Good morning, Jon and Jacqui. Jacqui, do you feel it is fair that we should be extraditing our citizens to other EU countries without first establishing whether they would have a case to answer in a British Court?'

Jacqui Smith: 'Well, Leslie, in my opinion and that of the government, the EAW is considered a great success! It secures the transfer of criminals and terrorist suspects across European borders in much shorter time frames than in the past. It is to the advantage of both governments and police agencies throughout Europe. If say a terrorist bomber was sent back from Italy under the European Arrest Warrant, it would mean that...'

Les: 'But we aren't talking about terrorism, we are talking about the protection of British citizens. Take the case of a young Londoner, Andrew Symeou, who is to be extradited to Greece without the evidence first being...'

Jon Gaunt: 'Sorry, we are going to have to leave you there, Leslie, and the next caller is...'

The speed at which the call was dropped was impressive, especially for a live radio show. I could imagine the Home Secretary pulling an imaginary blade across her neck as soon as she heard Les say my name. Jon Gaunt, a fearsome and argumentative presenter who hosted a radio show that is often controversial, had been silenced in a fraction of a second. He'd encouraged no debate on the subject, which was unusual. We wondered if he'd been notified in advance that during any talk concerning the EAW he was to cut it short if my name was mentioned. We will never know – what we do know is that Jacqui Smith was well aware of the case. Her refusal to speak publicly on the subject spoke volumes.

9

THE HEARING

It was 30 September 2008 – the date to which my extradition hearing had been adjourned. It was a long, stressful and emotionally strenuous day. Overlooking a courtroom full of lawyers and journalists, I sat in the defendants' dock for the fourth time. Sitting there, alone, I was at least confident in knowing that there was no case against me whatsoever. I just hoped that the judge had the courage to go against the EAW and consider my innocence. He was an older judge who hopefully wanted to end his career with a bang and use his common sense to prevent a possible miscarriage of justice.

My name was the first to be called out to testify. It was a scenario that I'd repeatedly thought about since being on bail. I assumed that my heart would race or I would feel shaky and nervous, but I actually felt pretty confident because I had absolutely nothing to hide. Mr Hiles sat to the right of the witness box – I could see him in my peripheral vision as I stood and took the oath.

During my barrister John Jones's questioning, I explained to the judge my whereabouts on the night in question. I reiterated the statement that I'd made to a solicitor in 2007, explaining that I was in a nightclub called Bad Boys that was over 200 metres away from the Rescue nightclub. On the strip of Laganas in

Zante, holidaymakers are able to walk freely in and out of the bars or nightclubs with no entrance fee or security check. On the night, my group of friends and a group of girls went into the Rescue nightclub at around 4 a.m. for about fifteen minutes on the walk back to the hotel. This was three hours after the attack had allegedly occurred, and we stayed near the front bar area only.

The prosecuting barrister, Peter Caldwell, cross-examined me. He was curious as to why my friends and I had made statements with a solicitor in 2007. I told him that my mum had sought legal advice after Chris Kyriacou and Charlie Klitou had told us what had happened to them, and that it was suggested we do it to record our memories of the night in case anything were to happen in the future. He seemed to think it was suspicious that we'd documented our memories of the night in question as opposed to a different night. I knew of the date of the attack because Chris and Charlie were interrogated about it! Then I told him that a statement outlining my whereabouts on the wrong night wouldn't have been much help if I were to stand wrongly accused of the crime – which I assumed would have been obvious.

I remember being unhappy with Chris and Charlie's testimonies. They both explained what had happened to them in the police station, but I felt like they didn't get across how bad their treatment truly was. They were nervous and trying to face their fears in court. It was a horrible feeling knowing that my life may have depended on their testimonies. On the other hand, Georgina Clay (one of the holiday reps) was firm and descriptive in her testimony. I remember her clarifying that the Zante police were trying to intimidate her at her place of work. She told the court that she was at the police station when Chris and Charlie were held and that she was not allowed to speak to them, but she had mouthed, 'Are you OK?' to Charlie, who had shaken his head and mouthed back 'No.' She explained that Charlie's face had swollen up once he had left the police station and that she had called the British Consulate. Apparently, the chief of police and the hotel manager were very close friends, and he aggressively shouted at the consular representative, forcing her to leave the hotel because she was apparently trespassing. I couldn't believe it!

The hearing lasted hours and John Jones had put a firm argument across. Our argument that the EAW was invalid because the Greek authorities had failed to summon me was challenged. John Jones stated that, as part of the Greek judicial system, the process of summoning a suspect to appear before the investigating magistrate for questioning is part of the procedure initiated by the Greek public prosecutor. The EAW must be used only when the requesting state is trial-ready. In other words, the requesting state must not use the EAW as a summons for questioning but only once the investigation has been completed and the suspect is extradited to stand trial. However, Peter Caldwell argued that I was a fugitive. If one is defined as a fugitive, an EAW can be used in such a case. Thus, the EAW *was* valid.

John argued that I was *not* a fugitive. I had no knowledge of the attack, as I was not present at the time. We provided travel documents, showing that I did not leave my holiday early as the judge had previously implied. The prosecutor stated that it didn't matter if I had left the island when I had booked to leave or not. Without having the opportunity to examine the evidence against me, or for me to present my defence, the Greek authorities had decided that I was a fugitive – so we must trust them. The way I understood it, was that my innocence or guilt would determine whether I was a fugitive trying to prevent facing justice. It was something that could not be determined until the trial had finished and a verdict pronounced – in Greece. Proving my innocence would be the only way to prove that I was not a fugitive, and the EAW wouldn't allow us to do that!

There were times in the hearing where I had no idea what they were talking about. At times I sat there in utter confusion, attempting to understand the legal jargon as best I could. There was a short break and my solicitor John Tipple approached me in the defendants' box. I remember him saying, 'Don't worry about the prosecutor, he's just very good at stringing together long and complicated sentences!' He was trying to make me feel better, even though I knew that the counter-arguments were technically valid.

I was frustrated to my core; it was almost as though no human common sense could be heard in court. When we returned from the recess the judge informed the court that his ruling would be given on 30 October.

As I left Westminster Magistrates' Court, I once again found myself walking into a barrage of photographers, reporters and TV news cameras.

10

THE RULING

The day of 30 October arrived and I returned to Westminster Magistrates' Court for the verdict. Sitting in the defendants' dock, I listened to District Judge Purdy's ruling. Adrenalin ran through my veins as he walked into the courtroom. I could feel every pulse and hear every swallow. After rising and confirming my name, he began to speak:

> I stress this court is exercising an extradition jurisdiction pursuant to part one of the Ex. Act 2003 i.e. the European Arrest Warrant scheme not a trial jurisdiction. Thus I am not permitted, never mind inclined, to make any factual finding of guilt or innocence. If any court is to make such a determination, it is to be a Greek court.
>
> [First argument – the validity of the warrant:]
>
> First, the EAW is clear, a warrant was issued. Secondly, that being so, absent an abuse of process finding relying on blatant irregularity, this court has no jurisdiction to enquire into the process leading to the issue of a domestic warrant. To my mind Mr Caldwell [prosecution] must be right.
>
> [Second argument – the passage of time:]
>
> While I hear the Defence concerns, they all seem to be matters

properly aired at a trial. On the material before me I find myself agreeing with the prosecution, I find 'by reason of the passage of time' it would not be 'unjust or oppressive' to extradite Andrew Symeou.

[Third and fourth arguments – against my human rights and an abuse of process:]

As already found, the investigation process may well be heavily, perhaps correctly, challenged and rigorously tested at trial. Evidence currently relied on may be excluded altogether. Such matters are the stock in trade of criminal trials. I reject, on the instant facts, any proper basis for holding that an abuse of process has occurred.

I cannot but observe that this case has attracted a degree of press and public interest. One young man sits in the dock, another is dead. Emotions inevitably run high. Allegations abound and the truth is an all-too-easy casualty. Therefore it is incumbent on the court to ensure a dispassionate appraisal of the issues relevant to the extradition proceedings and this specific Greek judicial request. I make no apology for the lengthy recital of those matters necessary, in my judgement, to explain my ruling. Accordingly for the avoidance of doubt, despite his characteristic panache, I reject the various challenges Mr Jones mounts on behalf of Andrew Symeou. For the reasons given I order extradition to Greece in respect of this EAW.

I didn't feel my heart drop – I thought my heart had stopped altogether. For the few moments after I heard the words, I thought I was dead. What hurt the most was that I had convinced myself that I was going to win. The truth was on my side and our arguments were legitimate, but it was made clear that the court had no power to prevent my extradition. District Judge Purdy asked me to rise and confirm that I had understood the ruling. I took

a while to mumble the word 'yes', before slowly walking out of
the courtroom. My legs were trembling so much that I almost
fell over. I met with my family, friends and girlfriend in the pas-
sageway of the courts. In disbelief and devastation, we hugged
and cried together. It was the same as when we'd cried together
on the day I'd first made bail – only this time we knew that our
fight for an investigation would be almost impossible.

╫╫

Private Eye magazine published an article after seeing the evidence against me. They described it as 'flawed, contradictory and
in places ludicrous'. Yet the judge claimed there was absolutely
no abuse of process on behalf of the Greek authorities "on the
instant facts".

We did everything that we possibly could for the British
authorities to investigate this evidence, but it didn't work. My
family lobbied through every avenue for the Greek authorities to
apply for Mutual Legal Assistance. Our local MP Joan Ryan was
eventually a great help to us, and had written a letter, which we
asked the deputy ambassador at a meeting in the Greek embassy
in London to pass on to the Greek authorities. Sabine Zanker
from Fair Trials International came to support us too, and the
deputy ambassador assured us that he would do everything in
his power to help – but of course nothing came of it. My parents
even flew to Zante to speak with the investigating magistrate
and show her all the evidence that we'd accumulated. We were
nothing but open and honest. I couldn't understand how, in the
twenty-first century, in *Europe*, this could have been allowed to
happen. I felt absolutely powerless.

After losing our argument in Westminster Magistrates' Court,
we appealed against the ruling and took it to the High Court.

Our only ground for appeal was that there was clearly an abuse of process by the Greek authorities. After more painful adjournments and delays, in May 2009 we discovered that I'd lost again. The court ruled that there was no abuse of process, regardless of the flawed, contradictory evidence.

We battled against my extradition to Greece for over a year, trying our hardest to get the British authorities to look into the case. Innocent with no criminal record, and having never been questioned in the investigation, I was to be extradited to Greece at the age of twenty. Everything that we had feared was about to become reality.

11

THE STRENGTH

I remember the day when I was told that I was to be extradited. We didn't have to go to court to find out, it was my lawyer who told us that it would be happening. I'd just returned home from Riya's house and I peered into the living room to say hello. Everyone seemed quiet and drained. I could tell that something was wrong.

'What happened?' I asked. Nobody spoke; my mum just wiped away her tears. She attempted to tell me, but the words didn't come out. I walked into the kitchen where my dad was sitting. 'What happened?'

He took a deep breath. 'Andrew, the appeal was rejected. The extradition is going ahead.'

It took a while to comprehend the words. I bit my lip, trying desperately to stop my eyes from streaming. 'How long?' I managed to utter.

'Within ten days.'

I felt like my world was ending, and my instant reaction was to leave the house. I hunted for my car keys in a state of erratic dread. I needed to drive somewhere, just to escape. Everything around me was moving too quickly and I felt faint. My mum became hysterical – she didn't want me to drive in such a volatile state. My car keys were in my pocket the whole time. Teresa grabbed me before I could run out of the door. 'Slow down! Your parents are already in a bad way, think about how worried they'll be if you go off driving like a lunatic. Just give me the keys. Why don't you call Riya or one of your friends to pick you up?'

'OK,' I said. I don't even know if I made eye contact with her before running out of the house. I walked to the petrol station in the rain and called my friend Alex on the way. 'It's happening. They're extraditing me within ten days,' I told him. It was only when I heard myself say the words that I began to well up.

'Are you serious?' he asked.

'Why are we so shocked? Why didn't I think this would actually happen? They're gonna put me in prison.' I could barely speak.

'Andrew, listen, mate.' He paused for a while, unsure of what he could say to make it any better. He exhaled. 'What happens happens. You're ready for this, you may not know it, but you are. You've been preparing for this shit for over a year.'

'*Prepared!?* When I get there I might be handed to the officers who beat Chris and Charlie and pinned this shit on me! Think about it! They're gonna fucking kill me!' I cried.

'Andrew! Listen to me, they aren't gonna kill you man. Don't be stupid. Don't think like that. Just calm the fuck down. You don't realise how strong you are. You have to accept that you'll be in a cell for a while before making bail. We'll all come round a bit later; don't do anything stupid. Go and see Riya!'

Over the next few days, my family managed to persuade me that everything would be OK. I'll always remember the words of my uncle Andy, Michael's dad, the night before I was extradited. He called me into the garden and said:

Michael always made out he was fearless and strong, but inside he was weak. In hospital, when he heard that things weren't going well for him, however weak he was, he was overcome with an overpowering strength. I'd never seen him so strong. '*I am going to beat this*' was his mentality. When it comes down to it, you don't realise what strength you have. There will be many ups and downs. However difficult it is, whatever you have to go through for this to be over, you will find the inner strength.

He gave me a wooden cross on a thread that had belonged to Michael, which was to stay with me in Greece.

However many times my family and friends told me to be strong, it was his words that gave me strength throughout my journey. You can't prepare for the unknown, or know how you will deal with what *could* happen, all you can do is focus on today's worries, and have faith that you will have the strength to endure anything that may happen tomorrow. There will always be times of weakness – but it is in the darkest moments when you realise how strong you really are.

12

WALKING THE MILE

The day of 23 July 2009 began very differently from the way it ended. It wasn't a typical summer's day – the sky was awash with translucent grey clouds and it sometimes looked as though it would rain at any moment. I wasn't nervous; I didn't have the usual sickening feeling in my stomach and my mind wasn't overwhelmed with negative thoughts. I lied to myself and decided that I didn't give a fuck any more. *Whatever happens happens*, I thought. A blast of nerves ran through my body when I saw Sim's cab outside. He'd come to take us to Belgravia Police Station where I'd be transferred to Heathrow Airport under arrest. I was told that all I could take was a medium-sized bag, so I had packed a blue Nike sports bag to join me throughout my journey. I made sure to pack a notebook and pen so that I could keep a journal, and I took the first book that I picked from the bookshelf in our study, *The Da Vinci Code* by Dan Brown.

When I walked onto the driveway, I didn't look back. Before I got into the cab, I walked up the road and sat in Riya's car with her for a while. I held her in my arms and couldn't find the right moment to let go. At what point do you say goodbye? We'd been through so much, and we didn't know how long it would be before we could be together again. It was a hug that I wished would never end, and I only allowed myself to shed a tear without her seeing. I had to stay strong for her, as she'd been for me.

'I have something for you,' she stuttered. She wiped a tear from her cheek and handed me a brown envelope. 'I want you to open it when you get to Greece.'

'Thank you, I will. You know, I'll probably only be there for two weeks and I'll make bail back to the UK!' I told her and half smiled.

'Andrew, it's time to go,' I heard my dad calling.

I could see her eyes watering up before they trickled with tears. She couldn't find the words to respond – we both knew, in spite of my joking, that I would probably be away for a long time. Up until that point in my life, kissing her goodbye was one of the most difficult things that I'd ever had to do.

When we drove off, I watched Riya driving behind us through the rear window. The emotion only really hit me when we finally went our separate ways – we turned right and she continued straight. Just like that, she was gone. I had no clue when I would see her face again. The image of her driving behind us stayed with me for a very long time.

The cab journey to Belgravia Police Station was spent in silence. I couldn't even look at anyone directly in the eyes and I doubt my family could either. When we arrived, I remember walking up and down in the corridor, waiting to be taken to the airport and dumped on a plane. An officer from Scotland Yard's extradition unit walked in. I recognised him; it was Jamie, who'd arrested me over a year earlier.

'Andrew, I'm afraid it's time to go. I can't tell you what's going to happen in Greece, but I won't be handcuffing you,' he said. I nodded, finding it almost impossible to let any words pass my lips. I hugged my family and our eyes welled up.

'Andrew, we're on our way to the airport now. We'll find you in Greece,' my dad stammered. 'Just remember, you're innocent.

Always be on your best behaviour. Being rude won't get you any-where – just play the game. They can take away your rights and treat you badly, but they can't take away what's in here,' he cried while pointing at my head.

My mum grabbed me by the cheek. 'Listen to me, whatever they do to you, never sign anything. If they beat you, don't sign anything! You take the beatings, OK? If they threaten you or threaten to hurt your parents, don't sign anything! Do you under-stand me? We can look after ourselves.'

'I love you, everything's going to be fine. Don't be scared,' Sophie said. Almost in an instant, they were gone. I didn't look back when the police car doors closed. I couldn't look through the window and watch my family fade into the distance. After everything we had fought for together, we'd parted ways. *I don't give a fuck*, I remember kidding myself.

When I knew that my family were out of sight, I looked back and wiped away the silent tears.

'Andrew, when we get to the airport, we aren't going to hand-cuff you. Usually, we would – in some cases maybe even put you in an airport cell, but we're gonna take you for a coffee,' one of them said to me.

'Thanks, I really appreciate that,' I replied. 'So what's gonna happen after we go for a coffee?' I asked.

'Well, we're meeting Greek police officers there and we will hand you over to them,' one of them answered.

'Andrew, I really feel sorry for you, mate. I can't believe they're extraditing you,' Jamie said. I appreciated the comment and thanked him. I couldn't believe that the words were coming out of his mouth. I knew they were just doing their job and that they could see that I was a threat to no one.

Being extradited was a surprisingly normal process. In hind-sight, it was just like catching a flight, only with police officers

instead of a partner or friends … and going to jail after landing instead of a plush resort.

Jamie approached three plain-clothed Greek officers in the
terminal. I shook all of their hands, which probably confused
them a bit. I don't know if they expected to see me being escorted
in handcuffs with a rude demeanour, but they seemed slightly
puzzled.

We were early so the Scotland Yard officers took me for a
coffee, as promised. The Greek officers sat on a table close by;
they must have been thinking, *what the hell is going on?*

'Seriously, Andrew, this is ridiculous, mate. There's no way this
would stand in a British court,' Jamie said to me sympathetically.

'What can I say? Our government signed up to something
ridiculous that allowed this to happen,' I replied.

He ignored the comment and I noticed him look over to the
Greek officers a few tables away from us.

'What do you think?'

'About them?' he asked. 'I think they're all right, they seem
fine.'

'I'm crapping myself, I've never been extradited before,' I said
sarcastically. Both of the officers chuckled, not having a clue how
to respond.

We conversed over a coffee and it came to the point where
I almost forgot that they were the officers handing me over to
the Greek authorities. Jamie told me about his career and how
he'd become a police officer, then worked his way up to Scotland
Yard's extradition unit. 'It's time to board, Andrew,' he said. I felt
faint as soon as I heard the words. The more I pretended it wasn't
happening, the easier it was to accept.

I have a vivid image of walking towards the gate. It was a tunnel,
and it felt as though I was on death row walking the mile. I was
drained, and I had an emotion-fuelled headache because I had no

idea what was going to happen once I landed. I stood next to the aeroplane door, wishing that I didn't have to walk through it.

'Good luck Andrew.'

'Jamie – thanks,' I said.

I shook both of their hands. The other officer nodded as though he was saying, *you can do this*. As soon as I stepped onto the plane, I felt the vibrations of the engine running through my body. I smiled at the air hostess, as I would on a normal flight, then was escorted to the very back of the plane and told to sit in the left-hand window seat. Two of the Greek officers sat next to me and one sat in front. I studied them for a few moments; the officer next to me had quite a kind face – I didn't find him threatening. The officer next to him had a cold, evil look in his eyes and the officer in front of me was older, maybe fifty-five years old and seemed to be smiling a lot of the time.

'So what do you think of London, great city, eh?' I said.

'Yes, we went to Buckingham Palace and Big Ben, we saw it all!' the officer next to me responded in perfect English. 'I was looking at your Facebook group, you have thousands of supporters!' he said.

'I saw your sister speaking on YouTube,' the evil-eyed officer inputted.

'Yes, I saw that too,' the officer next to me said. 'You know, it won't be eighteen months in jail. I think maximum three months and you will come back home,' he said casually.

Three months! I thought. I couldn't bear thinking about what could happen in three whole months.

'We'll see,' I responded while taking a big gulp from the bottle of water that I'd bought before boarding. There was an awkward pause for a few moments.

'You know, not all Greek police are like them,' the officer next to me said.

I was quite shocked by the comment.

'Of course not. They ruin it for all of you, now you all have a bad reputation!' I said. The evil-eyed man and the officer next to me both smiled; the one in front had already fallen asleep before the plane had even taken off.

'You're right,' the officer next to me said. 'It's like the policeman who shot the fifteen-year-old boy in the riots in Athens a few months ago as well. They are all arseholes.'

I'd forgotten about the story that was all over the news. A Greek police officer had shot a fifteen-year-old boy at point-blank range and the Greek public had been protesting.

The plane began to head slowly towards the runway. The engine roared and we began to shake. Before I knew it, the plane began to accelerate. My head pounded with tension, I shut my eyes and massaged my temples to try to release the pain. The friction between the plane's wheels and hard runway stopped – I knew that the next time the wheels touched the ground I'd be in Greece.

卌

I can visualise my extradition so vividly even though it feels like an eternity ago. I had no idea where I was going to be taken, how I was going to be treated, how I would feel or how long it would take for me to finally clear my name and go back home to my family. Despite the many 'unknowns', there was one thing I could be sure of: it was going to take a great amount of inner strength to endure whatever was to come.

I'd been battling for justice like I'd never battled before, and I felt like I'd already been through so much. In truth, it was just the beginning.

PART II

You have power over your mind – not outside events.
Realise this, and you will find strength.
– Marcus Aurelius

23 July 2009, the *Daily Telegraph*

STUDENT ACCUSED OF GREECE NIGHTCLUB KILLING EXTRADITED

Andrew Symeou, a student accused of killing British teenager Jonathan Hiles in a Greek nightclub, was extradited on Thursday. Symeou denies the allegations and says he was not even in the nightclub at the time of the alleged attack on Mr Hiles.

Mr Symeou, 20, from Enfield, north London, is accused of manslaughter following the death of Mr Hiles in a nightclub in Zakynthos on the island of Zante in 2007.

He fought the extradition, with his lawyers saying the evidence against him was fabricated and obtained by Greek police through the violent intimidation of witnesses.

Symeou denies the allegations and says he was not even in the nightclub at the time of the alleged attack on Mr Hiles, 18, from Llandaff North, Cardiff.

Earlier this year he failed in his bid to get the High Court to refuse his extradition under a European Arrest Warrant.

He won permission to take his appeal to the House of Lords but the Law Lords last week refused to hear the case.

Symeou flew to Greece from Heathrow Airport on Thursday morning after surrendering to police at Belgravia Police Station in central London.

Campaigners against Symeou's extradition fear he could be held in jail for months before the case is heard. Symeou himself has said he is worried he will be beaten by police.

Jago Russell, chief executive of Fair Trials International, which is supporting Symeou, said: 'It is a tragedy that, despite the serious flaws in the case against him, Andrew Symeou has been sent to Greece.

'We hope the Greek courts will do a better job of delivering justice than the British and that this young man will not be forced to spend months in Greek jail before his case even comes to court.'

His father, Frank, said the time spent fighting his son's extradition had given the family the opportunity to gather information about the case against him and challenge the evidence held by Greek police.

'Without this extra time, Andrew may by now have been in a Greek prison convicted of a crime he did not commit, based on evidence obtained by torture and that had been fabricated and manipulated by the investigating police officers.

'Andrew is ready to face his accusers, confident in the fact that he is innocent and that the case against him has no foundation in truth.

'This whole nightmare has tested Andrew in ways that most of us could not imagine. Yes, it has been extremely difficult for him and the stress has taken its toll, but he has shown great courage and strength of character.'

Symeou is charged with striking roller-hockey player Mr Hiles hard in the face, causing him to lose consciousness and fall off a dance podium at the Rescue nightclub in Zakynthos while on holiday in July 2007.

Mr Hiles, who represented the Great Britain roller-hockey team and also played ice hockey for Cardiff Devils' junior team, suffered a severe brain injury and died two days later.

Symeou, a Bournemouth University student, said he did not know of Mr Hiles's death until he returned to England and was never interviewed by the police.

His lawyers allege that two of his friends who remained on Zante were held for eight hours without food or water and beaten, punched, slapped and threatened by officers until they gave statements implicating him in the death.

The pair immediately retracted the statements on their release and informed consular officials about the treatment they received.

13

THINKING OF YOU

I could see mountains beneath me as I stared through the aircraft's small window. It was slightly smudged from where my head had been leaning on it. *Ding* – the seat belt sign lit up; I looked down and realised that it had been fastened for the entire flight. The plane began its descent and I'd never dreaded anything as much as I dreaded that landing. Everything that I'd feared for the previous thirteen months was coming true, and floating in mid-air for an eternity was a better, but far less realistic option.

'What's gonna happen to me?' I asked one of the officers.

'Well, there will be some policemen waiting for you who will take you to the police station. At some point you will be taken to Patras. After that, I don't know,' he answered.

Peering out of the window, I watched Athens get closer and closer. I buried my face in my hands as the aeroplane's wheels hit the runway. When the plane slowed down and came to a halt, I looked out of the window and saw five police cars and a police van on the ground. There must have been at least seven uniformed police officers holding machine guns. They stood in a row and sported the same intimidating posture: legs in line with their shoulders, machine guns held in both hands from bottom right to top left, loaded and ready to use.

A bout of nerves ran through my body. 'Are they *all* here for me!?' I asked the officer next to me in surprise.

'Yes, I think so,' he answered.

'Will they handcuff me?'

'I'll ask them not to, don't worry, they are good guys. They are funny!' he said.

I appreciated the fact that he was trying to comfort me, but I wasn't comforted at all. They were there to lock me up, and I didn't expect them to be telling any jokes.

Passengers on the aeroplane exited first, all of whom were totally oblivious that there was a person on board under arrest. When the plane emptied, the officers who I'd flown with stood me up and walked me towards the back door of the aeroplane. Two of the armed officers from the ground had boarded the plane. The officer next to me opened his mouth as though he was about to speak to them, but the armed officers didn't give him the chance to say anything. Within a few moments they'd cuffed me and dragged me down the stairs that led to the ground. It all happened so quickly – my heart was pounding. As soon as I stepped off the plane I was overwhelmed by the sweltering heat – it must have been forty degrees. There was no breeze, just hot, petrol-fumed air. They pulled me down the steps so quickly that I almost fell over.

When we reached the ground, the officer slid open the side door of the small police van that was parked in between two police cars. He pushed me into a cage in the back of the vehicle and slammed the gate shut. He pulled open a rectangular section of the cage door.

'*Ela* – Come,' he said.

Luckily I could get by with basic Greek. I turned around and he gestured for me to put my hands through the gap so that he could take the handcuffs off me.

There were two short rows of metal benches and an old man

smoking a cigarette was sitting on one of them. I sat on the bench in front of him and then closed my eyes, taking a deep breath of the warm, smoke-filled air. Only a little bit of light shone into the van through a few small holes.

The van's engine turned on and the whole vehicle began to vibrate. The man put his hand on my shoulder and said something in Greek that I couldn't understand – he was speaking too fast. I turned around and looked at him. He initially appeared to be old, but I saw he was probably only in his fifties when I had a closer look. He looked like a frail, broken man with balding grey hair, and the few teeth he had were yellow and crooked.

'*Pos se lene?* – What's your name?' he asked.

'*Andro,*' I told him, which is what my grandparents have always called me. His facial expression told me that he was confused.

'*Eisai Ellinas reh?* – Are you Greek boy?' I understood.

I told him I was a Greek Cypriot from London and that my Greek wasn't very good at all.

'*Andro?* This name is not Greek!' he said to me in English. '*To onoma sou einai Andreas!* – Your name is Andreas!' he said.

'*Andro* … yeah, it's Cypriot I guess.'

He pointed to himself as a child would before an introduction. 'Yiannis Economou,' he said. I remember the name because it sounded Cypriot and like the word 'economy'. From what I understood, Yiannis was serving a twenty-year sentence for trafficking cocaine.

'*Pou pas?* – Where're you going?' he asked.

'*Patra,*' I told him.

'Ahhhh,' he said, then tutted.

My stomach sank as soon as he began to tut. '*Ti?* – What?' I questioned.

'*Tha sas gamisoun stin Patra!* – They're going to fuck you in Patras!' he said.

'No no,' I said, shaking my head. 'No fucking!'

'*Dekapente hronia ekana stin Patra fylaki* – I did fifteen years in Patras Prison,' he blurted while holding up his hands and gesturing ten, then five. '*Deka pente!* – Fifteen!' he said, smiling and exposing his few nicotine-stained teeth.

'Only police station, no prison!' I said in broken English. I attempted to help him understand with hand gestures, but I don't think that he did.

The journey to the Athens transfer jail could have been forty minutes, in which time I'd become drenched in my own sweat and dehydrated. When we arrived, a policeman slid open the van door and let us out of the cage. An officer grabbed my arm and handcuffed me before stepping out onto the concrete floor. I looked up and noticed that we were in some kind of underground car park. I had my blue Nike sports bag around my shoulder, some money in my pocket and my mobile phone, just in case I found the opportunity to call my family. They escorted both of us up a flight of stairs, where we were made to stand in a corridor. For the first time, I stood before a group of Greek police officers. After fighting the extradition for over a year and knowing what the police were capable of, standing there was surreal. They placed my bag on the floor, then they frisked me and took my mobile phone, my money and box of medication.

'*Ti ora?* – What time?' I understood him asking.

'*Octo* – Eight,' I replied.

A skinny officer took a pull of his cigarette and said something that I didn't understand while pointing at my bag. I used my initiative, opened it up and took out some clothes, an empty journal, a biro pen and the envelope Riya had given me. He grabbed my arm and escorted me to the end of the hallway, and Yiannis Economou was taken in the other direction. On the left-hand side was a barred gate.

'*Anixe!* – Open!' the officer shouted. I remember his colleague taking ages to acknowledge him. This seemed to irritate him. '*Anixe, reh vlaka!* – Open, you idiot!' There was a buzzing and clunking sound, which unlocked the gate for a few moments. He pulled it open and pushed me in, shutting the gate behind me.

I stood at the top of a long, thin corridor looking at a cracked, concrete floor and large barred windows along the right side. Jitters ran through me because I could hear men talking and shouting. They emitted the foul stench of a used ashtray and body odour, which lingered in the stuffy heat. On the left were five cells next to each other. I looked into the first cell, which was empty. In it there were five concrete beds, a few of which had thin mattresses to sleep on. Some of them were made of broken-up yellow sponge, but some were covered with a dirty green material – it looked disgusting. I looked back at the officer behind me, catching him just before he walked down the hallway. I was about to open my mouth to ask him which cell I should go into when he said, '*Opou thelis* – Whichever you want.'

As I walked past the second cell, I could see in my peripheral vision that it was full of men, which made me anxious. The doors of the cells were unlocked, so we were free to walk up and down the hallway. I walked into the next empty cell and I hoped that no one would come in. It was the first time that I'd been alone since I'd landed in Greece, and the first thing that I did was sit on one of the concrete blocks and hold the brown envelope that Riya had given me. I took a deep breath and slowly opened it, sliding out a photograph of us together. We were both smiling, both happy – we had no worries in the world back then. I welled up, but smiled to myself because it meant so much to me. I turned the photograph around and she had written 'thinking of you' on the back. My heart melted as I read the words – I lost my face in my hands and there were quiet tears.

14

DAY 1

Journal extract – Day 1 – 23 July 2009

So the journey begins. 5 beds per cell – stinks of stale smoke. Managed to get myself a free cell and hoping no one comes in at any point. There is a big group of prisoners next door to me. Who knows why they are here? I'm scared to even go to the toilet and walk past them. The floor in this cell is disgusting, dirty concrete and looks like compressed ash from the many years of prisoners flicking their cigarettes. Prisoners must have got pretty bored as the walls are covered in writing. One big word 'ALBANIA'. I wonder where he is from?

I put down the pen and took a brief moment to look at the writing and pictures that ex-detainees had drawn on the walls. I remember a huge illustration of a naked woman with long hair, lying on her back with her legs apart, touching her vagina. Her arms were out of proportion in comparison to the rest of her body, but other than that it was actually quite a good attempt. It'd been drawn with a blue biro, but the detainee who'd drawn it had managed to give the illusion of her hair flowing in the wind; he'd made a huge effort.

Someone else had drawn a picture of a skull with hypnotic eyes. Underneath was written 'so much cocaine in my brain'. The walls were covered in what looked like Arabic, English and some Greek writing. I remember reading a badly spelled poem: 'Some hate one, some hate tow (I think he meant 'two'), I hate one, I hate you.'

The mattresses were covered with a dirty, green material with a few whitish stains – I didn't want to think about what they were. As much as I beat the mattress with my palm, it wouldn't stop filling the air with dust. It seemed to be never ending, so I unzipped the cover at the tip of the mattress and pulled out an old, rectangular, yellow sponge. I didn't have a sheet to cover it, or any kind of pillow. I just lay down, closed my eyes and attempted to unwind, however difficult it proved to be.

'*Fileh mou* – My friend,' I heard. I opened my eyes and sat up. A guy, who was probably in his thirties, was standing in the cell with me. '*Café?*' he asked, holding a Nescafé *frappe* disposable plastic cup. It was the kind that had sachets of coffee and sugar inside; all you had to do was mix it with a bit of cold water and shake with the lid on to make a cold frothy coffee. I stood up, took the cup and thanked him. He introduced himself as Alex. I remember him offering me a cigarette, which I accepted. He told me that he was an illegal immigrant and was being deported back to Albania in two weeks' time.

Journal extract

I thought I would go and thank them all so I wouldn't look like a tosser. They ended up inviting me into their cell to drink the coffee and smoke. I just about got by with my little Greek. They didn't seem aggressive in any way. I am officially nicknamed 'o Anglos' (Englishman). I'm wearing an England T-shirt as well to top it off. Who knows, I could have been sitting in a room full of paedophiles, rapists and murderers – but my guess is drugs.

As I followed Alex into the cell next door, I looked up and noticed about ten sweaty men sitting on the concrete beds, most of whom were smoking and drinking a *frappe*. I could see that they had stocked up on food and drinks, like croissants, water and coffee, which made me think that they had been in the transfer jail for quite a while. I can only remember the faces of three men from that first day – a chubby, old Greek man called Dimitris, Alex the Albanian man and a man whose face reminded me of my mechanic back in London.

Dimitris must have been at least sixty-five years old and whenever he asked me a question, he would refer to me as '*paidi mou* – my child'. He told me he was going to Patras Prison for selling drugs, but he didn't look like the kind of guy to be involved in that kind of illegal activity – he looked more like a typical granddad!

Alex took the Nescafé cup from me, filled a quarter of the cup up with water and handed it back. *Shake it*, he gestured. I sat on the concrete bed and shook the cup, still concerned about the men surrounding me, most of whom were staring. Alex took the coffee cup from me and topped it up with bottled water.

They were bombarding me with questions, but my answer was usually: '*Den katalavo* – I don't understand.' I managed to ask Alex in Greek where the toilet was. He pointed down the hallway and gave me some toilet paper, which I appreciated. The toilets reeked and looked like they hadn't been cleaned in days – the stench of sewage was horrific. The toilet was on floor level and I'd never seen anything like it – I was baffled. It was an oval shaped bowl with a hole in the floor and two grips to put your feet on either side. It should have been white, but it was dirty and brown. I had to take my shorts and underwear off to squat, which was annoying because there was nowhere to hang them. I was multitasking, balancing and making sure my clothes didn't touch the floor, which was covered in piss. No soap, of course.

I walked back past the cell full of men and planned to go and sit on my own, but Alex insisted I sit with them. A policeman began to shout from the top of the hallway. '*Symeos Andreou!*' It sounded similar to my name, but wasn't my name. I thought that there may have been another Cypriot there, as 'Andreou' is a Cypriot surname. '*Symeos Andreou!*' he shouted again. Nobody in the cell moved, so he must have been calling for me. I walked out of the cell and over to the officer. The door buzzed open and he gestured for me to follow him down a long hallway, which made me tremble a little because I had no idea where I was being taken. I saw other sections of the transfer jail where people were being held as we walked past. I saw an old toothless man screaming, shouting and banging on the bars. There was even a woman in another cell, screeching – she sounded like a witch, but could just have easily been on crack. The officer led me into a room and sat me down on a chair. I looked up and I could see just enough to make out the outline of my lawyer George Pyromallis sitting behind a perforated metal panel. As soon as I saw him I could feel myself about to well up – it was a familiar face.

'Andrew, is everything OK in there?' he asked.

'No, not really,' I told him. I remember holding back tears and hoping that he had some good news.

'I should be able to get you out by Monday; you'll be transferred to Zante to speak with the investigating magistrate. Once you're there, I'm hoping she'll grant you bail,' I remember him saying.

I took a moment to figure out what day it was. *Is it still Thursday?* I thought. The day's unusual events had left me confused. I couldn't believe that I had been saying goodbye to my family and Riya only hours earlier. 'Yeh … I really hope so,' I said.

'You just have to be patient. It's not a big prison in here, where the big guys run everything, this is just a transfer jail.'

I spent the majority of the evening lying on the dirty mattress and staring at the ceiling; there was a heavy tremor inside of me that wouldn't go away. Every now and then I'd look at the picture that Riya had given me and allow my eyes to swell to the brink of tears.

At some point in the evening the officers gave all of the detainees a disposable plastic bowl of *fassolia* – beans – with stale bread and an orange that I forced down. After I ate I remember standing in the hallway and leaning my arms on the plastered windowsill, trying to avoid the cigarette ash. I stared through the barred window and watched the sun set behind a mountain in the distance – probably one of the same mountains that I'd seen from the plane. It looked far more soaring and intimidating from the ground. When witnessing such a beautiful view, a Londoner can feel only like he is a long way away from home.

I walked back to my cell and lay down. Before attempting to sleep, I summed up my first journal entry:

'I wish I knew how this story will end, or maybe I don't. It's time to go to sleep. I know tomorrow is going to be a tough day. I can't even cry here because everyone will hear.'

15

PATRAS AND ZAKYNTHOS

Journal extract – Day 2 – 24 July 2009

I'm one day closer to Justice. I can't even describe how much I miss everyone. Grinding your teeth helps stop the tears. I can't even think of good times because it's just making me emotional.

In the afternoon we were made to pack our things and stand in a row in the hallway. There were about ten of us being transferred to Patras and the officers handcuffed us together in pairs. I was cuffed to the man who looked like my mechanic, but with fewer teeth and lots of tattoos. They took us out of the hallway and down the metal staircase into the underground car park. A few officers were asking questions and becoming irritated because I couldn't understand them. The Greek dialect was also very different from the Cypriot, which made it even more difficult to follow!

There was a large, dark blue, coach-sized police vehicle in front of us that already held some prisoners from other jails. We were taken into the back of the coach where four of us were uncuffed and crammed into a cage that should have fitted a maximum of only two people. Thin metal walls surrounded us with small holes for air. In the cages were two metal seats facing each other with only a little bit of space in between them. Two of us had to stand while the other two sat because there wasn't enough room for four men. When standing up, we'd bend our knees and hunch our backs because the ceiling of the cage was quite low. We alternated for the delayed four-and-a-half-hour journey to Patras with our bodies squashed together. It was forty-degree heat and the men stank of body odour. Then again, so did I; I hadn't had the chance to shower and was wearing the same clothes as the previous day. The other three prisoners smoked throughout the journey, regardless of the lack of space or fresh air. When the coach drove over a bumpy bit of road, my arm would sometimes be burnt with the tip of a cigarette.

If I peered through one of the holes in the side of the van, I could just about see a beautiful blue sea and lofty mountains in the distance. It's as if they'd made the holes just big enough to give us a teaser of glorious freedom.

About an hour into the journey it dawned on me that I'd left my money and mobile phone in the possession of the transfer jail police officers. Before boarding the police coach, the officers must have been asking me whether I had any possessions to collect. I couldn't understand a thing – my mind had been elsewhere and I'd completely forgotten about it. I would have kicked myself if I'd had the space around me! Having my mobile phone would have been the only chance to contact my family in Patras, if the police there were to allow me.

'*Reh*, Tony Blair,' as one of the men in the cage referred to me. '*Ti ekanes?* – What did you do?'

I tutted. '*Tipote* – nothing,' I answered.

He laughed. The other two in the cage smiled with him. '*Gamise ta reh! Kaneis mas den ekane tipota!* – Fuck, man! All of us did nothing!' he said, winking with his left eye and blowing out smoke. His right eye was lazy with a glazed cataract.

It was hours later when the vehicle had come to a stop. I was the only one to be taken out of the cage and handcuffed. Finally being able to stretch my legs outside, I was guided to the top floor of Patras Police Station via a flight of external stairs that looked like a fire escape. They dumped me in a cell that was already occupied by another man who looked a bit like Sean Penn – the same curved nose and slim lips with a trimmed, brown moustache in between.

I had no access to a clock, so I started to lose track of the hours passing. At one point, an officer opened the cell door and gave us both something to sign. 'Sean' took the pen and offered his signature. I asked what I would be signing for, but the officer kept silent and wouldn't tell me. I remembered my mum's words: '*Don't sign anything!*'

'I'm not gonna sign it unless you tell me what it is!' I said.

'Don't sign it then!' the officer said in perfect English. He shut the door, locked it and walked down the corridor for a moment. When he came back, he slid open the letterbox-type hole in the cell door and called Sean Penn over. The officer handed him an envelope, which had about €5 in it.

'If you sign it they give you money for food!' said Sean.

The police stations didn't provide food or drinks for detainees – instead they purchased food from a local kebab shop.

'*Kyrie Astynome* – Mr Policeman (the respectful way to address an officer, which I'd picked up in the transfer jail), I'll sign it.'

'You don't wanna sign it remember? You don't wanna eat,' he mocked before turning around and walking back down the corridor towards his office.

'I just wanted to know what it was!' I shouted to the back of him. 'For fuck's sake,' I mumbled to myself.

'He's an arsehole. Don't worry,' said Sean Penn. He took his wallet out of his pocket and showed me a wad of fifties inside.

Journal extract (written a few days later)

The guy was Albanian, but could speak English. I didn't realise how many Albanians lived in Greece. He told me he was in for something that happened ten years ago. He was doing a friend a favour by giving him a lift home on his motorbike. It turned out the friend had shitloads of stolen goods in his bag. They were randomly stopped by the police and the guy ran off leaving him in the shit. I told him my story and he replied, 'Wow, that's one fucked-up story!'

The police in Patras were absolute cunts, they don't care one bit. I was standing by the little hole in the door saying 'Signo-mi Kyrie – *Sorry Sir', but they walk past the door and blank me, or hold up their hand. Didn't get any water for hours.*

It took a while for us to get the attention of one of the officers. When we finally did, Sean offered him some money to buy a range of sandwiches, kebabs, *frappes*, fizzy drinks, bottles of water and packs of cigarettes. I ate one of the sandwiches and tried not to drink too much, but he insisted that I did. I appreciated it and thanked him for the generosity. It must have been at least 5 p.m. and if it wasn't for him, I probably wouldn't have eaten or drunk anything for two days.

It wasn't long before Sean Penn was released from the cell and I was on my own. Later that evening I managed to get the attention of one of the officers and asked him if he could open my bag and hand me my journal to write in.

'This is not a market place, this is a police station,' he said. The comment frustrated me – I was desperate for the escape that writing had started to give me.

'Sorry sir, I didn't explain myself properly. I wasn't looking to buy the notebook, I already own it.'

'Do you think you are funny?' he said in his thick Greek accent. 'Why won't you give it to me!?'

'I am a policeman, I do not have to answer to you,' he blurted.

┼┼┼┼

Journal extract – Day 3 – 25 July 2009

The policeman woke me up at 3 a.m. Finally, I was allowed some clean clothes to wear. He said, 'It's going to be Monday when you see the judge.' Hearing that I would definitely be in custody for another two days was a crap feeling.

I carried all my stuff out of the cell and he told me to put it all on top of my bag, rather than inside it. He cuffed me, then made me pack my bag. He could easily have let me pack it before being cuffed. They all stood around and watched me attempt to do it, dropping my possessions. They laughed at me, saying, 'Kane grigora, Angleh malaka – Do it fast, English wanker.' I just about managed to pack it when he got annoyed and did it himself, deliberately scrunching up the envelope Riya had given me and squeezing my toothpaste in the bag. My clothes were covered.

They put me in the same kind of small police van that I was put in when I first landed in Greece. I was by myself, locked up in the back. There were lots of seats, but he pointed at one at the front and said, 'Sit there, and only there!' I didn't know why. I later realised that the air con hole above me was the only one without a protector, the kind in cars that allow you to change the direction of the airflow. He turned the air con on and I was freezing. I had been sweating from the heat and it just froze onto my skin.

After a while a policeman opened the cage door and asked if the air con was OK. I asked him to turn it down and gave him the hand gesture to say 'down, not up'. The bastard purposely turned it up. I closed all the other air holes and sat on the other side, even though he told me not to.

We had parked on the ferry, waiting for it to move – it must have been two hours before it did. With the engine turned off, the icebox suddenly became a sauna. I sat for hours, listening to the bastards laughing and joking. The sun began to rise. Looking out of the little hole at the side of the van – I could see blue sea and land. We had arrived in Zante.

A police car had been waiting at the marina to escort us to Zakynthos town police station in Zante. It was only 500 metres away, but the police insisted on driving in front of the van with flashing lights and sirens on. *Neeeeee noooooor, neeeeee nooooooor – big criminal coming through.* You would have been forgiven for thinking that they were holding Osama bin Laden, not Andrew Symeou, the student from Enfield. There wasn't even any traffic.

I was exhausted, but still filled with a numbing fear. There were only three cells in the police station. I walked past the middle cell; it was filled with about six or seven men who could just about fit inside. I was taken to the cell on the far left, which was already occupied by one man. It was about 3 metres wide by 4 metres deep and a solid concrete bed was covered with flea-infested, dirty blankets. Unlike Patras Police Station, the entrance to the cell was made up of vertical metal bars and a gate, as opposed to a solid steel door. The outside wall – opposite the entrance – had a small rectangular window that was welded shut. Outside it was forty degrees, so the heat in the cell was almost unbearable.

Journal extract

The other man in the cell sparked up a cigarette and took a huge pull. He looked at me and threw the box in my direction;

I assumed he was offering me one so I took it and thanked him. I asked him, 'Yiati eisai mesa – Why are you in here?' He put his hand to his nose and sniffed, so must have been something to do with cocaine. It wasn't long before he was released and I was alone.

I started to read The Da Vinci Code. *I brought it with me from home and the officers allowed me to have it inside the cell. About twenty minutes had passed and I could hear a female voice – I could have sworn that it was my mum. But the woman whose voice it was began to speak quickly in Greek and I realised that it wasn't her. My heart dropped. Suddenly a woman walked in front of the cell bars. It took a while to process, but it was my mum. Seeing her standing in front of me just brought all of the emotion back. I had got myself into the 'prisoner' frame of mind – I was in the zone. I couldn't process it. I couldn't get up to go and speak to her; it took a few seconds to walk towards her and hug her through the bars.*

I'd only been in police custody for a few days, but I had always had a close support network around me before my extradition. I was treated well by police officers in my own country – they'd refused to handcuff me and told me that the extradition should never have gone ahead. To then be treated like an animal in a foreign land (after a year of fearing it) was such a drastic transition that I fear my words won't do it justice. I wasn't merely held in a series of police cells waiting to be released, I constantly dreaded what the next day would bring. I reminisced about my past and questioned whether my future would be taken from me. Since my extradition, I'd been facing the journey alone and was forced to change my mentality. There had been no one around me to pick me up and it was completely draining to stay strong without them. But the moment I saw my mum standing in front of the barred cell gate, all of that strength I'd built since I was dragged to Heathrow Airport days earlier had crumbled away.

I was shaking as I squeezed her arm. No words can describe how comforting it was to see her. I knew that my family was there to pick me up, like they had always been. Not everyone's mother would be standing there like she was.

It wasn't long before my mum was asked to leave, then a police officer approached my cell and gazed at me through the bars like I was a caged animal in a zoo. '*Ehoume CCTV, xeris?* – We have CCTV, you know?' he said smiling.

'Take it to the judge then; we can show it to her so she can let me go home,' I said.

The officer's smile became malicious as he walked away.

For the remainder of my time in Zakynthos, the police allowed my parents to see me for a few minutes a day at specific visiting times. They came back a few hours later and my mum told me that the officer had also mentioned something to her about CCTV of the alleged attack. Her response was exactly the same as mine: it needed to be included in the investigation because it was a crucial piece of evidence that would clear my name – if it even existed.

My parents had brought me a sheet and towel, so it was an incredible feeling knowing that I could finally have a shower after four days in the heat. My dad called Riya on his mobile and passed the phone to me through the bars. I could hardly hold the phone because I was shaking so much. 'Just stay strong,' I remember her saying softly.

There was no toilet in the cell, so when I needed to go I'd have to stretch my arms through the bars and wave frantically at a camera in the hallway. Eventually, one of the officers would acknowledge the live feed on a screen in the office and come to let me go. Sometimes I would be waving at the camera for over an hour – and I knew that they were just sitting there drinking coffee and smoking. I could hear them only metres away, laughing and completely ignoring me! There was one time in particular when I'd been waving at the camera for at least an hour. I was absolutely desperate to go to the toilet. I began to shout at the top of my voice, '*Kyrie Astynome! Kyrie Astynome! Toualeta!* – Toilet!' I could hear one of the officers laughing with his friends in his office, so he must have been able to hear me. After a while, a few of the men in the neighbouring cell started to shout too, saying things like, '*Ade, gamimeno! Afiste to paidi na paei stin toualeta!* – Come on, fucking hell! Let the kid go to the toilet!'

The officer walked into the hallway of the jail, still sniggering about something that his friend had just said. As he approached the cell, he slapped on an angry frown and started to shout at the men who'd tried to help me. I believe the officer said something like 'Who do you think you are telling me what to do? I'm the policeman, not you!' He approached my cell and began to unlock the gate. 'Ten seconds, no more,' he said in English.

16

WE NEED GUNS

It was a long, hot and sweaty time spent locked up in Zakynthos town police station. I'd memorised every bit of graffiti marked on the cell walls, and I can still remember them. One detainee had written 'TONI MONTANA', the name of the infamous Cuban drug lord brilliantly portrayed by Al Pacino in the film *Scarface* (spelled incorrectly of course). He seems to be the fictional character that most small-time criminals idolise, regardless of the fact that he murders his best friend and ends up dead. I also remember reading '*PATSI! GOUROUNIA! DOLOFONI!*' – which was written in its rightful Greek lettering. I learned what these words meant on my second day in Zakynthos, when a man called Sakis Sofos was thrown into the cell with me. Sakis looked a little bit like a Greek Mel Gibson in his thirties: he had the same short, neat brown hair, which was slicked back exposing his defined widow's peak hairline. He pointed at each word one at a time and translated them for me.

'*Patsi* – this is what we call cops. *Gourounia* – pigs, they are fucking pigs! *Dolofoni* – killers, that's what they are my friend! Fucking murderers.'

I'd always known that the word for 'police' in Greek was '*astynomia*'. But Sakis told me that the slang word '*patsi*' had derived from the word '*patsa* – slap', and is a direct reference to the brutality with which they may enforce the law. It just goes to show how common police brutality is in Greece. Of course, 'not all Greek police are like that', as argued by the police officer from the aeroplane when I was extradited days earlier. Nonetheless, I found it bizarre that the frequency of police violence in Greece had actually influenced the slang word for 'cops', and it was one of the key reasons I stood wrongly accused of murder in the first place.

Journal extract – Day 4 – 26 July 2009

His name is Sakis Sofos and he works in the motorbike shop down the road from the police station as a mechanic. He told me why he was here and he spoke enough English for us to communicate. He and his wife are divorcing; they have a daughter together and he pays the wife €80 a week. He even voluntarily showed me his cheque book for proof! He said that his wife always wants more money for their child, but uses the money for herself.

He told me his life story and it was fucked up – abandoned at the age of eight, he was forced to bring himself up and work. He started off working at motorbike shops, working for very little money. He ended up selling weed, then cocaine, then heroin. By the age of twenty-five he was addicted to smoking the stuff. Once he settled down with his wife and had his daughter, he stopped everything. When he was selling heroin, he was earning €20,000 a week. Now he said he earns very little again.

He went to his wife's place to pick up his daughter. She asked him for more money, but he didn't have it. He was in the driver's seat of the car with his daughter sat next to him. His wife tried to grab his wallet, which was in the car. He grabbed

her arm and pushed her head into the steering wheel causing
the horn to sound.

Sakis acted out what had happened, using a pillow that he'd brought in to the cell as a prop of his wife's head. He thrust it into the wall and held it there. 'I fucking grabbed her hand and pushed her head; all the neighbours could hear the car going *beep beeeep.* Then I said to her, "You have no idea what I will do!"' His wife told the police what had happened. According to Sakis, she'd exaggerated the story, saying that he beat her and threatened to kill her.

'*Gynaikes, ti na kanoume?* – Women, what you gonna do?' Sakis smiled and shrugged his shoulders.

Suddenly, without any prior warning, a policeman opened the cell gate and handcuffed me from behind. He took me outside of the police station into a police car. 'Where am I going!?' I asked him.

'The court,' he replied.

'I thought that was tomorrow!?'

'Now! It won't be long,' he said. My dad was planning to bring me a shirt and trousers in the morning. The sudden change of plan was very frustrating. Now – for the judge's very first impression of me – I would be wearing flip-flops, shorts and a vest. She would be considering my bail, so I wanted to look as presentable as possible.

I was put in the back seat of the police car with my hands cuffed behind my back. We drove for about thirty seconds to the court down the road, where I sat in a hallway filled with policemen. A few of them surrounded me, holding machine guns to intimidate me. I could sense one of the young ones staring at me for ages, waiting for a glimpse of eye contact. I didn't look at him; I couldn't help but wonder whether these were the investigating officers who had pinned the crime on me. At the time I had no idea what those officers looked like.

My parents, who must have been told by George Pyromallis that I'd be seeing the judge briefly, walked in. My mum approached one of the older police officers and said, 'What's all this for? Are the guns really necessary?'

'*Etsi einai* – That's how it is,' he replied.

'You don't need guns,' my mum insisted.

'It's written down.'

'Where is it written?'

'In the papers, it says he is dangerous and we need guns,' he slurred.

'He isn't dangerous and you don't need guns. Where were these papers from?' she asked.

'From London,' the officer lied.

I saw the investigating magistrate for a brief moment only. It was just to present myself to her and confirm my name. It wasn't until the day after next when I went back to the court to make my first official statement. When I walked into the hallway of the courthouse for the second time, the officers didn't have guns. The same policeman approached my mum. 'You're right, we don't need guns. *Einai ena kalo paidi* – he's a good kid,' he said. The police had started to realise that I wasn't dangerous at all.

Journal extract – Day 5 – 28 July 2009

I woke up earlier than Sakis so I could prepare myself to see the judge. When Sakis woke up, straight away he sparked up a fag. His sister came to visit him and he asked her to get two frappes and two tiropittes [cheese pasties]. I said, 'No, don't be silly,' but he was the kind of man who wouldn't take no for an answer.

It was time for me to go; this time I could wear a shirt and trousers at least. Just before I put my shirt on I was standing in my boxers, and one of the officers walked over to the cell and asked me if I was ready. I smiled at him, 'Yeh I'm ready let's go,' I said. He laughed, so I think he realised what a stupid thing it was to say – like I'm going to go to court in my underwear.

They cuffed me again with my arms behind my back and told me to get in the car. Sitting in there, I could feel my shoulder about to dislocate.

I saw George Pyromallis waiting outside the court when we parked up. I nodded to him and he waved back. I stepped out of the car and was taken into the court and up the stairs again. I had a good chat with my parents and George after they finally took the cuffs off. I was surprised to see the cocaine guy from my first day in Zakynthos, who was strolling around the courts – he looked a bit lost.

It was finally time to see the investigating magistrate, so I walked into the room and took a seat in front of her desk. She was very young for a judge – quite pretty. She looked like Apollonia from The Godfather *– Michael Corleone's first wife when he runs away to Sicily. The one who accidentally gets blown up in the car because Michael was supposed to be driving. Anyway – she asked me about the sequence of events on the night in question, which I told her. I explained I wasn't even there! This took a good hour. She said, 'Is there anything else you would like to add?' I was thinking, Wow, where do I start? I told her everything – what I have been going through and how the end to this nightmare is in her hands. I told her everything under the sun that had to be said, but most importantly that the Hiles family deserves to know the truth and that I do not deserve to be held in custody any more. I could tell by the look in her eyes that she believed me. At some points I became emotional because it's been such a long road.*

When I left the room I told my parents that it had gone very well. George told me that once the investigating magistrate had spoken to the prosecution judge, I would then have to go in and answer a few of her questions too.

The judges were in the room for a good twenty minutes. I saw 'Apollonia' walk out – it was time to go and answer to the prosecutor.

You could tell that she was a smoker because of the ring of wrinkles around her thin lips. She must have been in her forties, no younger. Her hair was dyed blonde with mousy-brown roots. She didn't ask me to sit. I stood in front of her with George to my left and a translator to my right. She had the chance to ask me as many questions as she liked, but she asked me only one thing: 'Why did it take two years to come back to Greece!?'

Through the translator, I explained to her that it had been only one year. It took a year after Jonathan's death for an EAW to be issued. I told her that I appealed the extradition because I could prove my innocence and feared pre-trial detention. I wanted the case to be properly investigated, and was willing to fully cooperate without any unnecessary prison time on remand. I wasn't trying to prevent justice; I was trying to prevent further injustice.

Her response was loud and abrupt – she seemed to be speaking twice as fast as the average person. She and George argued in Greek to the point where they were almost shouting at each other. My eyes swung between them as though I was witnessing a fierce game of tennis. My heart raced in anticipation – her decision would change the course of my life. The only thing that I understood George shouting was: '*Pou nomizete oti tha trexei makria? Vrazilia!?* – Where do you think he will run to? Brazil!?'

'What's going on!?' I asked George frantically.

'She wants to put you in prison,' he said quickly before continuing to argue with her. I felt my knees about to give way. I contained myself from an emotional outburst and took a deep breath. It wasn't over yet – the investigating magistrate still had a say in whether I would make bail.

When we left the room I remember seeing Sakis sitting down, waiting to speak to the prosecutor for his own case. He could see that I was in a bad way – but I still shook his hand, knowing that I would probably never see him again. My mum began to cry when George told her of the prosecutor's wish to put me in prison pre-trial. My great-uncle Andreas owned a flat in Athens that he was willing to let me live in, so even bail in Greece wouldn't have been a problem. However, the prosecutor couldn't understand why I'd appealed the extradition in the UK – it made no sense to her. She seemed to have convinced herself that I would run away at the first chance! But if that were the case, I would have done a runner months earlier instead of taking a taxi to Belgravia Police Station and handing myself over to the authorities to be extradited!

The anticipation was unbearable and my legs fidgeted. I needed to know the outcome, but dreaded hearing the words at the same time. The investigating magistrate and the prosecutor sat in the room together for at least another twenty minutes. I could hear them arguing through the door, but couldn't make out the words. I believe that the investigating magistrate was pushing for my bail and the prosecutor was opposing it. The investigating magistrate walked out of the room, past us and back into her own office.

'Come on,' said George. We all followed her into the room and I sat down. I desperately needed her to tell me that I would be released until a trial. She spoke in fast Greek, really quietly. I couldn't understand. My mum could. She stood up and I watched her eyes fill with tears.

'You didn't make bail,' George said.

╫╫

Life doesn't always go to plan. We all at some point hear things that we don't want to hear, or have to do things that we just don't want to do. Bad things happen – and we may have no control over them. The only thing that we have some control over is our reaction. When I found out that I was definitely going to a Greek prison, my instant reaction was to wail. I wailed so loudly that every person in the building could probably hear me – but I didn't give a shit. My heart was broken and I was being taken away from my life for no reason. I couldn't bear the thought of being held in a Greek prison, especially without knowing how long for. I didn't want to face the reality of the situation; I felt incapable of doing so. I was a strong-minded person, but I wasn't some streetwise kid who could deal with things like prison. I'd done nothing wrong – all that I had ever wanted was a thorough investigation so that I could be vindicated of the crime and there could be a possibility of finding the real culprit. Instead, I'd been given a terrifying prison sentence. To say that it was unfair is an understatement: it was a gross miscarriage of justice.

I was in a state of utter shock, shaking with teary eyes. 'I'll give you money! However much you…'

'No Andrew!' George interrupted me.

'Please, it wasn't me,' I stammered. The investigating magistrate handed me a pen and some documents. She couldn't make any eye contact – I could tell that she didn't want to lock me up. This decision came from the prosecutor, who knew very little about the case.

'You have to sign here, Andrew; all this says is that you understand the decision,' said George.

I held the pen in my hands and looked at the small wad of Greek documents in front of me. I stared at it for a moment and took a breath, stopping myself from any more tears – but I couldn't do it.

'No!' I screamed while bursting into another flood of tears. 'I can't. I can't do it. I don't understand the decision!'

'Andrew, you have to do this,' George added.

The sense of injustice that had been burning inside of me for months was ready to erupt. 'Do I? Do I really!?'

My attention flipped to the police officer who was standing in the corner of the room. The translator standing next to me flinched as I swung my arm out to point at the officer with a full arm stretch. I heard gasps of surprise in the room. 'What … is this guy gonna beat me into signing it!? That's how it works here!' I roared.

I was sent out of the room to calm down without having signed the document. Sitting in the hallway of the court, I continued to sob as loudly as I could.

Prison.

I couldn't even process the thought.

It was dawning on me: I'd be locked up in a foreign prison for days – weeks – months – maybe longer. It was real. It was actually going to happen. Fuck. I couldn't even begin to imagine what it might be like.

My hysteria wasn't purely out of fear; it was also out of frustration. The decision was exactly what we'd been fighting against for over a year; it was disgraceful and inhumane. Granting me bail wouldn't have changed the prosecutor's life in the slightest, but her choice to lock me up changed the entire course of mine. I was a twenty-year-old student of good character and with no criminal record. I was an innocent man – all I had ever asked for was the chance to prove it.

17

FIFTEEN MINUTES

I fainted in the hallway of the courthouse, and I'd never fainted before in my life. The next thing I remember was waking up in a hospital to the sound of screams. I could hear them coming from the hallway; two women were crying in states of distress. I opened my eyes and witnessed a nurse rushing down the corridor pushing a hospital bed. It carried a man covered from head to toe in blood and my hair stood on end at the sight. It was as though I'd woken up in hell already.

I was startled when I noticed a group of police officers standing to my left. Confused, with blurry eyes, it all came flooding back. After being briefly examined, the doctor said that it was fine for me to leave, so the police officers handcuffed me and I had to walk slowly through the hospital like a criminal. Staff members and people in the hospital hallway were watching and it was humiliating.

As soon as we were back at the police station I was thrown back into the cell – trapped physically, but also in my own mind. I couldn't stop shaking and my head pounded with deadening fear. It was difficult to absorb the news, especially as I was alone. I walked up and down the cell in an erratic state of panic and kept repeating to myself, *It'll be OK, it'll be OK*. Claustrophobia began to get the better of me; it was as though the walls were closing in. I didn't want to sit down, I didn't want to stand up; all I wanted was for it not to be true.

After a few hours of what I can only describe as self-inflicted mental torture, a police officer opened the cell gate and moved me to the cell next door, which was already full of six or seven men. I was in a vulnerable, numb state and the officer didn't hesitate to make my situation worse. It was unbearably hot because the window was welded shut – and it didn't help that we were all squashed together, the majority sleeping on the concrete floor. Being in that situation – just after discovering that I would be thrown in a foreign prison for a crime that I knew I hadn't committed – added to the torture that I'd already inflicted on myself. It was ridiculous to squeeze us all in there because there were two empty cells in the police station, one on either side – it made absolutely no sense. My parents later told me that one of the officers insinuated that he would take a payment to move me back to the cell on my own. He tried to take advantage of the situation, believing that he could make a profit out of my family. My mum considered paying him, but refused. She's a woman of principles and didn't want us to be labelled as those who give bribes. Instead, she returned to the police station with bottles of soft drinks and treats for everyone in the cell – ensuring that the officer could see. I'm proud that she did that; I'd rather have suffered than give the officer anything.

There wasn't enough room for us all to lie down. When night came, two men had to sleep with their backs up against the wall in a sitting position. When finally drifting off to sleep I dreamed of my old manager from Superdrug (where I used to work part time). It's strange that I still remember the dream, and I have no idea why she made a cameo appearance in it. She locked me up in a dark underground dungeon with a group of people. An unknown person was swinging a knife violently and chasing me. The person slaughtered everyone in the dungeon before going missing. Light shone in from the ceiling, where I could see my ex-manager opening a door. 'Look what you did!' she shouted. I was the only one left, surrounded by corpses.

I woke up in a puddle of sweat. Most of the men in the cell had been woken up and were staring at me. The one closest to me was wide awake, smoking a cigarette. 'Why do you scream like this?' he asked in broken English.

It took me a little while to realise what had happened. 'Sorry,' I mumbled.

'You shouted, "It wasn't me, it wasn't me!"'

It was very difficult to mentally prepare myself for prison. I was a trembling mess and I couldn't come to terms with it. I had absolutely no idea what to expect. The only thing I had to go by was films, and the depictions of prison that I'd seen were terrifying.

The next day my parents convinced the chief police officer to let them bring in a psychiatrist to prescribe me some medication. I was given pills and liquid drops that were taken orally. I have no idea what the hell they were, but I spent the next two days in Zakynthos Police Station as high as a kite. Luckily I'd been moved back into the cell on my own, but felt sorry for the men in the cell next door. The way they were being treated was outrageous, and I couldn't think of any reason for it other than racism. 'Why don't you put a few of them in here?' I said to one of the officers – who ignored me.

When my dad came to visit, he told me that I was being taken to a young offenders' prison rather than a maximum-security prison, which sounded far better. With the medication in my system and the knowledge that I'd be locked up with young offenders, I began to think more positively. Once I was settled in the juvenile prison, it would just be a waiting game before the trial. What I wasn't looking forward to was the transfer via Patras again.

The drugs that the psychiatrist gave me were too strong. When I was transferred back to Patras I was completely spaced-out, which made the journey far more enjoyable. I'd been so depressed and anxious that my emotions flew to the other end of the spectrum and I was overcome with joy – it was as though the drugs were a release. The police officers put me into the back of a small police van on my own. The journey was about three hours long and I sang the entire way, even when we were parked on the ferry. I sang – very badly – at the top of my voice so the police officers on board could hear me. My repertoire included some '90s pop songs and Bob Marley classics, but I also performed my own version of Queen's 'Bohemian Rhapsody', Peter Andre's 'Mysterious Girl' and rapped the whole of 'Forgot about Dre'. I really pissed them off.

By the time I reached Patras I'd sobered up. I was thrown into the same cell that I'd been held in a week earlier and was then told that I would be leaving for Athens in 'fifteen minutes'. I sat for fifteen minutes – ready to go. Hours passed and I was still sitting there. The sun went down and a policeman finally unlocked the cell door. '*Ela* – Come,' he said. I followed him out of the cell, assuming that I was being transferred to Athens, but he put me in another cell with three Romanian men – Leonarde, his brother Constantin and Remos. In the end, it wasn't fifteen minutes that I waited – it was four days. On each of these days I was told that I would be transferred to Athens at some point, but the *patsi* were just toying with me. The days passed extremely slowly and the four of us were crammed in together with no space to walk about. I tried my hardest not to let claustrophobia get the better of me, like it had in Zakynthos Police Station days earlier. I just lay on one of the bunks and did nothing else but stare at the ceiling for the entire four days. It's funny how many contradictory thoughts can pass when someone has too much time on their hands. I would convince myself that the juvenile prison would be absolutely fine and that I'd sail through before clearing my name in court. Then I would start to worry: what kind of young offenders could be in this prison? Perhaps they were far more immature than adult prisoners and would make my life absolute hell.

Journal extract – 3 August 2009 – Day 12

It was a very small cell with two bunk beds. Only one of the Romanian guys, Leonarde, could speak English, which he said he had learned from TV. He was all right I guess. He was short but looked like he went to the gym all the time. He was covered in all these stupid tattoos; there were lots of different-coloured animals all over his body. He even had one of Disney's 101 Dalmatians on his arm. What would possess anyone to do that to themselves? Anyway, he told me he got caught for doing an insurance scam for €150,000 and that the police there beat him for no reason.

There was no shower in the cell, just a hole to shit and piss in with no flush – so it stank. It was a long four days. After being locked up for over a week, to then be locked up with these guys was painful.

They [the police] woke us up this morning at 5 a.m. and put us in the police coach. I was locked up in my own little cage this time, unlike the first time when four of us had had to squeeze in. I thought I was going to the under-21s prison, which I think is called Evalonia, or Avlona … something like that. But I find myself in the same transfer prison I was in when I first landed in Athens. Tomorrow is when they will take me to the young offenders' prison and I have no idea what to expect.

18

HOW TO GET HIGH WITHOUT DRUGS

4 August 2009, Avlona, Attica

The next morning I was transferred to Avlona – about an hour's drive north of Athens. Five prisoners and I were escorted off the vehicle. I was handcuffed to an African man who must have come from a different transfer jail. We walked towards the wide, off-white arch that loomed over the entrance into the complex. I remember squinting at him, using my free arm to block the sweltering sun out of my eyes.

'*Milas Anglika?*' I asked him – but my question was ignored. I repeated it in a language that he may have been more acquainted with: 'So you speak English?' He was probably more likely to speak English than Greek; I don't know why I hadn't asked him in my mother tongue the first time.

'Yes. We speak the same language. I am fed up with everyone talking to me in the Greek language. I am Nigerian, I understand nothing.'

We walked through the gate onto the site, practically hand in hand. I glanced at the arch above me, which when translated into English said 'Special Juvenile Detention Centre Avlona' in thick black lettering. *This isn't real prison*, I thought, attempting to downplay the situation. After almost two weeks of being held in scorching police cells and filthy transfer units, all I wanted was to go home. I'd become weak from dehydration, not even able to clench my fists. In the roasting forty-degree heat, I could have passed out again – just like I had in the Zakynthos courthouse.

The guards uncuffed us as we entered a holding cell that was already filled with a few other young offenders. I took another look at the Nigerian man without the glare of the sun obstructing my vision. He was clearly not younger than twenty-one, and looked like he could have had teenage children! I asked him how old he was and he told me that he was twenty-eight – but he looked older than that. He lit a cigarette. 'You know, you are not a real man until you go to jail.'

I nodded my head and gave a subtle smile, but I didn't really agree with him. I told him that Avlona was a prison for offenders under the age of twenty-one and asked him why they'd brought him there. He seemed surprised, having no clue that it was a juvenile prison.

'It is?' he asked.

Over the next few months I would see far more grey hairs, wrinkles and receding hairlines than you'd expect to find in a young offenders' prison. But without a passport, illegal immigrants living in Greece appeared to pass for whatever age they wanted to be.

A man walked into the holding cell and introduced himself as Costas 'the male nurse', and was the spitting image of the actor Tim Curry. He began to ask each of us medical questions in either Greek or English. When he asked about the recreational use of drugs, the African man looked to the ground as though he was an embarrassed child. Costas asked each of us one by one whether we took drugs.

'And you?' he asked the man.

'*Heroini*,' he replied.

It was the first time I'd ever met an active heroin user. I pictured him strapping a belt around his bicep and tightening it with his teeth. I imagined his vein throbbing and injecting himself with the translucent brown liquid – like in films.

Some time later, a prison guard escorted me into a small room where I experienced the first of many strip searches. I had to take off all of my clothes, which was degrading, but I knew it was a procedure that they had to complete. The guard looked as though he hated the situation as much as I did.

'*Archidia* – Testicles,' he said – trying extremely hard to ensure that we didn't make any awkward eye contact. He checked me while I held them up, and then asked me to bend forward so he could look to see if there were any drugs in my arse. I put my sweat-drenched clothes back on and he began to rummage through my possessions, throwing away anything that could possibly contain illegal substances. Having been found with no weapons in my sports bag or drugs in my anus, I began the dreaded walk to my cell. With each step that I took, I became more overwhelmed with anxiety. I was taken down a corridor to the right that had off-white walls with dry, cracked paint that was a nicotine-stained yellow.

By this stage, my nostrils had become accustomed to the stench of stale cigarette smoke and warm body odour. The sound of pigeons fluttering and cooing resonated in the hallway. I looked to my left – the top of the entire wall had a series of rectangular, barred windows that started at the beginning of the hallway and continued all the way to the main wing. Each window had a dirty, translucent plastic shutter in front of it – and several pigeons had become trapped in between the shutters and the steel bars. The ones that were alive were suffering slowly – so it seemed that I wasn't the only one who was being held there unjustly. A few pigeons were dead and rotting, which left a slight stench of decaying flesh in the corridor.

At the time of my arrival, the *Parartima* wing was empty – inmates were either locked up or were working in other areas of the complex. It was a thin hallway with only ten cells; five on each side. There was also a large, shared cell of about ten prisoners, which they called '*thalamos*' – and many of the inmates housed there were from adult prisons. They'd been transferred to Avlona because they were tradesmen and the prison would use them for free labour.

I'd been allocated to cell five. On my walk down the corridor I noticed that the floor was uneven and slightly indented, which left a pool of backlogged sewage water in front of cell one. I had to walk through it wearing flip-flops. The water surrounded my feet, which was the closest I'd been to showering in the six days of forty-degree heat. I'm sure it was infested with germs, but at least it was cool and soothing. I imagined myself jumping into a swimming pool and dunking my head under to hydrate my skin.

My cell was empty because (I would later find out) my cellmates were working as cleaners in another wing. When the guard slowly opened the heavy metal door, the first things that I noticed were the colourful towels that covered the majority of the cell walls. They were suspended from the ceiling for decoration and each one had a different image on it. There was a Native American Indian surrounded by a map of Canada, Warner Bros' Tasmanian Devil and many others. It gave me an impression of the kind of people that my cellmates were – they'd clearly made an effort so that the cell would be a less depressing place to live – it was a good sign. What I couldn't figure out was how were they able to stick the towels to the ceiling without them falling down?

The prison guard pointed to one of the top bunks and closed the large steel door behind him. I heard him insert the key, making a loud clunking sound as he turned it. I dropped my sports bag and pushed it under one of the two metal-framed bunk beds, which met to make an 'L' shape.

A sheet hung from the ceiling over a doorway, which led to a wash area. There was a sink, a shower basin, a hose and a toilet at floor level that you had to squat over to use. I walked in and drenched my face with chilled water. When wiping the water from my eyes, I noticed a great deal of pornographic images stuck on the walls of the toilet area.

After showering myself with a cold-water hose and changing into a clean pair of shorts and a T-shirt, I jumped up and pulled myself to my bunk (there were no ladders). I tried to avoid leaving a distinctive wet footprint on my unknown cellmate's bed, which was directly under mine. I remember lying there and grinding my teeth – it was what I would do when trying to stop myself from sobbing. I turned to my side, feeling the roasting sun burn the back of my neck through the wide, steel-barred window above me. I allowed my heart rate to decrease to a regular pace and my body sunk into the thin, rigid mattress beneath me. I was exhausted – but every time I reached the brink of unconsciousness, the reality of what was happening would hit me. I would suddenly open my eyes and have to take a fast, gasping breath – it was as if I was being suffocated by my own anxieties. I thought of being at home with my family again. Only then was I able to drift off into a light sleep – into my own world, where everything was OK.

Then I heard voices.

When I opened my eyes, three other young men were in the cell with me. They introduced themselves as Fivos, Christos and Yiannis. I jumped down from the top bunk and took a seat at the small plastic garden table in the middle of the cell.

Fivos was the only one who spoke English. He was broad and tall with a defined nose and jawline. He told me that I was lucky to be put in a cell with 'the Greeks', then pointed towards the cell next door. 'You're lucky you weren't put with the stinky Somalians,' he said.

'If I was lucky, I wouldn't be here my friend,' I told him.

He smirked awkwardly. Fivos didn't seem like the kind of guy to smile very often. 'We are all unlucky. *Yiati eisai mesa reh?* – Why are you inside, man?'

When asked this question in prison, the best thing to do is give away as little information as possible. Don't attempt to defend your innocence, because nobody cares. I was yet to learn this. On my first encounter, I told him that I was innocent and I briefly explained my story to him. He laughed and looked at the others, telling them in Greek what I'd just said. The three of them sniggered together.

'*Nai kalo!* – Yeh sure!'

Christos looked at me and said something far too fast for me to comprehend. His voice was quite high pitched and yappy like a Greek Chris Tucker. Fivos translated for me. 'He said all of us did nothing! Everyone here is innocent!'

I'd heard that before. 'So why are you inside?'

Fivos told me that he was caught with a gun and a copious amount of cannabis. 'I had one friend who was a fucking *roufianos*.'

'What's a *roufianos*?'

'A rat! He told the police everything to save himself. *Ti na sou po? Malakas einai* – What can I tell you? He's a wanker.'

I nodded and lit a cigarette that Christos had offered. 'What about these guys? What're they in for?' I exhaled.

'Christos … well, he is an arsehole. He stole half the fucking cars in Athens with no gloves! Yiannis did the same.'

I looked over to Christos who was nodding and smiling. For a guy with such a tough face, he had a smile that turned him into some kind of jolly cartoon character. He was of medium height, quite defined and muscular with a short crew cut and several black prison tattoos. The most distinctive was the shadow of a scorpion on the outside of his left forearm – there were also two curved, oriental-looking symbols on his chest, one above each nipple.

He made a gun shape with his thumb and index finger, then pointed it to his head and twisted it. '*Malakia*,' he said, which quite literally means 'wank'. The gesture was another way of admitting that his crimes were stupid things to do. Actually – it seemed like the word *malakia* is relevant in most sentences in a Greek prison. If someone steals your cigarettes, that is a *malakia*. If you lose your telephone cards, that is a *malakia*. If a judge sentences you to life in prison, that's a big *malakia*. If anything bad happens, if you embarrass yourself, or if someone says something that's untrue, there is only one appropriate word. What I found quite funny is that they all seemed to call each other *malaka* – 'wanker' when we would say 'mate'. It sounded strange, like hearing an English guy say to his friend, 'All right, wanker?' 'Yeah, not too bad, tosser, how are you?'

Christos grabbed a sheet from his bed, wrapped it up like a rope and twisted it. He held it tightly with his fists and looked at me with his animated smile. As he did so, I became aware of the tattooed letters on each of his knuckles, which spelled out '*ΜΑΦΙΑ* – mafia'. Fivos spotted where my eyes were directed and laughed. 'That used to say "*MAPIA* – Maria", his ex-girlfriend, but she fucking dumped him so he changed it to mafia,' Fivos said.

I nervously chuckled as Christos stood up and began to walk over to my side of the cell. Fivos put his arm out, stopping Christos in his tracks.

'And you see this *Kinezika* – Chinese shit?' Fivos pointed to each of the oriental-looking symbols that were tattooed on

Christos's chest. 'He did this to himself here a few months ago. This one means "life" and this one means "death", but he is stupid. He did it in a mirror and now they are both fucking backwards!'

I thought it was pretty funny, but I also found it incredible that he knew how to tattoo another person, let alone himself. Catching me by surprise, he tried to wrap the sheet around my neck.

'*Ti kanis reh?* – What are you doing, man?' I blurted.

He was breathing in and out rapidly, giving me the impression that he wanted me to copy him and hyperventilate.

'Christos wants to do a trick,' Fivos told me while lying in his bunk.

'*Ohi reh!* – No, man! He wants to do it!' I said anxiously, pointing at Yiannis. Yiannis was tall and thin with a shaved head. He didn't look like a typical Greek; he was darker toned and looked like he could be Indian.

'*Pame* – Come on then,' Yiannis said. He started to hyperventilate, taking deep breaths as fast as he possibly could. As the air rapidly flowed in and out of Yiannis's lungs, Christos loosely wrapped the sheet around his neck. After a minute of quick hyperventilation, Christos pulled both ends of the sheet as hard as he could, strangling Yiannis with all his might. I could see the veins in Christos's arms throbbing – his solid bicep was bulging. He had angry eyes and his teeth were clenched tightly together as though strangling Yiannis was a therapeutic way to release his anger. I witnessed the entire thing, unsure of whether to be more confused or astonished at what was happening. What disturbed me most was the colour of Yiannis's face. I didn't think it was possible for a human's face to become so rich in different shades of blue and purple. Fivos lay in his bottom bunk – he didn't seem to care that Christos was killing Yiannis. I turned my head back to witness the strangling. It had been going on for far too long by this point.

'*Ade, kani* – All right, enough,' I said, but everyone ignored me. The strangling continued and Yiannis fell to his knees. He began to make gagging noises and was clearly desperate for an intake of oxygen. Christos pulled the sheet even tighter.

'He's killing the guy!' I said to Fivos, but he just looked back at me and gave a closed-mouth chuckle. My heart began to race a bit – I was about to witness a murder. 'All right all right, stop *reh*!'

The gagging noise stopped. After giving the sheet one last tug, Christos loosened it and Yiannis collapsed frontwards. His left cheek slammed onto the dirty concrete floor. There was a pause. No sudden intake of breath.

'He's dead.' We all looked down at his motionless body. I looked at Christos. 'He's fucking dead,' I said.

The gleam in Christos's eyes told me that he'd realised something was wrong. He slid his bare foot out of his flip-flop and gave the unconscious Yiannis a little nudge with his big toe to check if he was alive. Fivos sat up, finally taking notice of what was happening. Before I had the chance to check his pulse, Yiannis took a deep gasp of oxygen and began to shake. It looked as though he was having some kind of fit. Strands of saliva trickled from his mouth and he began to murmur like a zombie and crawl all over the floor. At this point Fivos and Christos burst into laughter.

It took Yiannis about a minute before attempting to bring himself up to his knees. He repeatedly tried to stand up, but kept falling back down to the floor. His face was covered with his own drool and his glazed eyes met mine for a brief moment. He looked straight through me, as though he had no idea I was even there. After a few minutes he managed to bring himself to his feet – then stumbled all around the cell and fell onto the plastic garden table like a drunk, knocking over the plastic ashtray that was filled with grimy water and cigarette butts. When finding his feet he sat on the edge of Fivos's bottom bunk and stared into space. He was silent. Christos tapped Yiannis's face with his palm, but it was more like a subtle slap. He lit up a cigarette and passed it to Yiannis who took it, but remained in a euphoric state. Before managing to take a puff, Yiannis held the cigarette in his hand until half of it had burnt out. He finally managed to bring the cigarette to his lips – he took a long drag and the ash fell onto his lap. Holding the smoke in his lungs for a moment, he exhaled. '*Imoun sto spiti mou reh* – I was in my house, man,' he mumbled. Yiannis began to tell us how amazing the experience was, that he'd hallucinated and believed he was at home. In fact, he loved the experience so much that he did it again – straight away. Only this time Christos strangled him with his bare hands. I don't think Christos or Yiannis really considered how danger-ous the stunt was. They thought it was hilarious.

That evening I lay on my top bunk facing the wall – the first night of many. I tried to convince myself that it wasn't so bad and that I wouldn't be there for long. Thinking about my family – thinking about Riya and my friends – I wouldn't allow myself to get emotional. *Man up*, I repeated in my thoughts. I took a deep breath and filled my lungs with warm, smoke-polluted air. My cellmates didn't seem like a threat to me, they were just a bit nuts.

There was a small TV in the corner, which was connected to many speakers that had been mounted around the cell in card-board boxes. Fivos told me that Christos was a genius when it came to electronics, so other inmates would trust him to fix their electrical appliances. When asked to fix another inmate's televi-sion, he would sometimes steal the internal speakers. He'd cut round holes into small cardboard boxes that the speakers could fit in. He mounted the speakers in them by burning the tips of drinking straws with a cigarette lighter and dripping the melted plastic between the edge of the speaker and the box, which acted as a strong adhesive. When I was told that, I realised that it was melted plastic straws that were used to stick the colourful towels to the ceiling in the cell! I was impressed – my cellmates seemed to be imaginative and resourceful.

I turned around and could just about see the small television in the corner of the cell that my cellmates were watching. The volume was far too loud because of Christos's DIY surround-sound system. I still remember the documentary that was on, which was in English but with Greek subtitles. It was about a Swiss woman called Elisabeth Sulser who supposedly had 'fused senses'. Apparently, the sensory area in her brain was overactive, causing all of her senses to trigger at the same time. For example, she claimed that she could 'see' sounds. Whatever sound she heard, depending on the frequency, she would see different strands of colour in her peripheral vision. I remember her saying something along the lines of: 'When a dog barks, I might see green. When a car drives past, I might see pink. If a telephone rings, I can see blue.' Then Christos let out the loudest fart I'd ever heard.

'*Kitrino!* – Yellow!' he shouted.

On that note, I rolled over and forced myself to sleep.

19

LAS VEGAS

The next day I woke up to the familiar clunking sound of a guard opening the cell door. There was a moment of confusion – it took me a few moments to remember where I was. I felt numb when it finally dawned on me.

'*Symeou!*' the guard shouted in his heavy Greek accent while poking my leg with the master key. He clapped his hands and motioned for me to hurry up. '*Pame, pame!* – Let's go, let's go!'

I was taken out of the Parartima wing into a small office where I was presented to a woman who introduced herself as Zoe, the social worker. She must have chain-smoked three or four cigarettes in the fifteen-minute period of me being there. I looked around the room, noticing a number of religious icons hanging on the walls. A clock presented a faint outline of Greece; the sound of the second-hand ticking from island to island resonated in the room. Her desk was messy and the ashtray overflowed with lipstick-stained cigarette butts. She asked me to fill out an application form and list the family members that would be visiting me. The entire thing was written in Greek and I had to ask her to translate it. I took the forms that she'd placed in front of me and began to write. Every pen that I attempted to use either wasn't working or was so faint that you could hardly see the writing.

'Do you have any other pens? These pens don't work.'

She smiled and lit up another cigarette, almost ignoring my question. A strand of her mousy-brown hair hung in front of her face. She brushed it behind her ear with the claw-like red nail on her index finger. I shook my head to myself and took a deep, stinging breath of the air-conditioned, recycled smoke around me. I had to press the pen down as hard as I could, as if to carve the letters into the paper itself. I handed her the forms along with the broken pens. She filed the documents and placed the useless pens back into the pot on her desk, which really frustrated me!

'My lawyer told me that I should be here for only about five days, so there won't be many visits. My bail appeal is on 8 August.'

Zoe smiled, exposing a few nicotine-stained teeth. She gave one big nod, resting her double chin against her chest for a brief moment. Smoke exited each of her nostrils like a dragon. 'You will be here a lot longer,' she said, chillingly, while taking another puff of her cigarette.

I left the office and walked back down the corridor towards the Parartima wing. The comment left me irritated. Who was she to tell me that so confidently? How could she have known? She wasn't a lawyer or a judge! I refused to believe her.

There was a barred gate that prevented prisoners from entering or exiting the wing. I stood behind it, completely unaware of how to open it. An African prisoner walked up to the gate and stood next to me. He was short and light-skinned with an unusual hairline that began at the top of his head. 'You have to shout "*ypallileh*",' he told me. We looked over to the guard sitting about 30 feet away from us. In front of him was the bright red button that controlled the gate's lock.

'*Ypallileh!*' the African man shouted.

The prison guard must have heard, but chose not to acknowledge him.

'*Ypallileeeh!*' he shouted again, prolonging the last syllable. A deep buzzing and metallic clonk meant we could push the gate open and walk through.

'What does it mean?' I asked.

'I have no fucking idea,' he responded with a twang of an American accent. I had a feeling that he'd picked it up from American television shows. 'Where're you from? Australia or some shit?'

'England.'

He had confused, squinted eyes that avoided contact with mine. 'What the hell are you doing in Avlona? What did you do?'

I briefly explained why I was there, but I didn't go into too much detail, remembering what Fivos's response had been when I did a day earlier.

'And why should I believe you?' he asked.

I ignored the question and dismissed it with a smile. 'Well, why are you here then?'

'I was in Omonia Square and some police found a big bag of heroin in a trash can. They said it was mine.'

'Was it?'

'It wasn't mine,' he slurred.

We stopped in our tracks while I lit a cigarette and offered one to him. 'And why should I believe you?' I exhaled.

His eyes swung towards me. It looked like he wasn't happy with what I'd just said – then he smiled. I lit the cigarette for him that he'd put between his lips.

'You know what the police officer said to me? The one who arrested me?' he took a big puff of his cigarette, holding it between his thumb and index finger like a spliff.

'What did he say?'

'"Well, if it's not your drugs then it belongs to one of your brothers" – you know what he's saying right?' He gazed at me, waiting for me to ask as we stepped into the hallway of Parartima.

'What was he saying?'

'He's saying all us fucking *arapides* – niggers are all the same. It doesn't matter whose it was.' He shrugged his small shoulders and walked through the puddle of water on the floor. I looked down and noticed that he was wearing brown sandals; they were slightly too big for him and it didn't help that one of the buckles was broken. In addition to what he was saying, something as insignificant as a broken buckle made me feel sorry for him. As he shut the door to cell one behind him, he told me that his name was Jamal and that he had a chess set if I ever wanted to play.

The cell doors were left open for a few hours in the morning and a few hours in the afternoon, which allowed us to walk freely around the wing and courtyard. Almost all of the young offenders held a *pegleri* – coloured beads that had been threaded on a piece of thick black cord (like mini dumbbells). They were all different colours, deep blues and emerald greens. Some were even semi-precious stones threaded on thin stainless steel chains that glistened in the sun. The prisoners would throw the beads between each finger, swinging them from the pinky all the way up to the thumb. The beads quickly ran up and down their hands in an almost therapeutic motion. Every now and then, the beads looked as though they were floating in mid-air, defying the laws of physics. But they would always catch them and continue to twirl them gracefully between their fingers without having to think about it. I would often see prisoners with one leg crossed over the other, multitasking with their beads in their right hand, cigarette and *frappe* in their left.

Christos had a *pegleri* lying around the cell that he let me use. I spent the next few days walking up and down the courtyard smoking cigarettes, drinking *frappes* and practising with it. At least practising with the *pegleri* gave my mind something to focus on. It was a welcome distraction from the negative thoughts that plagued me: *How long will I be here for? When will I finally clear my name?* As I attempted to twirl the beads between each of my fingers, it was easier to bury every worry that I had deep into the recesses of my mind. At first I would frequently drop it, having to pick it up and start over. As the days passed I became better and better, catching the cord when the beads swung over my index finger.

┼┼┼

I was told that a judicial council would review my case upon five days of my arrival. I don't know why, but I'd convinced myself that they would be releasing me. Maybe it was because I couldn't deal with not knowing how long I would be held there. The five days had long passed. I'd got into the routine of waking up, speed walking through the wing and shouting through the barred gate. '*Ypallileh!* Have the papers arrived?' The *ypallilos* – staff member – would always give an upward nod and tut, which is the cultural equivalent of us shaking our heads to say 'no'. Each day I would wake up hoping that it was the day of my release, but each day I was let down. I started to accept what Zoe the social worker had told me; it was going to be a long time and I had no choice but to settle in there.

It didn't take long to get to know most of the guys in Parartima. It was the smallest wing, where the guards tried to keep the Greek prisoners together – 'away from the gypsies and Albanians' as Fivos had said. There were still quite a few Albanians and Romany gypsies in Parartima, but the majority of the guys were Greek and it felt like they were all either a 'Dimitris' or a 'Georgios'. The ones whose names I didn't know (or couldn't remember) I'd nicknamed in my head. For example, there was 'telephone guy', because he was always using the payphones, or 'shit tattoo guy' because he was covered with uneven prison tattoos that looked like a child had attacked him with a permanent marker.

One day I sat on one of the stone benches in the courtyard – I remember feeling the raging sun begin to burn my forehead and cheeks – and I read the graffiti that adorned the tall, concrete walls. The names of Greek football teams like AEK, Olympiakos and Panathinaikos covered them, along with other Greek writing like '*Gamo tin astynomia!* – Fuck the police!' The walls that surrounded the courtyard had metres of spiralling barbed wire mounted on the top of them. Old, deflated footballs and basketballs were wedged within the metal. If you looked just above them, you were able to see a stunning, rocky mountain in the distance that was coated in a blanket of leafy, green trees.

An inmate called Georgios from cell nine, opposite mine, came and sat next to me. '*Pou eisai alani mou?*' he said. I translated it as 'where are you my homie?' – or something similar to that.

'*Fylaki, esi?* – Prison, you?'

Georgios smiled. 'No *reh*, where are you *in your mind?* What's up?'

I was picking up the slang terms, *slowly slowly*.

His English was reasonably good, which surprised me because he was from a small Cretan village. There were guys in Avlona from cosmopolitan cities like Athens and Thessaloniki who couldn't speak a word. Georgios and his best friend, also Georgios, had been caught with a hefty amount of cannabis and had both been held in Avlona for nine months. They reminded me of the Greek version of Ant and Dec – probably because they weren't very tall, and usually strolled around together – almost inseparably. 'You will see with time what it is really like here,' Georgios said.

'What do you mean?' I asked.

He crossed his right leg over his left and started to twirl his *pegleri* from finger to finger. 'You see this guy?' His eyes pointed to a guy at the other end of the courtyard. It was Marios – one of the guys who'd invited me into his cell on my first day for a *frappe*. 'You met him yet?'

'Yeah.'

'What did he tell you he was in prison for, *Andrea*?'

'Theft, I think.'

Georgios burst into laughter, accidentally dropping his *pegleri*. 'No *reh*. He raped a kid! Twelve-year-old boy! When he first came to Avlona we beat him every fucking day. But now we can't; the guards protect him.' Georgios spat on the ground in disgust while bending down to pick up his beads.

I looked over to Marios across the courtyard. He was sweaty and overweight with long oily hair that stuck to his neck. I couldn't believe that I'd sat down and had a coffee with this guy, completely unaware that he was a paedophile.

'And you know how fucked up the system is?' Georgios continued. 'Drugs is the worst in all of Greece. Men who sell drugs to feed their kids are worse than what this *hondro poustanos* – fat faggot did. *Den pistevo reh* – I don't believe it, man.' He spat on the ground again. '*Gamise ta* – Fuck it.'

My heart fell into my stomach. Hearing him say that the system was 'fucked up' made me worry about my own case. I needed a strong system to help me fight against the injustice, not a 'fucked-up' one.

Georgios continued his rant; his voice became louder and caught the attention of some other inmates in the courtyard. 'Look, you see this fucking guy!?' He pointed with his middle finger, making it quite obvious to those around us. It was the one who I'd nicknamed 'telephone guy'.

'This guy was in the army. On his last day he was in a bar with his army friends or something like that. He wanted some girl, but she told him "fuck you" in front of all his friends. They all laughed at him so he walked into the women's bathroom when she was in there alone. He stamped on her head till she was dead *reh*.'

'On her head?' I repeated.

'Her head *reh malaka*. Her fucking *kefali*,' he reiterated, tapping his skull.

The guys in Avlona may have been bigger criminals than I'd thought. I started to understand why Fivos and Jamal reacted the way that they did when I told them my story – it was difficult to believe a word that came out of anyone else's mouth. Although, the thought began to dawn on me – how could I know whether Georgios was telling the truth either? Maybe he was misinformed. How could I know?

'*Reh Georgio*, we have to get out of this fucking place,' I said.

He nodded and smiled, continuing to throw his *pegleri* up and down his fingers.

I stared at the mountain in the distance. 'Man, you don't get that where I'm from,' I said. If I gazed at it for long enough, I could almost mentally block out the barbed-wired walls and imagine myself standing at the peak of it – freedom.

'*Poly omorfo* – very beautiful,' he added. Georgios and I stared at it for a short moment as if we could run towards it. '*Reh Andrea*, you know when I'm out of this fucking place, you know where I wanna live?' he asked.

'Where?'

'Las Vegas, man.'

'Las Vegas, eh?'

'Yeah. Everything about Las Vegas is amazing: the lights, the women, the casinos … the party,' he winked.

I nodded in agreement and offered him a smile. 'I've never been,' I told him. 'Maybe one day, if I don't go down for twenty years!' I said, sarcastically.

'Yeah,' he responded. 'But where is Las Vegas, man? Is it in America?'

'Yeah, it's in America,' I chuckled.

Georgios and I sat outside for another hour. I began to build a picture of what his life was like in a small Cretan village, not too far from the party town of Malia. He told me far-fetched stories of the family vendettas, organised crime and corrupt policing that happen in their small community. He made it sound like the Sicilian village of Corleone in the 1900s, the way it was portrayed in *The Godfather: Part II*. He said that he made a living from selling drugs and prostituting women. He wouldn't pay the women, he would rent a house for them to live in, buy them everything they needed, prostitute them and keep any profits. They were all Eastern European women; he told me there was no way he would ever prostitute a Greek girl.

Georgios was very homophobic, claiming that he wanted to behead all the homosexuals in the world. Regardless of his severe homophobia, he also believed that it was fine to fuck a man because the one getting 'fucked' was the only '*poustanos* – faggot' in his eyes. It seemed as though his belief was that a real man has sex with absolutely any human being with a pulse; a real man can have sex with another man, because he has power over that man and dominates him with masculinity. He told me that a boy in his village was gay, and that all the boys used to 'fuck him'.

He said, 'Maybe you drink a bit too much, maybe you take a bit too much drugs, you see a *kolo* – bum, you get a *gavla* – boner. It happens!'

I admit that I did find the statement quite funny, but I'll never understand his twisted view. I'm not homophobic in the slightest and I found the contradiction to be ignorant and pathetic.

He was really racist too, and said things like, 'Black people make me sick. They should bring back slavery.' I couldn't believe my ears. When I asked him what black people had ever done to him, he answered, 'Nothing, I don't care, they should clean my feet.' He even said, 'If I ever saw a fucking Turk, I would stab him. I hate Turks,' then he would conclude his rant with 'but the Turks ... *perrrr* ... they have very beautiful women.'

It was the first time in my life that I'd ever heard such racism. It seemed like he actually wanted to hurt people because of their ethnicity. I was never really exposed to serious racism growing up – then again, my upbringing was completely different from his. In his village there was a clear divide between the Greeks and ethnic minorities. On the other hand, my school in north London was filled with kids from many different ethnic backgrounds. Whatever ethnicity, or whatever the colour of someone's skin, being British was always the common denominator.

After speaking with Georgios, I contemplated whether he was a bad person or not. I don't think that he was; I knew that he held these strong views only because of the life that he'd led. It made me speculate what a 'good' or 'bad' person really is. If he'd lived a life similar to mine, he probably wouldn't have had these unsettling opinions. He'd also probably know where Las Vegas was before deciding that he wanted to live there.

My conversation with Georgios made me wonder what I would have been like if we'd swapped lives. What if I'd led a life like his? We'll never know! Maybe most of us would have ended up a racist, homophobic, drug-dealing pimp too.

20

THE TONGUE

I would call my girlfriend Riya every day at 8 p.m., but there was always a long wait for the phones because lock-in would be at 8.30. There were only four payphones in Parartima and some inmates would talk for absolutely ages.

When waiting for one of the phones, Marios (the apparent paedophile) was waiting too. He asked me for a cigarette.

I ignored his request. '*Yiati eisai mesa reh?* – Why are you inside, man?' I asked.

He grinned, knowing that I'd probably been told of his real crime. He started to thrust his hips and smirk. '*Dodeka chronon* – twelve years old,' he winked.

'You're a sick cunt.' I knew that he wouldn't understand a word of what I'd said.

'*Reh Andrea, dose mou ena tsigaro!* – Andreas, man, give me a cigarette!'

'No,' I said. It couldn't be helped; there was no way I was giving him anything. A telephone had become free; I picked it up and dialled the UK country code and Riya's number that I'd memorised. For the entire conversation I could sense him behind me – staring.

In the main hallway of the Parartima wing, there was a big, plastic, cone-shaped speaker mounted onto the ceiling. If the guards wanted you for anything, or it was a visiting day, you would hear your name being called out. It was meant to be white, but was a blend of different shades of stained, dirty browns. A quarter of the cone had been chipped away, as though it was a pie and someone had cut out an uneven, crooked slice. It must have been there for years, having had the sound of thousands of prisoners' names resonate within it.

When one of the guards called for you, distinguishing your own name was close to impossible. They must have been cupping their hands over their mouths and standing 10 feet away from the microphone. To make the muffled utterances even more difficult to comprehend, they were pronouncing my name in such strange ways. So oddly that it wasn't my name any more. So on visiting days, I had to be on guard. I had to know that I would be called at some point and listen out for something that could potentially be my name. If not, I feared that I would miss the visit and my family would be sitting behind a pane of glass, holding a telephone and waiting for a son who didn't turn up. To prevent that from happening I would hover around the speaker and walk up and down the corridor, lightly spinning my *pegleri* between my index and middle finger. When passing another inmate, it seemed to be the norm to acknowledge each other with a wink.

Sometimes I would hear my name after fifteen minutes – other times I could be waiting for two or three hours. My family would travel for three hours from central Athens, having to take two trains and a taxi to the Avlona complex. Every time they visited, they would bring me three letters from friends and family who were supporting me at home. Reading them would either put a huge smile on my face or leave me with tears in my eyes.

I hadn't been in Avlona for very long, and already my entire body was covered in flea bites – my arms and legs, my chest and back, even my hands were covered. The mattress that I'd been sleeping on must have been infested. It looked as though I had chickenpox and I was in constant pain. My mum watched me in complete shock as I walked over to the glass dividing us and sat down. She wanted to tell the guards to give me a new mattress, but I told her that it wasn't as bad as it looked and I'd sort it out. I didn't want to irritate the guards too much and bring attention to myself. The last thing I needed was my mum complaining, because I knew that they wouldn't appreciate that.

After briefly explaining what was happening on the inside, I needed to know what was happening outside of the prison walls. My mum told me that a woman called Christine Sakali, who she'd met through the church, was supporting her greatly and would be driving up to Avlona to pick up my parents and take them to her house for a coffee. It was amazing that a completely random person could be so kind to my family.

'And what's going on with my bail appeal?' I asked.

My dad then told me that George Pyromallis's office had finally got through to the courthouse in Zante, who said that they had no record of any bail appeal at all. They'd forgotten about me, leaving me to rot. After hearing the news, any faith I did have in the Greek justice system disappeared completely. As difficult as it was to hear, I knew it was just as difficult for my parents to tell me. I struggled to digest more bad news, which seemed endless. I was the lowest I'd ever been and was trying desperately to pick myself back up – it felt as if I was being kicked back down and made to feel even worse. The only things getting me through were the visits from my family. I loved seeing them, even when the news was bad. We would have only half an hour to speak, or a bit longer if we were lucky. Whenever I saw them it felt as though I wasn't in prison any more. For those precious minutes, it felt as though there wasn't really a pane of dirty glass between us. I was on the same side as them – free. As soon as the bell rang and the visiting time had run out, I was overcome with sadness every time. I didn't want to go back to the Parartima wing. After each visit I relived my first day in Avlona all over again.

After that first visit I walked to the Chief Guard's office to ask him for a new mattress. Everyone seemed to refer to him as the '*Archi Fylakas*', and his office was similar to that of the social worker's; a number of religious icons were hung on the walls. He sat behind his desk with a cigarette in hand and the first few buttons of his shirt undone – he had thick chest hair and a gold crucifix for all to see. He was a real *manga* – geezer … a real lad. I showed him the hundreds of bites on my body, but he just shouted at me in Greek. I understood the words for 'outside' and 'broom'. Unofficial sign language helped me understand that he was telling me to take the mattress outside and beat it with a broom handle. He said it abruptly, and gestured for me to leave the office as soon as possible. I didn't want to risk another sweltering night of being bitten so badly. I don't know why he couldn't just have given me a new mattress; there was an entire room full of clean ones. When I asked the question, he became aggressive, shouting fast strands of Greek words that I couldn't understand even though he spoke perfect English. I told him that I didn't understand.

'I'll beat the shit out of you, maybe then you'll understand. *Ei-maste stin Ellada, milame Ellinika!* – We are in Greece, we speak Greek!'

I took the thin mattress into the courtyard along with a broom that we had in our cell. I hurled it over one of the bars that were there for pull-up exercises. I stood next to the hanging mattress like a baseball player, battering it with the broom and watching the brown dirt burst out of it with each strike. I heard some cheers, which caught my attention. A group of young offenders

were playing football and one of the inmates had scored a goal –
the 'posts' were painted onto the concrete wall. I stopped battering the mattress and took a moment to watch them. 'Shit tattoo
guy' was playing; he was a Romany gypsy called Costantinos,
but went by his surname – Paiteris. He had a rough face and an
oriental look to his eyes, which always had swollen, grey bags
underneath. His mouth was a constant frown, so when he did
smile it looked almost malicious.

Fivos had told me to stay away from him, saying that he was
the biggest *roufianos* in prison – 'You'll get into trouble if you
talk to him.' I'd seen Paiteris act like a *malakas* before – a few
days before he had stabbed another inmate's leg with a pen for
no reason. I felt sorry for the guy who was getting stabbed. His
name was Dimitris but everyone called him '*Tripa*', which means
'hole'. He was involved in a train accident when he was a kid and
doctors had to drill a hole in his neck to save his life. He would
often come into our cell for a coffee and a cigarette. I'd hear him
wheezing next to me and sometimes catch a glimpse of smoke
exiting his neck hole as he laughed. I don't know why Paiteris
did that to Tripa, I think he was just a very angry person. I'd
even caught Paiteris speaking on one of the phones to his 'wife',
shouting things like '*Gamo ta paidia mas! –* Fuck our children!' or
'*Poutana! Na sas skotoso! –* You whore! I'm gonna kill you!'

As I beat my mattress, I watched him playing football –
dribbling and running through people like a professional. He was
doing kick-ups and keeping the ball up with his knees while he
ran around the opposition. The ball was an extension of him; at
times it seemed as though the ball was stuck to his foot with an
invisible elastic band. He did 360-degree turns on one foot with
the ball held tightly between his other foot and the shin above
it. I witnessed him let the ball go from his shin and foot, propel-
ling it upwards and volleying it into the goal at full pelt. Such a

repulsive person was performing in a way that was so beautiful; it was amazing to watch. He could take on the entire opposition single-handedly, but wasn't tactically football-minded in the slightest. He'd probably learned these skills in the streets rather than football training on Sunday mornings – it seemed like he had no sense of teamwork whatsoever. I imagined what he could have been like if had been trained from a young age – maybe he would have been the next Cristiano Ronaldo.

I continued to beat the mattress as much as I could and then took it back to my cell. It probably made little difference. Still, I threw it onto my bunk and made my bed, ready to test it that night. Some time later (it may have even been the next day) I walked over to cell one with Fivos, who was going to play chess with Jamal.

I sat down on Jamal's bunk while they set the board up.

'What the fuck is all that?' Jamal asked, referring to the flea bites covering my arms and hands. He had an unnecessarily exaggerated look of disgust on his face while pointing at me like a schoolboy bully.

'Bites, what do they look like?'

'Like you are fucking diseased, man,' he responded.

Fivos moved a white pawn. 'They've eaten you alive, you must have sweet blood,' he added.

Jamal lit a cigarette – it almost looked like a novelty large one because he was such a small guy. He took a long drag and moved the black pawn opposite. 'I've been here for a year and I've never had one bite,' he said.

Fivos laughed. 'Yeah, that's because your blood is black and stinky.'

Jamal would hear stuff like that on a daily basis. He made out as though it didn't bother him when everyone was around. When it was just the two of us, I asked him how the comments made him feel and he told me that it made him 'very angry and upset' – understandably. He was thirty years old and all of the guards knew it. He was sent to Avlona only because he claimed that he was seventeen. In fact, he told me that his name wasn't even Jamal, it was Mohammad and he was a Somali illegal immigrant from Syria. When he was arrested in Athens, he said that 'Jamal' was the first name that came to mind. He had a job in Avlona as a cleaner. In return, the guards looked after him, giving him cigarettes and pre-paid telephone cards to call his family, who were scattered all over the world. He would rarely use them; most of the time he would exchange them for more cigarettes. I would often hear his name being called on the muffled speaker for him to clean their offices – no surname, just '*Jamalli … Jamalli!*' One guard even used to take him outside of the prison walls and make him clean his car. I'm pretty sure that this wasn't allowed, but it didn't surprise me that the guards made up rules as they went along. A few days earlier I'd seen Jamal walking with one of the guards out of the wing; he must have been about to start work. The guard looked at me, patted Jamal on the head and patronisingly said, 'He's a very good little black boy, isn't he?' Jamal wouldn't react to the racist remarks, he always remained calm and silent – but I noticed that he found it more difficult to hold his tongue when my cellmate Christos spoke to him. Christos refused to call him by his name – instead he would refer to him as '*o mavros* – the black' or '*arapis*', which means 'nigger'. His favourite phrase, which he also used to say to me, was '*gamo to spiti sou!* – Fuck your home!'

One night I discovered that Christos was more insane than I initially thought. He woke me up at four o'clock in the morning and was shouting something in Greek that I didn't understand – waving his hands around. I told him to go back to sleep, but he kept on poking me with a stiff piece of thin wire. I managed to wake myself up and slid off the top bunk.

'*Ti thelis esi?* – What do you want?' I asked him. I softly massaged my temples, having no idea what he was yapping on about.

Fivos, who was lying in his bunk, translated for us. '*Christos* says he wants you to pierce his tongue.'

I rubbed my eyes, hardly able to see. 'He wants me to pierce his tongue?'

'Yes,' Fivos said, sitting up.

'He wants *me* to pierce his tongue?'

'Yes *reh*! I told you already, he is an arsehole!' Fivos said, chuckling.

'With what? This wire?' I asked.

Fivos shrugged his shoulders while Christos nodded and opened his mouth, gesturing how he would like me to pierce his tongue.

'You can't just stick dirty wires through your tongue.'

Fivos and Christos briefly argued the point that I'd just made between themselves. 'He said it's fine, he's done all of his piercings himself,' Fivos translated.

I lit a cigarette. 'Listen, tell the guy that the tongue's a muscle; he might hit a nerve end or vein. It's not the same as an ear lobe, or an eyebrow … or whatever else he's pierced.'

Fivos took a deep, irritated breath. They argued for a while, shouting fast in Greek. I saw Yiannis turn around in his bunk to face us, open his eyes and softly close them as if to say, *I'm trying to sleep here, guys.*

'*Christos* doesn't care, he wants to do it,' Fivos said.

'If he does it wrong he could bleed to death or never be able to talk again. It's a fucking stupid idea.'

Fivos smiled. 'You're telling me? Of course it's a stupid idea!'

I couldn't help but laugh at the absurdity of it all. 'Tell him it will get infected, man! Where did he even find this wire? On the floor?'

Fivos let out a subtle snigger that reflected mine. 'I don't know. *Trelos einai reh!* – He's crazy, man!'

In spite of my advice, Christos was adamant that he wanted to go ahead with the piercing. I made Fivos tell him not to blame me if he lost the ability to talk.

Christos held a lighter underneath the wire, moving it up and down and claiming that the flame had killed all of the bacteria. He held his tongue out and pulled the tip with his index finger and thumb to expose the veiny base. I caught a whiff of his smelly breath. There were little bits of food in his mouth, which made me realise that I hadn't seen him brush his teeth for the whole time I'd been in Avlona. I started to poke the middle of his tongue with the wire, avoiding the most obvious vein that I could see. I jabbed a little bit harder, but it was going to take a lot more force because the wire was quite blunt. I pushed as hard as I could a few times without penetrating – he let out a little moan with each poke. The wire pressed into the bottom of his tongue; I poked even harder. As soon as I saw the metal wire begin to pierce through his tongue, I couldn't go through with it. I felt like I was going to be sick. Christos casually pulled the wire out of his tongue so that he could smoke a cigarette. He claimed that his mouth now tasted of lemon, but he must have been confusing it with the taste of blood. He poked Yiannis with the wire, waking him up to finish the job.

'You know what's gonna happen now?' Fivos asked me, once I'd returned from heaving over the toilet hole.

'What?'

'He's gonna do it wrong, man; Christos is gonna punch him.' Fivos had been locked up with them for quite a few months – he must have seen something similar happen in the past.

I remember the stifled screams as Yiannis gripped Christos's tongue with his left hand and rammed the wire into the tongue as hard as he could with his right. Christos let out a screeching moan that sounded like a closed-mouth roar. Almost automatically, his right fist smashed the left side of Yiannis's face. There was a crunching sound. Yiannis fell to the ground and Christos continuously kicked him. I wrapped my arms around Christos as hard as I could, pulling him away from Yiannis.

Rather than going upwards, the wire had gone into his tongue horizontally. Almost the entire six-centimetre wire was inside of his tongue, but the tip of the wire had failed to poke out of the top. Instead, it was almost touching the back of his throat. Fivos burst into laughter as Christos sat down and struggled to pull the wire out of his tongue before lighting another cigarette. He was mumbling swear words directed at Yiannis, unable to talk properly. He ended up staying up all night, trying to pierce his own tongue.

When I woke up a few hours later, I noticed that he'd fallen asleep with the wire successfully threaded through. His lips were faintly covered in blood, as though he was wearing red lipstick. When he woke up he attempted to put the 'tongue bar' (the piece of jewellery) into the pierced hole. I have no idea where he'd found it. It didn't matter; his tongue was probably three times its original size and it all seemed to be a huge waste of time.

++++

Christos's tongue seemed to return to a normal size after a few days, despite the hundreds of cigarettes that he'd chain-smoked since 'the incident'. Yiannis wasn't happy, though; I was given the impression that he couldn't handle another night of Christos's antics. I didn't blame him; I myself had started to get worried. Who could have known what the guy was capable of? I'd already witnessed him almost strangling Yiannis to death and piercing his own tongue with a dirty wire!

Yiannis soon made a complaint to the *Archi Fylakas* about Christos, which was a complete *malakia*. I found it strange because they were friends from the outside who had both been caught stealing cars together. The guards moved Yiannis to cell nine with Georgios (the drug-dealing pimp), his friend (also Georgios) and a convicted murderer called Mihalakis. Rather than Christos losing his temper and beating Yiannis senseless, Yiannis was invited back into our cell for an 'intervention' where lots of abusive language was hurled at him. Once Yiannis was sent back to his new cell to think about what he'd done, Fivos told me that Christos wanted to celebrate the fact that Yiannis had left. It'd been decided that we would be brewing our own alcohol. I was quite concerned, as being caught with alcohol in Avlona would have resulted in a six-month prison sentence; but at the same time I had no control over what they did. I had to go along with it.

'Don't worry, we've done this many times,' Fivos reassured me.

Christos asked me if I was a *roufianos* – a rat.

'*Ti nomizis reh?* – What do you think, man?'

We could buy many things in Avlona from the *pakali* – grocers, such as coffee, cigarettes, pre-paid telephone cards and necessities like toilet paper. We could even order fruit, vegetables and pasta. I'd never really bought anything other than the necessities, but for my first order, each of my cellmates and I had chipped in for the ingredients to brew alcohol. Fivos ordered lots of sugar, I ordered several cartons of orange juice, Christos ordered lots of cigarettes (not an ingredient, but essential nonetheless) and Makis (our new cellmate who was arrested for stealing a motor scooter) ordered lots of apples. The last ingredient was free: every morning we'd be given two long loaves of bread that looked like huge baguettes.

I copied Fivos; he'd written his shopping list with his name and inmate number on the top. We walked to the front of the wing, where we posted our shopping list in a little post box. To order groceries like this, inmates would need to be financially supported by people outside of the prison. The guards would accept cash from friends or family of the inmate, which would be deposited in a 'prison account' because no cash was allowed. It was all very sloppy, as other inmates ran the accounts. Sometimes they would steal a few euros out of each one to buy whatever they wanted. I regarded this as a kind of unavoidable 'prison tax'. Once the order had been processed, there would be a specific day when the guards would fill an empty room near their offices with the groceries. We'd go to collect them, which was chaos because there were so many inmates and sometimes we'd have to wait for hours.

Our groceries had arrived a few days after we'd ordered them inside big, blue plastic bags the size of black bin-liners. It was 9 p.m. As soon as one of the guards shut the cell door behind him and we heard the metallic clonk of the key turning in the lock, we immediately started to mix the concoction that would soon be fermented. The others had borrowed a few utensils that had been circulating Parartima. For example, Christos managed to find a miniature, portable electric hob and a pan big enough for Fivos to boil sugar water. Makis and Christos crushed up all of the apples while I was instructed to rip the crust off the loaves of bread that we'd collected and make a perfect sphere out of the dough-like interior. We lined up four of the big plastic bags, which we would be using to brew our alcohol. We poured in all of the ingredients, plus the orange juice that I'd ordered. Once everything was in the bag and ready to ferment, Christos let out all of the excess air. He made sure that all of the ingredients in the bag were airtight, forming a perfect blue ball that was filled with sugary juice, mushy apples and bread. Fivos knotted the very top of the bags, allowing room for alcoholic fumes to later fill the bag.

Christos placed the sack of ingredients into his sports bag

and we hid it in the small gap between the two bunk beds. We covered it all with sheets and towels, so that the guards wouldn't see it when they came to lock us in.

'So ... now what?' I asked Fivos, who was looking at me with a big grin on his face.

'Now, my friend – we wait.'

21

INTO THE WILD

I still had no idea if the bail appeal had happened, or whether the courthouse in Zante had conveniently forgotten about it. Alison Beckett from the British consulate came to visit me, but she had no further news on the matter. The topic of conversation was generally about the Greek justice system and how unbearably slow it is. I remember Alison having a kind smile, which almost made me forget that what she was telling me was awful for my case. When I took a moment to digest what she was saying, my chest quivered. I was given the impression that I was just a random document among thousands of others that would probably get lost!

'Andrew, you're going to have to be very patient,' I remember her saying sympathetically.

I'd started to accept it as true, when all I wanted to do was clear my name and go home. But, to be honest, I'd started to get used to life in Avlona (even though my cellmates were possibly insane). It wasn't easy to settle there, but it would have been far easier to endure if I'd known how long I was going to be incarcerated for. It was like running a marathon and being absolutely exhausted all the time because I had no clue as to how far away the finish line was. The finish line was my home, and I was determined to do whatever it took to get there.

Alison had brought a few newspapers and books for me to read, which was very nice of her. One of the books was called *Into the Wild*, which was a true story about a young man from Virginia who gave all of his money to charity, changed his name and hitchhiked around America. He travelled to Alaska and attempted to survive in the wilderness, but in the end was found dead inside a derelict bus. I read the book in two days and it was a great form of escape. When incarcerated, there's nothing more uplifting than the fantasy of being in the great outdoors – it was something that I'd visualise thereafter to get myself through each day. If I closed my eyes and imagined freedom, I could smell air as fresh as a mountain breeze. I didn't need any kind of drug to escape my reality, or Christos to strangle me and deprive me of oxygen until the point of hallucination. All I had to do was close my eyes and think – really hard.

As soon as I'd finished the book, I met a new inmate called Arnas Pakrosnis from Lithuania. He was tall, skinny and blond, sticking out in Parartima like a sore thumb. I invited him into cell five to meet Fivos, which I thought he would appreciate because Fivos also spoke English. When Arnas sat down, he noticed the book on the table. He told me that he'd seen the movie adaptation and it had inspired him and his friends to hike into the wilderness just outside of Kaunas (the second-largest city in Lithuania) with a bottle of vodka and 'a big fucking bag of weed'. They camped out there for days, just to get away from the stresses of everyday life for a short while.

Arnas explained that he'd been caught trafficking a huge amount of drugs on a boat from Turkey to Rhodes. At first I thought it was a stupid thing to do – was the money really worth the risk of life imprisonment? The more he told me, the more sympathetic I became towards him (and feeling sympathy for an inmate was a rarity in Avlona). He told me that his dad was in debt to a group of crooks, but had died of a heart attack and left his family with the debt. The crooks approached Arnas and demanded their money, but Arnas and his family had no idea where any of it was. When he told them that he was only nineteen and had never seen that much money in his life, they forced him to do a job for them and threatened him with a gun. They said that they would kill his mum and sister if he didn't. I attempted to put myself into his shoes. Would I have done it?

'Why didn't you go to the police!?' I asked him.

He smiled. 'I don't know what the fuck it's like in England, my friend. But in Kaunas, that would be suicide!'

It seemed as though he had no choice. Arnas told me that the crooks flew him to Turkey, where he was told of an address to meet someone who would give him a suitcase and boat tickets from Turkey to Rhodes – then from Rhodes to somewhere in Italy. The plan was to transport the drugs to Italy via boat to clear his father's debt. When he entered Greece, the border security searched random suitcases and his was one of them. He described to us the guilt that was written all over his face, and beat his chest with a closed fist to show how fast his heart was pounding. The security guard found no illegal substances in his suitcase and let him go. Delighted that he'd managed to get away with the first part of the crime, Arnas walked out. Just as he was about to leave the area, something must have dawned on the security guard who had searched his suitcase: the clothes in the suitcase didn't belong to Arnas – they clearly weren't his size and some of the items were women's clothes with the price tags still attached to them. When the security guard called him back, his heart palpitated more and more. They emptied the suitcase and lifted it slowly, realising that it was far too heavy. In front of his eyes, they sliced open the base of the case with a Stanley knife and found six kilos of pure heroin. Now, here he was, an inmate in Avlona, talking to me and Fivos!

Arnas and I went into the courtyard and walked up and down, chatting and smoking cigarette after cigarette. It turned out that he was a student like me and it was his first day in Avlona. I noticed that he was walking quite stiffly, as though filled with apprehension. As the hours passed, I could sense that he'd relaxed a bit, which I'm glad that I'd helped him do. The sun began to set behind the towering mountain in the distance – it left the Parartima courtyard with a cool, tranquil atmosphere. Arnas and I sat with another inmate called Socrates, who spoke some English and told us that he had been arrested for threatening his wife with a knife after catching her cheating on him.

'They will probably take me to *Korydallo. Perrr*... that fucking place,' he said while shaking his head.

'What's that?' I asked. It was the first time I'd ever heard the word.

'Man, you don't know about Korydallos? You didn't hear about Vassilis Paleokostas? The guy who escaped from Korydallos Prison in a helicopter this year!' he said in broken English.

I shook my head.

He continued. '*Reh*, it's the fucking most crazy jail in all of Greece, maybe even Europe.' His facial expression said it all; he was trying to hide the droop of his cheeks and subtle headshake with a delicate smile. Socrates was facing a possible transfer there, and he was definitely crapping himself.

When I asked him why they would be transferring him, he told me that it was because he'd be turning twenty-one. My heart fell into my stomach when the words reached my ears. I always had faith that I'd be released before my twenty-first birthday, but it was beginning to look unlikely. I only had a month before I would be too old to be in Avlona and I'd still heard nothing about the appeal for bail. Illegal immigrants like Jamal were thirty years old and had no proof of their real ages. They were able to stay in Avlona for years, yet I was facing a possible transfer to one of the worst prisons in Europe for my twenty-first birthday present! I asked Socrates if there was any way we could stay in Avlona after our birthdays. He told me that if we sign up for the prison school, they wouldn't transfer us because it was for our 'education'. I was relieved that there was a possible loophole. It was decided that I'd be signing up – and maybe it was a chance to further improve my Greek.

We stayed in the courtyard until the evening food was served. Like every evening in Avlona, inmates from the other prison wings had brought the food in wide metal cauldrons that they would push on a set of wheels. It was their job – I just tried not to think about them cooking it. Usually it was *fassolia* – beans, or *fakes* – lentils that we would eat with plastic cutlery. Sometimes it would be spaghetti, but it would be slimy and cold. They would put on a plastic glove, grip a load of it and slap it into our plastic Tupperware containers, which wasn't a very appetising sound. Once we'd collected our food, we'd take it back to our cells and the guards would lock us in for the night.

On this particular evening, we'd been served *fassolia*. I remember walking into the cell, placing my plastic container of *fassolia* onto the table and being shocked to see Christos lying on his bunk with electrodes connected to his body – jolting because he was electrocuting himself. Over the previous week, I'd started to realise how intelligent Christos was, not necessarily in an academic way, but in terms of electronics and DIY. I'd already watched him turn a normal CD player into a CD MP3 player somehow, and now he'd created his own 'Slendertone' machine. It was slightly too powerful though, and probably very dangerous.

Since before I'd arrived in Avlona, Christos had been sneaking into other inmates' cells and ripping the wires out of their electric fans. He had stolen loads of them, leaving other inmates to bake in the scorching summer heat. He'd dissected his portable hi-fi and connected eight wires to specific components on the main circuit board. He'd attached them by burning the ends of plastic straws, holding them like a soldering iron and using the melted, dripping plastic to stick the metal wire to the circuit board, which then hardened like solder. He'd been careful to ensure that the metal elements were touching, as plastic doesn't conduct electricity like solder does. To my surprise, it seemed to hold and actually work. He'd collected eight of the circular foil seals that you peel from the lids of fresh cans of instant Nescafé, which he then attached to the other end of each of the long wires. The best way to imagine his little portable hi-fi is like an octopus with skinny wire legs and metallic foil shoes.

Christos had licked each of the circular foil seals and slapped them onto his body – four on his abdomen, two on his chest and one on each of his biceps. It caused him to be electrocuted when the music played, but he claimed that the shocks were strengthening his muscles. What was funny was that he was being electrocuted to the beat of the music! With each kick, snare and bass note, electrical pulses would shoot through the wires into the circular foils and shock him. What was even funnier was that when the volume was turned up, the shock would be more powerful. The song that he would repeat over and over again was 'My Love' by Justin Timberlake – adamant that the beat was 'very good for his muscles'. We tried turning the volume up to full blast and Christos started to jolt and shake uncontrollably to the rhythm, and the speakers in his homemade 'surround-sound system' almost burst. Christos had a huge grin on his face. His abdominal muscles and chest were tensing as though a doctor was shocking him with a cardiac defibrillator. His arms were hopping like a puppet and his hands were jerkily opening and closing to the beat of the music like a dancer from a Bollywood movie.

Christos's body relaxed when the volume was turned down. Fivos then rapidly switched the volume from silent to full blast, and back down to nothing, and then to full blast again. The three of us were overcome with laughter because we'd finally found a way to control Christos.

I was the lowest that I had ever been in my life – wrongly accused of murder and caught up in what is possibly one of the slowest, most inept justice systems in the world. I had no idea if I would be granted bail, and had the fear of being transferred to one of Europe's worst prisons hovering over me. Nevertheless, moments like that would never fail to lift my spirits.

22

A NIGHT TO REMEMBER

My lawyer George Pyromallis contacted the court every two days to find out when my bail appeal would be considered. Unsurprisingly, it was a question that remained unanswered. I'd been locked up for a month and a half and my family hadn't stopped fighting for my release. Along with many family members, friends and the charity Fair Trials International, they continued to lobby dozens of MPs and MEPs, outlining the injustice and pushing them to put pressure on the Greek authorities for my release. The Prime Minister, the Foreign Secretary David Miliband, the Lord High Chancellor Jack Straw, the minister for security Admiral Lord West and the Home Secretary Jacqui Smith, among many others, were constantly bombarded with emails and letters, pleading for intervention in my bail appeal.

Both of my parents had been flying back and forth from Athens to be close to me, spending each day in an internet café because they had no connection at my uncle's apartment. My dad's business was on the verge of failing because he couldn't dedicate enough time to it, and they were spending an absolute fortune on legal fees – it was a very difficult and stressful time for them. They had a meeting with the British embassy in Athens, who made it clear that they couldn't intervene, but would push for a meeting with the Greek justice minister. Alison Beckett from the British consulate told my parents some of the truths about the delays in the Greek justice system. She informed them of an ongoing case that involved two young children who had tragically died in a rented holiday bungalow in Corfu. They were poisoned by carbon monoxide that leaked out of a badly installed boiler and two Thomas Cook holiday representatives had been wrongly accused of causing their deaths. Several months had already passed and the trial was adjourned for a further six months. We feared that the delays in my case would be just as long. I would remain locked up until finally having the chance to defend myself – and the threat of being randomly transferred to Korydallos became one of my greatest fears. School or no school, I knew that the guards could probably do whatever they wanted.

╫╫

Journal extract – Day 50 – 10 September 2009

I'm an innocent man and sometimes it just gets too much. How do you stay strong and positive, but prepare for the worst at the same time? Have I gone through the worst? Or is it yet to come? There's no point in telling myself that this is too much and that I want this to end, or wonder why this burden has been put on me. All I can do is continue to do what I have been doing for the past fifty days. I have been caught in a trap. I have to go through the whole corrupt system in this country when I have already been through the UK system for a year. This is psychological pain. I can't describe these emotions, I can only feel them. I feel like I am being treated as though I am guilty. I can't even cry, even though I want to because there is always someone here. No privacy. All I can do is endure and continue to go with the flow. All I want to do is be with the ones who mean the most to me – everyone who has been with me throughout this.

Arnas and I started to play chess quite a bit with Jamal, and I began to notice that many things that came out of Jamal's mouth were lies. Accounts he would tell me about his life were funny – but clearly untrue. Some of the stories were definitely plagiarised from television shows or films that he'd watched since being in prison. He must have thought he was the only person in the world to have seen them. One time he said, 'You know Andrew, when I was living in Syria, me and my friend used to crash weddings to pick up chicks.'

'Yeah, I think there's a movie about that, mate – it's called *Wedding Crashers.*'

'Maybe,' he responded.

Another time he said to me, 'When I was a kid, my mother left me in the house and these guys broke in to rob us – so I set traps around the house to catch them.' He mentioned it so casually, as if I hadn't watched *Home Alone* on TV every Christmas since I was a kid. I would have preferred to listen to real stories about his life. I remember looking at him and thinking, *Who the hell is this guy!?* Surely he had a life story far more interesting than mine. He didn't need to lie. One day he opened up to me, admitting that he didn't choose his life and that he had no opportunities. He referred to himself as a 'wild animal'. I couldn't even begin to compare him to myself – the son of a man who designs cruise ship interiors and living in a five-bedroom house. It made me feel stupid for ever complaining about my situation. He was alone, and even when he was released he would have nowhere to go. No wonder he felt the need to make up stories. At least in Avlona he had a job; he had a purpose.

My cellmates and I would spend hours locked up during the day, which is when I spent my time reading and writing. A week had passed and Christos was still playing the Justin Timberlake song *over* and *over* again – I was absolutely sick of it! It would be on repeat all the time, continuing to 'tone' his muscles. I asked him to change the track, but he refused. The song became a form of slow, painful torture. When Fivos, Makis and I joined forces to tell him that it was *malakia* and that he was getting on everyone's nerves, he finally stopped the music. I could close my eyes and escape again.

Every now and then we would check the bag of juice, sugar, apples and bread. It had been a few days and the bag was beginning to fill with fumes, which was a sign of fermentation. One day I showed Arnas the bag. He'd become a good friend of mine and I trusted him. I told him that I would give him some of the alcohol if he wanted, but to keep it to himself. Jamal, who was his cellmate, would have been the worst person to tell. Apart from being very close to the guards, nobody seemed to trust him. Fivos said that he was a *roufianos* who would tell the guards anything for a packet of cigarettes.

Eventually the bag had filled with so much gas that it looked like it would explode. Christos opened the top of the bag, letting all of the fumes out. It left the cell with a potent stench – the perfect mixture of rotting fruit and alcohol. It took another day for the bag to balloon up again. Every time we let the gas out, it would fill up faster and faster, leaving the cell smelling more like alcohol and less like rotten fruit every time. After a few more days had passed, the bag would inflate every ten minutes.

Christos untied the top of the bag and alcoholic fumes hovered around the opening. He put his mouth over it and took a deep breath – inhaling as much of the vapour as his tar-ridden lungs could hold. The bag was handed to me. I was confused as to what we would be achieving by doing this. I copied him and put my mouth around the opening, sucking in as much of the gas as

I could. I held the fumes in my lungs, attempting to prevent the imminent cough that wanted to escape. As I exhaled, my world began to spin. I was overcome with a powerful rush and couldn't help but take fast deep breaths, unable to move for a short while. The high didn't last very long. I found it hard to believe that the fumes of fermented apples, juice, sugar and bread would have an effect that strong! The alcohol was definitely ready.

We were locked in for the afternoon. Makis and Christos used Tupperware containers to scoop the lumpy liquid out of the bag. They then filtered it through a plastic drainer into another container and then carefully poured the concoction into plastic bottles that we'd collected. We ended up with twelve litres. There was a big bucket that we'd use to wash our clothes, which we filled with cold water from the shower hose. We left the six 2-litre bottles in there to stay cool until the evening. When the *ypallilos* locked us in for the night, the four of us waited a few minutes to ensure that he'd left the Parartima wing. Fivos clapped his hands together. '*Ade pame* – Come on, let's go,' he said.

The four of us sat around the plastic garden table, smoking cigarette after cigarette and listening to hip hop music on Christos's homemade stereo system. We drank our prison-brewed alcohol out of plastic cups. It tasted like alcoholic orange juice and had bits of bread and apples still floating in it. I had an idea, which was to melt the bottom of the plastic straws with a lighter and pinch it, so that the hole at the bottom was a lot smaller and wouldn't let in the bits of apple and bread. Clearly, I was beginning to think like a prisoner. I was sitting around the table drinking with my cellmates, and I felt accepted – it was almost the same feeling as starting secondary school and managing to fit into a group. The others used my straw idea, and when finishing a cup we'd find a lump of orange pulp sitting at the bottom.

'*Reh*, I bet you never would have thought you'd be sitting here getting drunk with us in prison,' Fivos chuckled.

It was true – I could never have imagined it happening. Two months earlier, when I'd landed in Athens and watched a row of armed police officers ready to handcuff me, my mind would never have conjured up such a situation.

We all became merry and ended up jumping around the cell and doing silly dances. We caught a mouse, as there would often be some running around the cell. Christos ripped the live wires out of his fan and electrocuted it. Then we attached the home-made electrodes to Christos's neck and face, finding it hilarious as the shock in his cheeks forced him to smile uncontrollably to the beat of the music. In hindsight, it was all quite dangerous.

We made the most of a bad situation, which is something that we all should do when life deals us something difficult to get through; if we don't laugh, we'll only cry. I actually enjoyed myself that night, regardless of the circumstances. From the moment that I'd landed in Greece, there was a deadening numbness in my body and a tremor in my chest that wouldn't desist. But for those few hours it seemed like all my anxieties were lifted. We'd forgotten about our problems and were doing what all normal young people did. That night, we were free. I know it may sound strange, but I hold the memory close to my heart.

23

THE ACCUSED WHO PUNCHED THE VICTIM IN THE HEAD

Journal extract – Day 85 – 15 October 2009

It's funny how you can wake up one day, oblivious to what is happening behind closed doors. After over two months here I just found out that I didn't make bail, again. The judicial council bail hearing happened. A guard just came and opened my cell door and gave me something to sign. He said, 'You made a request to wait for court outside, but they said no.' Just like that. I always wondered how I would find out. It's crazy how you can feel OK and then so emotionally weak in an instant. I can't even call my parents until they open the cell door in a few hours. So I'm locked in here to think about it. How are you supposed to feel? I can't believe this has happened. I'm going to be inside for a very long time. It kills me just thinking about it. I just want my life back. This is such an injustice – it's unbelievable. What do I do? It's my 21st birthday tomorrow and I wish it wasn't. When will they move me to Korydallos? I don't know, but something tells me it will happen now. How could the bastards reject me? I don't even know the reason because I can't understand the document – it is all

in Greek. I can't think straight. I want to get the fuck out of here,
but now I know that it's not even an option any more. This is my
life for now, maybe for the next year or so. I feel so powerless and
there's no one around me to care. Just me, my mind and four walls.

When I found out the news I became detached from my own body – numb. The *ypallilos* eventually unlocked the cell door in the afternoon and I ran into the hall so that I could be the first one to grab a telephone. I slotted in a telephone card and quickly dialled my parents' number that I'd memorised. My hand was shaking and my chest stiffened for the first time in my life – I remember the agony as I attempted to take a breath.

It wasn't long before we discovered what the document said. George Pyromallis sent my parents a translated copy. According to the Greek authorities, I would 'naturally' deny the charge. My two friends Chris and Charlie were beaten by Greek police officers and forced to incriminate me. On this matter, the judicial council's verdict simply stated: 'During the principal inquiry relating the pressure and physical violence from the staff in the preliminary inquiry are deemed trite, since nothing of the kind had occurred.' I find it incredible that the judicial council was able to make this decision without investigating the matter at all.

The document stated:

In the light of the aforementioned facts and in particular of the aforesaid behaviour of the accused who punched the victim in the head, it is evident that his intention was to cause the aforesaid grievous bodily harm to the victim, owing to the vulnerable point of the body chosen, with the risk of his ensuing death, which indeed occurred. The resulting outcome, which was more serious than intended, that is the victim's death, is attributable to the negligence of the accused who, although like every sensible person finding himself in the same circumstance, and given his age, his physical and mental health and his personality, should and could have foreseen and avoided such an outcome, by not striking the victim in the head in the manner described, and specifically although he was aware that the violent blow to the head could cause the victim to lose consciousness and fall from some height to the floor and be killed, he attacked the victim and struck him as described, resulting in the most serious outcome, that is the victim's death which he neither sought nor accepted as a possible outcome of his action.

In the instant case, in view of the foregoing, sufficient evidence has emerged of the accused's guilt, and moreover the serious evidence of his guilt, which led to the issuance of the aforesaid provisional custody warrant, following a European Arrest Warrant, remains just as strong today, as he has no permanent abode in the country and it is very likely that if he were allowed to go free he would abscond abroad. Consequently, there is a lawful case for this Council to find that the appeal under consideration should be refused as to its substance and that the disputed Warrant should remain in force.

I was disgusted. After seeing the evidence against me, the *Daily Mail* had released an article about my case, stating, 'should the same evidence be put forward in Britain, the chances of it going to trial are so slim as to be laughable' – clearly the Greek authorities had a very different sense of humour. It scared the hell out of me – and I was given no chance to defend myself against the lies. The evidence was crap, the investigation's identification process was disgraceful, and I hadn't even been questioned in the police investigation.

Fair Trials International put my family in touch with The AIRE Centre, a charity that specialises in litigation before the European Court of Human Rights. Instantly, they lodged an appeal for my release on the grounds that my incarceration was illegal. Subsequently, Fair Trials International and Baroness Sarah Ludford MEP launched a campaign to the European Parliament in Brussels, fighting for mutual cooperation between European countries in criminal justice matters.

+++++

The days passed very slowly after being given this news. I was in a constant daze, fighting off negative thoughts. I spent my days either lying on my bunk and thinking or walking up and down the courtyard, spinning my *pegleri* between each of my fingers and thinking some more. My emotions would fluctuate; some days I would feel accepting, but on others the black cloud that loomed above my head would cause my chest to tighten like the skin of a snare drum. Nights started to become polluted with more nightmares than dreams. One night, my heart began to palpitate. I started to panic and felt chest pains. I sat up. The cell door was locked, of course – there was no one there to help me. I was sweating, and took fast, deep breaths. Everyone else in the cell was asleep. I was trapped! I had to calm myself down. I jumped down from my bunk and splashed my face with water and told myself that I wasn't having a heart attack. I looked up to the wall – there was no mirror. I hadn't seen my reflection in almost three months. I could feel that my facial hair was the longest it had ever been. I climbed back onto my bunk and lay there. The water cooled me off and I started to breathe slowly. I stared at the ceiling until I embraced the deep sleep that I craved. It had come to the point where the short bouts of sleep that I did manage to get became infested with images of Korydallos Prison and murder trials. My mind was no longer a place where I could escape just by closing my eyes. There was no escaping now.

24

A MIXTURE OF MADNESS

I'd turned twenty-one – too old to be in Avlona. The more that Korydallos Prison was spoken of, the worse it began to sound. I started to recall prison films like *The Shawshank Redemption* and *American History X*, praying to God that I wouldn't have to experience anything remotely similar. There were arguments and fights in Avlona, almost on a daily basis – but they were no different from any that we used to see in school. It was a drug-free, youth offenders' prison and I didn't feel psychologically strong enough to be transferred to Korydallos. More and more inmates had told me that joining the prison school would prevent my transfer, so I went to see Zoe the social worker to fill out an application form. My cellmates instructed me to take two empty ballpoint pens from Zoe's office, which wasn't difficult to find considering her pens never worked.

When I got back to cell five, I couldn't believe my eyes as Christos handcrafted a tattoo machine using everyday household items. I remember exactly how he did it and could probably make one now. He broke a disposable cigarette lighter and took out the metallic, spiralled wire that acted as a flint. Then he stretched the coil out to its full length so that it formed the shape of a rigid needle. Holding a flame underneath it, he moved it up and down in an attempt to sterilise it. He pulled out the plastic cap that covered the bottom of Zoe's pen and took out the tiny ballpoint at the very tip on the other end. It left him with a hard, hollow, outer casing and a flimsy, hollow, inner tube. Feeding the needle through the empty inner tubing of the pen, half a centimetre of the needle then peeked out of the tip of the pen instead of the ballpoint, and an inch poked out of the back. With a lighter, he melted the back end of the plastic inner tubing, squeezing it so that it fused with the needle.

Christos took apart our electric fan and extracted the small motor that propelled the blades. He used a long, plastic-coated wire and his plastic straw 'soldering' technique to connect the small motor to the base unit of the fan, which now stood alone. The back of the makeshift needle now poked out the rear of the pen, so he bent the very end to make a hook. The hooked wire was fed into a hole on the circular plastic output shaft of the motor – the bit that spins.

He used the cylindrical, outer casing of another empty pen, melting it in the middle and bending it to make a right angle. It hardened when cooled down and he attached one end to the side of the motor and the other end to the main shaft of the tattoo machine itself. He did this by wrapping both ends with plastic strands from plastic bags. He melted the plastic with a flame, and continuously wrapped it with more plastic, repeating the action until it hardened to form a motorised handle.

The tattoo machine was connected to the base unit of the fan via a long wire. The base unit had three buttons, which would normally control the speed of the fan, but now controlled the speed of the needle and how fast it would penetrate.

For ink, Fivos and Christos set fire to plastic telephone cards that no longer had credit to make calls. The ink that formed the pictures on the cards burnt, creating a thick black smoke. They held a hard sheet of acrylic plastic above the smoke, which was part of the tabletop in our cell. The thick, black smoke set on the acrylic sheet and formed a black powder when scraped off. When mixing the powder with a few drops of water, ink was formed. It was engineering genius and, as I say, I couldn't believe my eyes.

Christos then turned the newly handcrafted tattoo machine on full blast, and started to tattoo something on a part of Makis's leg that he'd shaved with a Bic razor. He continuously dipped the tip of the machine into the pot of ink and then softly pressed it into Makis's skin. I looked at the design of the tattoo, which resembled a small elf sitting on a mushroom. I asked Fivos why anyone would want to have an elf on their leg for the rest of their life – he told me that it is something to do with the 'psychedelic trance' music that they listened to. Before being in prison, many inmates had a habit of taking hallucinogenic drugs like LSD or magic mushrooms and going to psychedelic trance raves where they would 'trip' and believe that they were dancing with elves. In my opinion, the music was shit – Christos played some for me. They'd listen out for the little tweaking high-pitched sounds, which was apparently an 'amazing' experience when on drugs. But it didn't sound very appealing to me.

It took Christos a few hours to complete the tattoo and it looked fantastic. Christos had even added shading to create a three-dimensional effect, rather than looking like it was drawn on with an eyeliner pencil like those on Paiteris – the 'shit tattoo guy'. Christos asked me if I wanted one and without really thinking, I'd agreed to it. I actually trusted him for some reason, which was probably a stupid risk thinking about it now with hindsight.

I made him take out the needle from the tattoo machine and replace it with a new one from a different cigarette lighter that we had lying around. He asked me what tattoo I wanted and I told him that I wanted the five-dot tattoo that most inmates had.

The five dots that you find on dice represent four walls and the prisoner inside of them. Several inmates had it on their hands, their ankles or even their necks. But, jokingly, I told him that I wanted it on my arse. '*Tora oli i zoi mou tha einai piso mou!* – Now all my life it will be behind me!' I said. I shocked myself as the Greek words so casually exited my lips.

'*Entaxi, ade* – OK, come on then,' Christos said smiling, pressing button number three on the base of the fan, which switched the tattoo machine on to full blast.

'*Plaka sou kano reh!* – I'm joking with you, man!' I responded.

'Don't be a *kota* – chicken, you said it now you have to do it!' Fivos claimed. 'Left or right?'

I didn't actually want a tattoo because I'm not much of a tattoo kind of guy. In the heat of the moment, I thought it would be pretty funny to go along with. In hindsight – again – I'm unsure as to whether it is funny or actually moronic to have a tangible memory of Avlona stuck just above my left bum cheek for the rest of my life. Probably the latter.

┼┼┼┼

There's one last story I have about Christos, which I feel obliged to share – just because you don't see things like this every day. He'd decided to make a steering wheel with pedals for the PlayStation video games console. There were a few PlayStation consoles that were circulating the Parartima wing. Inmates would buy one – which would cost a few telephone cards – then they'd use it for a while before selling it on in an attempt to make a profit. Christos owned one and it was rarely played. The only game that he had was a car racing game called *Gran Turismo*.

Every now and then the guards would give us a banana with our meals, and the bunches came in large, rectangular cardboard boxes. When the bananas were finished, the guards would leave the boxes in the hallway for the prison workers to dispose of. Christos took one of the boxes with the intention of using it as the base of the steering wheel. It didn't have a lid and had many holes in it. He sat on a chair and placed the cardboard box on the floor in front of him with his legs inside of it, as though he was sitting at a small cardboard desk. The top of the box ended a few inches above his knees. He used a long, wooden broom handle as an axle for the steering wheel. He fed the stick through a hole at the top of the box, exiting a hole at the back of the box so that it sat at a diagonal angle. On the tip of the front end of the stick, he attached the circular caging of the fan that he had previously destroyed to make the tattoo machine. The girth of the wooden broom handle happened to fit perfectly into the hole in the centre of the circular fan cage, which now acted as the steering wheel.

For pedals, he used the centimetre-thick acrylic plastic that he'd used earlier in the process of making the tattoo ink. It was probably just under a metre squared. I sat on Fivos's bottom bunk and held it tightly between my knees while Christos used a long, thick strip of material that he'd ripped from his bed sheet to cut through the plastic. He'd twisted the strip of material, so it was thin and cylindrical. He pushed and pulled the strip in a fast, sawing motion. The friction caused a heat that allowed the material to melt and cut through the plastic. He cut out a big rectangle, which fitted perfectly at the bottom of the box. Within the rectangular plastic, he used the same 'twisted strip of bed sheet' technique to cut out three additional rectangles, leaving three pedals. He'd ordered a set of washing-up sponges from the *pakali* – grocery, which he cut into halves and wedged underneath the pedals where it met the cardboard flooring and stuck everything to the box with melted plastic. Just above the sponge, he'd stuck metallic foil on the back of each of the pedals and the cardboard beneath it. When the pedal was pushed down, the two strips of foil would meet.

Next, he opened up an existing PlayStation control pad. In the same way that he'd made the electrocuting hi-fi, he used plastic straws like a soldering iron – by burning the ends and dripping the melted plastic to keep the connections stuck together. He connected two wires to the metal underneath three of the main buttons on the PlayStation control pad, which were used for driving. Each button now had two wires connected to them. Christos connected one for each of the buttons to the foil on the back of the pedal. He attached the other three to the foil on the cardboard floor. When the pedals were pushed and the two strands of foil met, it would cause a connection in the same way as if the buttons were pushed on the control pad. I was extremely impressed, but was yet to discover if it would work.

He'd mounted the control pad at the rear of the box, just above the back end of the wooden broom handle. The analogue joystick controlled the direction of the car on the video game. He stole a chess piece from Jamal's chess set, melted the bottom and welded it to the tip of the joystick to make it longer. Jamal never found out that it was Christos who stole from him, but I'm sure he had his suspicions.

Christos then used a strip of material to create a mechanism between the extended joystick and the back of the wooden broom handle. When the steering wheel turned right, the joystick would turn left – when the steering wheel turned left, the joystick would turn right. The control pad had been mounted upside down, so that the PlayStation registered the directions as the same.

I'd watched him make the entire thing and was adamant that it wouldn't work, but I was wrong. It didn't just work, it worked flawlessly! He'd only started to make it the previous evening, and suddenly we had full control over the virtual car, being able to skid, drift around corners and win races on the most difficult setting. We sat for hours, taking it in turns to race.

If Christos had been given more opportunities in life, I'm confident in saying that he could have been the next Steve Jobs. I don't think he realised it, but he had a talent that many people don't have – an initiative and ability to create incredible things out of almost nothing. I believe that the greatest and most innovative inventions in this world are envisioned by people with minds that work in the same way as Christos's. He was resourceful and imaginative – feeling pride in everything that he'd ever made. Regardless of the fact that he may possibly have been insane and sometimes felt the need to pierce his own body parts with dirty wires, it was a tragedy that he'd been wasting such indisputable talent.

It has been argued whether an IQ test is a valid measure of intelligence, or whether intelligence is the ability to adapt to environmental changes and use resources successfully. I think we'd all have to agree that being able to make alcohol, a CD/MP3 player, a tattoo machine, an electrical muscle stimulator and full driving simulator hardware with nothing but everyday household items – using only a cigarette lighter, plastic straws and plastic bags – is pretty goddamn genius. As Aristotle said, 'There is no great genius without a mixture of madness.' Christos was a genius, even though he once asked me whether London was in New York. I doubt I'll ever meet another person like him again.

25

TIME FOR SCHOOL

It seemed as though the summer season jumped straight into winter and skipped autumn altogether – the vital crossover season that would have prepared us for the cold months ahead. The change in weather gave Parartima a completely different atmosphere. It was no longer unbearably hot and sticky, but had become cold, slippery and wet. Sometimes it rained all day – the smell of hot body odour and cigarette smoke in our cell had become overpowered by the stench of sewage, urine and faeces because our toilets would sometimes overflow. We had to hand-wash our clothes in a bucket and hang them on one of the many washing lines in the hallway, but it had become so cold that our clothes wouldn't dry. They were wet for days, leaving the entire wing with a musty and damp smell. We'd sit on chairs in the hallway of Parartima and look out into the courtyard. *Pegleri* in hand, we'd stare at the same green mountain above the barbed-wired wall and listen to the ambient sound of pattering rain against the stone benches and concrete outside.

I saw Costas, the male nurse, again – the one who looked like Tim Curry. Every inmate had to be tested for hepatitis and HIV, which was a very good thing. Thousands of mosquitoes had circled the wing throughout the summer and had bitten whatever piece of flesh they'd come into contact with. It seemed like Costas had never taken anyone's blood before. I opened and closed my fist and he slapped my inner elbow for ages, but still couldn't find the vein. After twenty minutes of slaps on both of my arms, I decided that we should stop trying – I was quite optimistic that I didn't have either virus anyway.

'Maybe we should stop,' I said.

'You want to stop?'

'Yeah, if that's OK.'

'Why, do you not trust me?'

I felt bad, but said 'no'. The truth was that I didn't really trust him at all. If he'd known what he was doing then my blood sample would have been taken within a few minutes. I'd never had any trouble having blood tests in the past, so I couldn't understand why it was so difficult for him.

An ex-heroin addict called Costakis was sitting on a chair waiting to be the next victim of stinging arm slaps. He'd witnessed Costas's inability to take my blood, so when it was his turn he said '*Dose mou to* – Give me it,' referring to the syringe. Costas handed it to the inmate, who managed to take his own blood in the first attempt. '*Koita reh, prepei na to kaneis etsi!* – Look, man, you have to do it like this!' he said.

᛭᛭᛭

'School' began in October. I would wake up at 8 a.m. and head to the building, which was connected to the prison. On the first day I was overcome with frustration because it was a stark reminder that I should have been in a lecture at university. Instead, I was in Avlona's very own '*proti gymnasiou*', which was the lowest class because my Greek was so poor. It was supposedly equivalent to Year Seven in a British secondary school, but I thought that Year One primary school level seemed a more appropriate description.

The classroom was a large, rectangular hall with a faint blue floor and off-white walls. There were two lessons that would go on in the hall at the same time – my lesson would be to the right end of the hall and another lesson would be to the left. Some of the inmates in my class had very little or no education, so they seemed to appreciate the opportunity to learn something. The guys in the other lesson (which was in the same room) didn't seem to care a lot of the time and would sometimes shout, scream and fight.

There were nine of us in my class and the tables were laid out in a 'U' shape. I sat on the right side of the 'U', at the very end – next to Arnas. The teacher stood to my right and in front of a whiteboard that was propped up against the wall. On the other side of the 'U', opposite me, sat Yusuf from Sudan. He was a big black guy who was chubby, broad and tall. I used to call him 'Biggie' because he dressed like the notorious gangster rapper: wearing Eckō tracksuits, Yankees baseball caps and plastic, gold-coloured chunky jewellery. Biggie really liked a pair of Nike tracksuit bottoms that I owned, and every few days he'd ask me if he could buy them. I said to him, 'If I sell these to you I might have to come to school in my boxers!' I only had them and another pair.

Next to him sat William from Nigeria, who'd just discovered that he'd have to serve a six-year sentence. On his first day in the Avlona school, one of the teachers asked him how he felt about his guilty verdict. With a straight face, he said to the class that he wanted to kill himself. Almost every morning when we walked in, Arnas would approach him, shake his hand and say, 'William, it's good to see you're still alive my friend.'

To William's right was Emmanuel from Kenya, who made it very clear to the class that he wanted to bomb the whole of Greece. Then there was Dmitry from Russia, who had a funny eyebrow twitch and turned up one day covered from head to toe in bruises. Next to him sat two inmates from Iraq whose names I can't remember, then Povilas from Lithuania – who like Arnas was caught trafficking drugs.

The school day lasted only a few hours. Lessons were about fifteen minutes long with a fifteen-minute 'cigarette' break in between them. We had an art lesson, whereby we were handed a piece of paper and asked to draw something. I wrote the words 'injustice, no logic' in big, shadowed, bubble writing. I showed it to the teacher, who nodded and said, 'Yes … very nice.' We had other lessons, like maths, English, music and PE. During our first maths lesson, the teacher wrote the number 666 on the whiteboard and asked the class whether we knew the number that came next. I was absolutely shocked because not all of the inmates in the class knew that is was 667. One guy thought the answer was 777; another thought it was 6666. I didn't think that they were morons – I felt sorry for them because they had never been taught something so simple. We also had a biology lesson, where the teacher handed out photocopied A4 pieces of paper with a picture of a chicken and a picture of a rock on it. The topic of the lesson was to discuss whether the chicken or the rock was alive, and Emmanuel from Kenya claimed that they were both alive because 'chickens move and rocks grow into mountains'.

It's strange to think that none of us could count when we were young children; imagine if we'd never had the chance to learn. None of us knew about tectonic plates in the Earth and how mountains are formed – we learned it in school! My time in Avlona's school was an eye-opener; it made me realise that I'd taken for granted the fact that I'd been educated – and I'd under-estimate the extent to which many people in the world are not. In a similar way to my conversation with Georgios (which made me contemplate our opinions on certain issues if we'd swapped lives), I wondered what life would be like if I'd led one similar to

Emmanuel. Would I honestly assume that rocks are alive? Could I honestly not figure out that the number 667 comes after 666? If Emmanuel had my life and went to my school, maybe he'd have a PhD by now – a higher qualification than I'll ever have!

Journal extract – Day 106 – 3 November 2009

> *One of the teachers from the 'school' called George teaches us maths. He has recently started to make it more challenging for me, which is good. Not just 2 + 2 = 4, but fractions and powers etc. … things that are easy but you have to work out, they actually stimulate a few brain cells! He is a legend – a very good guy. He has been researching my case. He printed the* Daily Mail *news article about me while I was in here so I could see it. Today he lent me an English book about positivity and accepting change. I'm going to finish the book I am on now and start reading it.*

By this stage I'd read many books and was a master of the *pegleri* beads. I could twirl them between my fingers from the pinky all the way to the thumb without even looking or thinking about it. My Greek had improved and I'd taught myself how to cut hair. My dad had bought me a cheap pair of hair clippers that were allowed into the prison once they'd been through security. He insisted on it because of something that I'd told him during our previous visit. One morning I'd woken up to a buzzing noise, which ended up being a fly caught in my beard. I hadn't shaved since being in London and he told me that I looked like Hagrid from the *Harry Potter* series. I shaved my beard with the clippers and asked Costakis (the guy who could take his own blood) if he could cut my hair. I told him exactly what to do, but he just shaved my entire head without telling me that he would. It was such a transformation that the guards barely even recognised me.

I knew not to lend the clippers to anyone, because they would disappear instantly and no one would have 'any clue what happened to them'. Instead, I would offer to cut someone's hair when they needed a trim – so I became the prison barber for a little while, even though I'd never cut hair in my life. I improved after my first few haircut attempts (which weren't very good). I would use a comb and the hair clippers with no protection to trim the hair because I didn't have any scissors. For the guys who had been in Parartima for longer than me, the haircut was free. I would charge a €4 telephone card to any new inmates, then I would go and call one of my friends in London, or Riya, who I would then call three times a week. It was a great feeling being able to contact them. They would always be shocked at how positive I sounded because I always made an effort to sound upbeat on the phone. They would never know how much my heart would break as soon as the conversation was over.

I was moved from cell five after confronting Christos for stealing a packet of my cigarettes. It led to a heated testosterone-fuelled argument that had been waiting to happen for some time. I'm not an aggressive person, but the build-up of frustration got the better of me. I lost my temper and called him a prick when I found out, so he gave me a stinging punch to the face and cut my eye with his silver ring. I started to breathe heavily as though I was going to explode, but considering that I'd been wrongfully charged with a violent crime, and that I could be transferred to Korydallos maximum-security prison with just one phone call – I took a deep breath and didn't fight back. I admit that it was difficult to control myself, but I knew that the *Archi Fylakas* wouldn't have hesitated to pass on information of violent behaviour to the judges, and probably exaggerate the story. The prosecution would be more than happy to use anything against me to defame my character.

With a bloody and bruised eye, I exhaled and unclenched my

fist. Locked in a cell for hours on end, we were in each other's faces for far too long; it was unhealthy. Our minds were polluted with the stresses of our pending court cases; they were constantly in our heads, desperately finding ways to escape. Sometimes it was impossible to bear because we had no privacy. I genuinely liked Christos. It was inevitable for conflicts to happen between us, but I wouldn't allow them to escalate to violence. It wasn't me, and a packet of Winston Classic cigarettes wasn't worth the potential consequences.

I wasn't a *roufianos* like my ex-cellmate Yiannis was; I just asked if I could move cell and didn't give the *Archi Fylakas* a reason. I must have caught him on a good day. He ended up moving me into cell one with Jamal, a Tanzanian man called Nico, and Arnas, which was lucky because he'd become a very good friend of mine. I slept on the top bunk above Jamal, which was next to a long barred window. It had a wooden shutter, but half of it wouldn't close at all.

Journal extract – Day 115 – 12 November 2009

The weather is getting worse. It's actually freezing, and sleeping next to an open window is painful. It's raining, which means my entire bed is soaked – it's so irritating. There's no heating, no hot water, just a thin blanket to sleep with, which is now very wet. Recently I have been sleeping in my Nike tracksuit bottoms (lucky I didn't sell them to Biggie), socks, a hoodie and a woolly hat because at night the temperature of the cell is maybe … 2°C? It's not going to get warmer, only colder as we start getting into December. Fuck, my hands are so cold I can't even write properly. I'm dreading having a shower.

Every day I made a request to the guards to fix the window shutter, but I would get the same answer: '*avrio* – tomorrow'. There were a few nights when I would wake up in the early hours of the morning, shivering because the bottom half of my body was covered in inches of snow. My clothes would absorb the icy slush, causing serious flu. Having the flu in a smoke-contaminated cell is awful, and it doesn't help when having to sleep on a wet mattress next to an open window. To make it even worse, we had no hot water. I told my mum about the situation when she came to visit me. She became angry and casually mentioned it to the guards on her way out, which I'd warned her not to do because I'd been held in the best wing of the complex for my entire incarceration. It was obvious that they didn't like it when inmates' mothers complained. They saw us as men, and if you're a man whose mum fights your battles for you, you're a *malakas*.

The next day I was told by one of the guards that the *Archi Fylakas* wanted to talk to me. I was escorted into his office. '*Thelete zesto nero?* – You want hot water?' he asked.

I didn't know how to respond. 'Erm…'

'Why don't I just move you to the other sector with all the Albanians … or you can go to Korydallos. *Ehoun zesto nero ekei* – They have hot water there,' he said.

I still didn't know what to say; I was speechless.

'*Fiye* – Leave,' he demanded.

Being transferred was a constant worry of mine, and it didn't help that Jamal overheard me telling Arnas that I'd turned twenty-one. Maybe I was paranoid, but I didn't trust Jamal at all; I feared that he would tell the guards and I didn't want them to be reminded that I was technically too old for Avlona. The management were lazy and sloppy, so if I attracted as little attention as possible, I would fade into the background and be forgotten about until my trial. The problem was that the guards were well aware of my presence – and after what the *Archi Fylakas* had said – it was clear that he was already pissed off with me.

Journal extract – Day 118 – 15 November 2009

The other day I saw the Archi Fylakas *beat the crap out of an Albanian prisoner. I knew it happened, I've heard it but never seen it. He was walking behind the prisoner and slapping him round the head. When the boy turned around he punched the boy round the face, again and again. Then another guard, who had nothing to do with it, saw and must have thought, oh yes, something fun to do. He jumped in and started punching him as well. I don't know what the guy did, but he was beaten pretty badly.*

26

IT DOESN'T MATTER HOW LONG IT TAKES

It was a chilly December day but the sky was a cloudless blue. School had just finished so I walked back to my cell and was locked in for the afternoon. I lay on my bunk and started to copy out a letter that I'd planned to give to Riya. She was flying out to Greece and I wanted her to have something tangible to take back to the UK. My handwriting needed to be as neat as possible, unlike the illegible draft that I'd scribbled on to one of the back pages of my notebook. I managed to persuade Zoe the social worker to allow three open visits with her, and it was all I'd been thinking about.

I heard an *ypallilos* slot the master key into the door and unlock it from the outside. It didn't seem right; it was slightly too early for lock-in time to be over. He opened the door and walked into the cell. '*Symeou. Ta pragmata sas, kato* – Your things, down.'

What things of mine are down? I remember thinking. I didn't understand what he meant exactly. '*Ti pramata?* – What things?' I asked.

'*Parei ola ta pragmata sas kato sto grafeio* – Take all of your things down to the office,' he abruptly elaborated.

My heart began to palpitate. 'What for?' I asked.

'*Etsei einai* – That's how it is.'

'What do you mean, "*etsei einai*"? Why am I taking all of my things to the office!?'

'*Etsei eipe o Archi Fylakas* – It's what the Chief Guard said.'

It felt like my heart was about to explode. I just wanted to be left alone so that I could finish copying out the letter I was writing.

He tried to rush me. '*Ade pame!* – Come on, let's go!'

'If you tell me why I have to take my things down, I will. I'm not doing it otherwise.'

He let out an irritated exhalation and left the cell, locking the metal door behind him. I heard footsteps and could see through the small peephole in the door that he'd walked out of the wing. Suddenly an eye peered back and startled me – it was Fivos, who'd been let out of his cell for his cleaning job.

'What the fuck's going on *reh*?' he said through the door.

'The *ypallilos* wants me to take all of my shit down to the office.'

'Maybe they are releasing you ... freedom!' he said.

It did cross my mind. We'd appealed the second bail decision – perhaps I'd won. I shook my head and waived the passing thought. 'They're sending me to Korydallos. I know it.' I had a gut feeling.

He was silent for a moment as if there were no words to say. '*Gamise ta* – Fuck. Hopefully not ... wait, don't go anywhere!' he blurted before being dragged to another wing to clean.

I nervously walked up and down the cell floor – back and forth. 'Won't you pack your things?' asked Nico, the Tanzanian man who lay on his bunk.

'Fuck that, I need to know where I'm going first,' I said.

I sat on the plastic chair and lit a cigarette – my leg shook with apprehension. I'd always known the transfer was a possibility, but I would never have been prepared for one of Europe's worst maximum-security prisons. The *ypallilos* returned. 'Why haven't you packed your things!? You have two minutes!' he said.

'Two minutes until what!? I told you I'm not going until you tell me. Am I being released?' I asked frantically.

'*Ohi* – No.'

'Am I being taken to Korydallos?'

Before he opened his mouth, there was a brief moment when I sensed his eyes acknowledge the agony in mine.

'*Nai* – Yes,' he answered.

He awkwardly looked away for a fraction of a second. I knew that the slight glance was his way of distancing himself from accountability for the decision.

I couldn't speak and my body froze. It was the same feeling as when I first discovered that I'd be sent to a Greek prison. I was alone and terrified in Zakynthos Police Station all over again. I'd finally begun to settle. Four months doesn't sound like a long time to live somewhere, but it feels like far longer when living in the wing of a prison. I couldn't bear the thought of being transferred to Korydallos Prison; I couldn't accept it as true – anywhere but there. I'd built up an idea of it in my head and it was like being told that I was about to go to hell on Earth.

'Collect all your things, you have one minute now,' uttered the *ypallilos* before walking down the hallway. He unlocked all of the cell doors in Parartima and inmates stepped out into the corridor to see what all the fuss was about.

My hands were trembling and I was forced to gather my things while trying my hardest to stop my eyes from flooding with fear. Being transferred to Korydallos was a nightmare of mine and it was becoming real. I could feel an emotional headache building up. It was cruel to give me only minutes to prepare for the move; I'd built a life for myself in Avlona. They must have known about the transfer for days but never told me a thing. As much as it hurt, I had no choice but to do as the *ypallilos* said. He walked back down to the office to wait for me, so I took the opportunity to quickly call my mum in a panic. It was visiting day, so she was on the train heading to Avlona with my auntie Georgina.

'Oh my God, they're moving him to an adult prison,' I heard her blurt to Georgina. 'Andrew, tell them to wait … I'll literally be there in five minutes to talk to them,' she said softly.

'Why would they listen to me? They don't care.'

I'd taken too long to pack my things. The *ypallilos* had come back to Parartima to rush me. I knew that if I didn't pack my things they'd force me to leave and I wouldn't have any belongings with me. Everything was so fast and I had hardly any time to think. I quickly threw my stuff into the Nike sports bag that I'd been living out of for the previous four months. There were some socks and underwear soaking in a bucket that I'd been in the process of washing, but I had to leave them behind because they were soapy and wet. I handed Arnas the self-help book that was lent to me. 'Make sure you give this back to George, the maths teacher.' I put my hand out to shake his.

He took my hand and then wrapped his arm around my shoulder and pulled me towards him. We embraced in a hug and he patted me on the back. 'Don't worry, man, it will be exactly the same as here. You'll be free soon. *Into the Wild*, remember?'

'I remember,' I stuttered.

'It doesn't matter how long it takes to happen, all that matters is that it will,' said Arnas. It was a phrase that I'll never forget. He'd become one of my best friends and I never saw him again. I didn't even have the chance to say a proper goodbye to Fivos. The time we'd all spent together in Avlona is something that we'll always share. We were never meant to cross paths, but we had, and in some strange way, I'm glad that we had. I never would have believed that leaving Avlona would be so emotional.

I walked through the Parartima hallway escorted by one of the guards. I wiped my eyes – they must have been puffy and red but I didn't let a tear run down my face. Some inmates moved to the left of the hallway to make way for us; some to the right. They watched in amazement as I walked past them like I was on death row walking the mile again. I was liked by many of the inmates in Parartima – a few of them made eye contact and softly nodded. It was their way of saying goodbye, good luck, you can do it, and acknowledging that the transfer was a complete *malakia*. I stood in the office for the last time. 'Why are you doing this?' I cried.

'*Skotoses enan anthropo, kai rotas yiati?* – You killed a man, and you ask why?' said the *Archi Fylakas*.

'I didn't kill anyone.'

'*Milame Ellinika!* – We speak Greek!' he bellowed, thumping his fist on his desk.

'Are you a judge?' I asked him.

He ignored me. I turned to Dimos – a prison guard who looked like Vin Diesel and had always been kind to me. After visits from my family he would often tell me that he thought my parents were very nice people. His face was serious, but his eyes told me that he knew it shouldn't be happening. 'Just let me stay. Please.'

He looked away, powerless.

'But I go to the school!' I argued.

The *Archi Fylakas* ignored me. I was escorted to the front of the complex where two police officers handcuffed me from behind and sat me in the back seat of a police car.

PART III

I learned that courage was not the absence of fear, but the triumph over it. The brave man is not he who does not feel afraid, but he who conquers that fear.
– Nelson Mandela

2 December 2009, BBC News

UK MAN IN 'INFAMOUS' GREEK PRISON

Campaigners say they have 'grave concerns' after a north London student on remand in Greece was moved to an 'infamous' maximum-security prison.

Andrew Symeou, 21, is charged with the manslaughter of Jonathan Hiles, 18, of Cardiff, who died on the isle of Zante in 2007, allegedly after being punched.

Mr Symeou, of Enfield, has been moved to Korydallos Prison in Athens, a jail condemned by Amnesty International.

Fair Trials International said it was 'horrified' at the move.

Mr Hiles, who was in Britain's roller-hockey team, died in July 2007 two days after falling off a dance podium in a nightclub.

Bournemouth University student Mr Symeou has denied killing him, saying that he was not in the club at the time.

He was extradited to Greece in July after losing a High Court battle and has been denied bail.

Mr Symeou was held at a detention centre for young people north of Athens until he was transferred to Korydallos Prison on Wednesday.

Fair Trials International Chief Executive Jago Russell said, 'Andrew, who was informed of the transfer only five minutes before he had to leave, is reportedly highly distraught.

'He has already been in jail for four months with no opportunity to clear his name.

'We are horrified that this young man has today been transferred to this infamous prison, and have grave concerns for his welfare.'

Human rights group Amnesty International and the European Committee for the Prevention of Torture have repeatedly expressed concern about Korydallos Prison.

Amnesty said inmates faced degrading treatment including poor hygiene in cells and a lack of fresh air, exercise facilities or prompt medical treatment.

27

STARRED UP

2 December 2009, Korydallos Prison, Piraeus

An Australian/Greek admin worker in the Korydallos Prison office took my photograph while I stood anxious and intimidated. I was allocated to the Gamma wing. 'You have nothing to worry about,' he said. The words didn't comfort me because I knew that they weren't true. I felt a constant falling sensation, like I was plummeting down a bottomless hole. However awful I felt, I had no choice but to hide my numbing fear with a sombre face and confident demeanour. I had to be as strong as possible; I couldn't show weakness.

The complex was a maze of corridors and I was expected to find Gamma by myself. My mind felt compelled to wander again and a silly thought suddenly entered my head: I could have blagged my way as an assistant psychologist interning from London and walked right out the front door. I started to reason with myself, as though I was seriously considering it. First, I was wearing tracksuit bottoms and Adidas trainers; for it to be believable I would have needed to find a psychologist and rob him of his clothes. Secondly, I was pretty fat at the time, so it would have had to be a fat psychologist that I robbed, otherwise his clothes wouldn't have fitted me. Thirdly, even if I had walked out, I wouldn't have been a free man. There was no escaping – even when using my wildest, stupidest imagination. I had no choice but to face it.

I stepped into Gamma wing and was immediately confronted by the echoing hum of wolf-whistles and men shouting. It was absolutely chaotic and I was instantly filled with fear. It wasn't like Avlona's Parartima (as Arnas had assumed it would be); hundreds of inmates roamed the wing and it was far larger, much more un-hygienic and daunting. A soaring ceiling covered a barred jungle of three-tiered levels, which hosted around 120 solid steel cell doors – each coated in dull orange paint. The ground floor was a wide, elongated hallway that was home to a number of dirty stray cats as well as many criminals. With broad, open-barred windows at the very end of the wing, pigeons made their way inside and perched on ceiling fans that no longer worked. The result was that the floor had blotches of bird and cat faeces scattered all around.

There were several men standing on the middle and top floors who leaned against the chest-high barriers. The barriers were made of steel bars, thickly covered with lumpy off-white paint – but were stained a nicotine yellow, chipped and rusting. The men watched over the ground floor as though they were standing on balconies; they could have been propelled over the side and fallen to their deaths at any moment. There were no safety barriers and it was extremely dangerous.

At the front of the wing was a staircase connecting each floor, which was open for inmates to walk freely on any level of the prison wing. Inmates were hanging around on the steps in groups – a threat to new inmates who needed to walk up or down the stairs. On the ground floor near the bottom of the staircase was a prison guard sitting at a desk.

With a plastic bin bag full of clothes in my hand, and my Nike sports bag over my shoulder, I looked down at the *ypallilos*, who was gazing back like a hawk.

'*Ti?* – What?' he said.

I rolled my eyes. 'I'm here to go to prison?'

'*Epitheton?* – Surname?'

'*Symeou.*'

He shuffled around some papers on the desk in front of him. '*Saranta ennea* – forty-nine.'

'Where is it?'

'*Proto orofo, aristera kai sti mesi* – First floor, on the left and in the middle,' he replied, pointing me in the correct direction without moving his eyes from the document in front of him.

My trembling nerves started to heighten. If it wasn't for my four months in Avlona I would have found it far more difficult to cope. I'd experienced entering a new prison before, and Avlona was a huge stepping-stone. Nevertheless, I could almost hear my own heartbeat increasing in speed – I was absolutely shitting myself. I took a breath and walked up the staircase, making sure that I didn't make eye contact with any inmates. I could hear different languages – what could have been Albanian and fast blurts of Arabic. My peripheral vision saw a group of inmates sitting on the stairs, but I didn't look at them. I looked forward and didn't move my head. Some were smoking and staring at me with curious eyes. A bulky man wearing a bandana hurried down the staircase, like an antelope running from a lion. He barged me as he passed and I almost toppled over. There was a hand on my shoulder behind me – I was startled, but the hand also stopped me from falling backwards down the stairs. I turned my head to the side and recognised the face. It was Leonarde from Patras Police Station, from before I was taken to Avlona (one of the Romanian guys who I'd shared a holding cell with for four days).

'You remember me?' he said, smiling.

I shook his hand in shock, as I expected never to see him again. 'Course I remember you, where's your brother and Remos?'

'Constantin is here.' Leonarde pointed to the bottom of the stairs where I could see his brother waving.

I gave him a subtle wave back. 'And how about Remos?'

'He's in Epsilon sector. But you will see him; he works in the kitchen and serves the food in Gamma sometimes.'

'And how is it here?' I asked.

He grinned. 'My friend. This is a hotel, didn't you know?'

'What time is check out?'

'You can check out if you don't hang yourself first,' he replied.

I ignored the comment. 'Forty nine ... you know who's in that cell!?'

'I don't think so. Come, this way,' he said.

I followed him up the stairs onto the middle floor, noticing that he strolled around like he owned the place. He turned his head towards me as we walked. 'I promise, you don't want to be living with the *Tsingani'* – Romany gypsies who are renowned for thieving in prison.

Looking around the Gamma wing I could already see that inmates generally stuck to their own kind. There were racial gangs, mainly of Romany gypsies, Albanians, Russians, Pakistanis, Africans, Greeks and even some Chinese.

'Here it is,' Leonarde said. He thumped his fist on the metal door, then pulled it open and peeked his head into cell forty-nine. '*Ehete ena kainourgio, kalo paidi* – You have a new one, good kid,' Leonarde said to my new cellmates. I couldn't see who was inside the cell because the door was obstructing my vision. Leonarde quickly whispered something to me. 'You're lucky, they are *Ellines* – Greeks.'

I walked around the door and into the cell where two men were sitting inside. It was half the size of Avlona's cells; absolutely tiny. Two metal-framed bunk beds met to make an 'L' shape, but there was no gap between them like there was in Avlona. There

was a small, rectangular, barred window at the other end of the
cell, which sat above one of the top bunks. Just to the right of
the cell door was a floor-level toilet, leaving the cell with the
potent stench of sewage. To make it worse, there was only a thin
half-wall to separate it from the rest of the cell. On the other side
of the thin wall was a sink and a small plastic garden table and
chair, which left only very little walking space. At the top of the
right wall was a long fluorescent tube light fitting with a plastic
diffuser. Underneath the diffuser must have been hundreds of
little cockroaches crawling around – I started to notice that the
cell was infested. I cringed when I spotted little cockroaches on
the walls, around the toilet and even on the cell door. It was difficult to believe that *four* fully grown men were expected to live in
such a small, insect-infested cell. It was inhumane. The cell was
too small for even two people to live in.

'*Ti krevati?* – Which bed?' I mumbled to one of the men.

He pointed to the bottom bunk that was free, adjacent to the
cell door against the left wall. There was a muscular bald man with
a goatee sitting on my bunk and playing with a *kombolloi* – beads
threaded on a looped piece of string – similar to a *pegleri*. I pushed
my bags underneath the bunk. The other man was sitting at the
table and peeling potatoes with a prison-made blade. I have no
idea what it was made out of, but it could easily have slit a throat.

'Come, let's go for a *volta* – stroll,' said Leonarde. We walked
down to the ground floor and wandered from one end of the
wing to the other – back and forth at a gentle pace. My temples
pounded, but I managed to prevent myself from bursting into
hysteria. Instead I put on a cool façade, covering the unbearable
tension inside of me; I think that I was even smiling sometimes.
I remember trying not to look anyone in the eyes and feeling
jittery, but walking with Leonarde was the best way to ease into
my surroundings.

There were plastic garden chairs and tables outside several cells. I could hear the knocking sounds of inmates throwing dice onto wooden *tavli* – backgammon boards. Some inmates were playing *skaki* – chess, and smoking or drinking *frappes*.

Two Chinese inmates were sitting behind a table outside of their cell and had created their own prison market stall. They'd handcrafted wooden objects out of kebab skewers and were selling them; their main products were cases for small disposable Bic cigarette lighters. The cases had been beautifully crafted, carefully glued together, filed down and varnished, giving the impression that they had been professionally manufactured in solid wood. Each of them exhibited a different painted design. Some were basic with black writing in different languages; others were coated with colourful religious icons, or pictures of things like dragons, cannabis leaves or naked women. There were a couple of full-sized backgammon boards for sale, which were also made entirely out of wooden skewers. It must have taken them months to make because the boards hadn't even been painted. They'd used a hot pan to burn thousands of skewers, so they had an entire spectrum of brown shades. The dark triangular markings on the face of the board were made from skewers of different lengths, which had been fried to a dark brown shade. Having been carefully filed down and varnished, the backgammon boards were left with a unique, striped texture and glow – but when you looked closely at the edges, you could see that it was made out of thousands of wooden sticks. I found it incredible and it reminded me of Christos in Avlona. With his ingenuity and their application, imagine what they could have made together.

'You know, I'm only walking with you so that people here can see you're with someone,' Leonarde revealed.

'Thanks.'

'Yeah, no problem.'

'When's your court?' I asked.

'I'm still waiting.'

'Yeah, me too. What kind of fucked-up system is this?'

'You will be here a lot longer than me. I'm here for a money crime, you're here for murder.'

The words were painful to my ears – sometimes I forgot why I was even there in the first place. Only hours earlier I was in cell one in Parartima, writing a letter to Riya. I was still in shock from the speedy transfer and desperately needed to think positively. I wouldn't be able to cope for the first few days if I were to get caught up in another negative spiral of my own fears and anxieties. Although Leonarde was trying to help me, comments like that didn't help at all. Positivity was the key, because the thought of possibly being locked-up for twenty years was a niggling thought that had been eating away at me for ages. Korydallos Prison was hell on earth, and I was paying for someone else's crime.

I returned to cell forty-nine and one of my new cellmates handed me a plastic container. '*Fayito?* – Food?' he asked. I copied him and took a food coupon out of an empty cigarette box that had been glued to the wall, to the left of the cell door. Earlier in the day, an inmate worker would poke his head into the cell and place the coupons in there, like a prison postman.

From the first-floor hallway I could see a crowd of inmates forming at the front of the wing, next to the stairs on the ground floor. I made my way to the back of the herd, where inmates began to push past each other like rugby players, desperate to make their way to the front. Within seconds I found myself in the centre of a smelly scrum of prisoners, being continuously pushed to the back like a *malakas*. The only way to make it to the front was to shove myself through them all and fight for my food, but I was too nervous to do that. A punch-up between two inmates kicked off and one fell to the floor – others kicked him as he screamed. It all happened so quickly – I gazed in surprise as the only *ypallilos* supervising the Gamma wing took a step back and waited for it to end. Was it going to be this dangerous, every day, just to eat? How could I possibly cope? I was exhausted just witnessing it. It was unfortunate that my first experience of queuing for food in Gamma was more dramatic than your typical day.

Inmates from other prison wings served the food out of huge metal cauldrons. Once the madness had finally died down, the injured inmate was carried out of the wing by a guard and another inmate. I'd made it to the front; the inmate serving the food scraped out the last scoop of *kritharaki me kreas* – barley pasta with meat, and let it drool into my plastic container. The lumps of lamb were all chewy fat, which floated in an artery-clogging river of red oil – I didn't even want to think about what else was in it. I took the food back to the cell, unable to bring myself to eat it. I was drained, nauseous, dizzy and powerless to calm the quivering in my chest. Going through the disturbing experience of collecting the prison food on my first day in Gamma wasn't worth the hassle. Just before lock-in, one of my cellmates took the leftovers to the ground-level hallway and splattered all of it onto the centre of the floor. Several other inmates would do the same. The middle of the wing would be covered in leftover food and families of stray cats would feast.

It was the first time that I'd had the chance to become properly acquainted with my cellmates. Stelios was a chain-smoker and *frappe*-drinker – a small, skinny man in his forties who looked a little bit like a Greek Robert Carlyle, although he was shorter and sweaty, with thinning hair. He was wearing a bright red McDonald's T-shirt, exhibiting the famous golden arches. But instead of displaying the fast-food franchise's well-known slogan 'I'm lovin' it', the T-shirt said 'I'm smokin' it', and had a picture of a cannabis leaf in the background. I think he had a mild form of Tourette syndrome, because he would often blurt out random meaningless syllables for no apparent reason, like '*pou le le le le!*' He spoke no English, only quick blurts of short Greek sentences. I could just about understand his story – he told me that he absolutely loved smoking weed and grew it on his farm in Rhodes. His whole family smoked weed – it sounded like his wife and kids were always stoned while he was out almost every night having sex with *poutanes* – prostitutes. He was in prison because one of his neighbours had stolen a few kilos of his hashish, so he chased him through the village with a shotgun and shot him in the thigh.

'Can you imagine *Stelios*, chasing the man with a shotgun?' Vasilis, my other cellmate, said. He was in his late twenties – tall and thin with a kind face. He mimicked Stelios waddling along, holding a shotgun and sticking his tongue in and out like Stelios would sometimes do. 'I call him the *savras*.'

'What's a *savras*?' I asked.

'It's a lizard: this guy just reminds me of a lizard – look at him! You'll notice that he does this thing with his tongue where he sticks it out sometimes,' he said. Vasilis was from Athens – an ex-heroin addict who was caught mugging an old woman for her purse so that he could buy drugs. He seemed like such a normal guy and I couldn't understand how he had ended up a heroin addict.

'It starts off as a little thing you do with your friends, then it starts to be every week … then every few days … then every day. It's an expensive habit and you will do anything for your next hit. Before you know it you're robbing someone's *yiayia* – grandma. *Malakia!*' he said.

'And what about now? Are you clean?' I asked.

'100 per cent clean. Even in prison I haven't. I was a *malakas* back then, now oxygen is my drug,' he said.

A new inmate called Ashmul had joined the cell while I was walking with Leonarde. He was from Bangladesh and, to this day,

I still have no idea why he was in prison. He spoke hardly any Greek and no English at all. Ashmul was a short, balding man in his thirties, with a big head, flat nose and pot belly. I'd been assigned to cell forty-nine just before him, and it was an unwritten rule that whoever had been in prison for the longest amount of time would be entitled to a bottom bunk. Vasilis was there for nine months before me, but preferred the top bunk above Stelios. I couldn't understand his preference at first, because it meant that he would have to keep climbing up and down. That night, I discovered why.

When the sun set and it was time to sleep, the lights were turned off and I stared at the rectangular light fitting attached to the wall. The hundreds of cockroaches underneath it began to disperse until there were none left. They scurried around the cell and made themselves at home in our beds. Tiny cockroaches swarmed the underneath of the top bunk. However much I tried to get rid of them, more kept coming back. I could feel them falling on me and crawling all over my body. I lay there in streams of silent tears because I was in hell, and desperately wanted my life back. My mind repeated, *I don't deserve this shit*, then I argued with myself, trying to give excuses for why I did deserve it. I needed a reason. I wasn't a murderer, I didn't kill Jonathan Hiles – but I deserved it because there were times when I may have acted selfishly in the past, or hadn't worked hard enough in school. I needed to go to prison to realise what I'd lost; to realise not to take things for granted; to realise that there is a lot to achieve in this life; to see the real world, not the middle-class bubble that I knew.

But I reckon one night there would have been enough.

28

THE KING OF THE GREEKS

I must have been far too exhausted for my sleeping mind to even conjure a dream, but the few hours of 'nothingness' at least offered some peace. My eyes opened and I couldn't help but gasp when I realised that I was in Korydallos Prison; it was far more difficult to bear than waking up in one of the police cells, or in Avlona on my first morning. There were cockroaches crawling on my face and I quickly brushed them off in a panic. 'What the fuck!' I blurted aloud. Luckily I hadn't woken any of my cellmates; it wouldn't have been the best way to start my first day in cell forty-nine.

It was early and the *ypallilos* hadn't yet unlocked the cell door. I lay there for hours, torturing myself with thoughts of the day ahead of me. Every negative thing in my life ran through my mind – the injustice of my extradition, the fear of life imprisonment – I even thought about my friend Michael like I'd always tend to do when things were bad. I sank deeper into my bunk, overcome with sadness and dread. I reminded myself that there were always people going through worse in the world – I just had to man the fuck up. The little cockroaches crawled around above me and I kept my attention on one, following it with my eyes. I let it crawl onto my finger – nothing to be afraid of.

An *ypallilos* unlocked the cell door. I shivered and I flicked the cockroach away. I stepped out of the cell onto the first floor hallway and lit a cigarette. Leaning over the chest-high bars, I overlooked a ground floor full of cats that would soon run away and be replaced with murderers, rapists and drug addicts. Inmates slowly began to fill the hallway to start their monotonous daily prison routines. After a few minutes, a herd of prisoners huddled near the front of the wing where a giant cauldron of watered-down milk was rolled in. I grabbed a plastic container from inside the cell and walked downstairs, thinking it would be a nice gesture to collect some while my cellmates were asleep. Within minutes I found myself in a ruck of prisoners again, all of whom were forcing themselves forward like animals and pushing me right to the back. I made my way out of the chaos and waited for it to be over. Once it'd calmed down, I collected the last dregs of milk and took it back to cell forty-nine. Stelios kept a box full of disposable plastic tumbler cups and straws under his bunk. I sneakily took a cup while he was asleep, but didn't take any of his coffee to shake up a *frappe*. I just filled it up with milk, wrapped up warm and made my way outside.

I was the first one in the courtyard that morning, a large, open rectangular space. There was a small, concrete area at the front with two wonky basketball hoops and sets of wooden benches under shelters on either side. The rest of the courtyard's ground was made up of grey sand and tiny broken-up rocks. As the hours passed, a group of Romany gypsies eventually began to play football on the gravel with a ball made of wrapped-up rags – some of them were barefoot and it was so cold.

Keeping myself to myself, I sat and hoped that no one would approach me. More inmates made their way into the courtyard and gathered into clusters of their own race. Ashmul came and sat with me for a few minutes – we attempted to communicate, but the language barrier was far too high. I noticed a few strange looks from other inmates. They probably thought, a white and brown inmate sitting together? Insanity! When Ashmul wandered back into the wing I heard a voice behind me that was deep and powerful. I couldn't understand the Greek words, but I knew that the man was speaking to me. I turned my head around to look at him – the first thing that I noticed was the five-dot prison tattoo on his left hand, which was the size of a baseball mitt. The man must have been in his thirties, bearded with a scar on the left side of his neck as though someone had tried to slice him with a right hook. He towered over me, broad and standing at around six and a half feet.

My heart began to palpitate. I lit a cigarette and didn't look at him. 'English,' I muttered, hoping that he couldn't speak a word.

'I said … I haven't seen you here. You're not an *Ellinas?* – a Greek?' he asked in his thick accent.

'*Kyprios apo Londino* – Cypriot from London.'

'*Milas Ellinika reh* – You speak Greek, man,' he said.

'Not as good as your English.'

'Here in prison, you are a Greek. You are one of us, unless you want to be fucking Albanian? Or are you a *Pakistanos* like your friend?' he chuckled – referring to Ashmul.

'I'm Greek.'

'You're with us now. *Onoma?* – Name?' he asked.

'*Andreas.*'

He pointed to his chest. '*Apollo.* Come to my *keli* – cell, whenever you want, number thirty-three. We will talk and drink coffee,' he said. He strolled off, back into the wing.

I had no intention of going to Apollo's cell for a coffee – he was being too nice and I had an uneasy feeling about it in the pit of my stomach.

The gypsies finished playing football, so I walked onto the

rocky part of the courtyard and circled it for a while. I saw an inmate shouting at the tall, concrete wall at the back of the courtyard. This guy's nuts, I thought. When I walked a bit closer I could hear faint, shouting voices responding to him. The wall at the back end of Gamma's courtyard met with Delta's courtyard, and the guy was arguing with someone from the neighbouring wing. Suddenly I noticed a rectangular package land a few metres away from my feet. Someone had hurled it from Delta into Gamma over the wall. The man sprinted over, grabbed the package and stuffed it inside his jacket before zipping it up and casually walking back to the wing – whistling. I looked around; there were no guards supervising the courtyard whatsoever.

Journal extract – Day 139 – 6 December 2009

I've been in Korydallos for three days now and it's been a living nightmare. The feeling of anxiety doesn't seem to be going away. I can do this, as long as the feeling starts to fade – my body feels numb. Yesterday the doctor here prescribed me Xanax and two other types of pills, so I'm hoping that the process of gaining consciousness in the mornings isn't as painful as it has been. You can do this, Andrew, it's nothing. You just have to keep yourself busy and the days will fly by. You are a soldier. Just do it.

Now I just want the days to pass. This is so stressful. I'm not going to make any friends here, not like in Avlona. Arnas was a good friend and now I've realised how important it is to have that. Here it is just me and my mind. At least I'm used to living the prison lifestyle. Vasilis speaks English at least – and plays chess. He's also been teaching me tavli (backgammon), but he's leaving soon.

The social worker here, Marios, told me he's going to try to move me to the 'Alpha' wing, which is apparently better. What

*if I get moved and it's shit? Who knows where this journey will
take me. What I do know is that things can't get any worse. Or
can they?*

My cellmate Stelios didn't seem to remember Ashmul's name. He
would accidentally refer to him as '*Moushmou*', or '*Moushmoul*', and
it had slowly evolved into the nickname '*Moushmoullo*'. Then he
would blurt out different variations like '*Moushmoullides!*' (which
could pass as a strange Greek surname) or '*Moushmoullopita!*'
(which quite literally means a '*Moushmoullo* pie'). I felt sorry for
Ashmul, not just because he had been assigned a stupid name, but
because he had no family outside of prison to financially support
him. To help out, we would sometimes give him cigarettes or phone
cards, and in return he'd clean the cell. Whenever he asked if it was
OK to clean, he would try to say '*Poro na kathariso?* – Can I clean?'
but because of his thick Bangladeshi accent, he would accidentally
say '*Poro na katouriso?*' which means 'Can I urinate?' However depressed I was, I couldn't help but find it quite funny.

Stelios tried to correct him. '*Kathariso!* – I clean!'

Ashmul attempted to repeat the word. '*Katouriso!* – I urinate!'

'*Ka-THA-riso!* – I CLEAN!' Stelios reiterated.

'*Ka-TOU-riso!* – I URINATE!' Ashmul struggled.

'*Ahhh Moushmoullo!*' Stelios said, shaking his head and smiling. He was still wearing the McDonald's T-shirt and I hadn't
seen him leave the cell yet. His days would involve sitting on
his bunk chain-smoking, drinking *frappes* and moaning. The majority of what came out of his mouth were complaints. Every
day he would list the same things about prison that he didn't
like and count them on his fingers. '*Ohi mastoura, ohi sex, ohi
kalo fayito!* – No weed, no sex, no good food!' He moaned about
the same things over and over again, especially about the heroin
addicts. They would continuously ask him for coffee or cigarettes

because they'd spent their own money on drugs. Desperate for more drugs, they would pickpocket and cause trouble. It made life in prison for everyone else harder than it already was.

╫╫

I'd been in Korydallos Prison for almost a week. The clunking sound of heavy rain pattered on the roof and echoed within the Gamma wing. When it rained the guards would shut the door that led to the courtyard – it left the wing overcrowded because no one was allowed to go outside. Rainwater leaked from several parts of the ceiling like dripping taps, leaving the wing slippery with a damp smell. The ground floor was heaving with criminals and it was muggy from an overload of body heat. Everyone was so crammed together, and it was the best opportunity for pick-pockets to act. Fights would often kick off and inmates would start to scream, shout and wolf-whistle in fascination at the men who were beating each other senseless.

'*Andrea, ela!* – Andreas, come!' Apollo shouted over a chaotic uproar of spectators. I tried to keep Apollo at arm's length, but he was adamant that I was 'with' him and his clique. I'd avoided him as much as I could, but I was put into a position where I couldn't say no. I walked into his cell.

'*Tsigaro* – Cigarette?' he said, offering me the box.

I took one and lit it. 'Thanks *reh*.'

'*Tipote* – Nothing.'

'You been in here a long time?' I asked.

'Ten years for a bank robbery,' Apollo responded.

'Oh … fuck,' I was lost for words.

He made the '*malakia*' hand gesture and continued. 'Then when I was let out I had no fucking money. I killed a man for €20,000 and now I'm back. Five months it's been.'

'*Gamise ta* – Fuck,' I replied. It made me feel uncomfortable knowing that he was a hit man – I wanted to get the hell out of his cell as quickly as possible! 'Anyway *reh Apollo*, I gotta go make a quick phone call.'

'*Katse reh malaka* – Sit my friend.'

'In a bit, man, I just have to call my girl quickly,' I said.

'Your girl? She is your Beyoncé?' he asked.

I had absolutely no idea what he was talking about. 'What do you mean *my* Beyoncé?'

'I have two Beyoncés, one's in Korydallos Prison for women, so I found another.'

'I think you mean "fiancée", not "Beyoncé", she's a singer!' I said.

'What?'

'You mean "*fiancée*". Beyoncé's the one who's married to Jay Z,' I told him.

'What are you talking about!?' he asked in his thick Greek accent. His face was stern and confused.

I tutted and smiled because I was nervous. 'Come on, you know *reh*. She was in the group Destiny's Child.'

He shook his head. 'No. She's not my fucking child. She is my Beyoncé,' he said with a harsh and serious voice.

'Oh, *your Beyoncé!* No, I don't have a Beyoncé, just a *kopella* – girlfriend. Why is your Beyoncé in prison?' I asked.

'She's a *poutana!* – whore! No one wants this for a Beyoncé.' His frown turned into a smile. 'They are all just fucking *poutanes* – whores – anyway. Not our mothers and sisters, but all the rest.'

I stood up. 'Anyway *reh*. I'll see you later.'

'*Pineis?* – You drink?' he asked, trying to delay my exit.

'No *reh*, I'm all right.'

'I don't mean coffee.' He put his index finger to his nose and sniffed. '*Pineis?* – you drink? *Prezza?*' – the slang term for heroin.

'*Ohi* – No,' I tutted.

'*Katse reh* – Sit, man.'

'In a bit, I've gotta go call her before she leaves her house,' I lied.

'She won't leave,' he pointed at me with his index finger. 'You are the one who wants to leave.'

My heart skipped a beat. 'I would love to leave. You really wanna stay in this fucking place?' I said smiling – attempting to generalise his words.

'*Ade reh katse!* – Come on, man, sit! This is an insult to me.'

I sat down on the bottom bunk.

'*Fileh mou, koita* – My friend, look.' He pulled out a tray from under his bunk that had two objects wrapped in tin foil. One was about the size of a tennis ball; the other was bigger – about the size of a small melon. 'You see this,' he said, pointing at the smaller one. 'This is €10,000. I sell this.' He unwrapped it, pouring out a pile of a brown, lumpy powder. 'There are kings in this prison. I am the king of the Greeks. No business is done without me knowing.'

I couldn't believe that he'd referred to himself as a 'king'; it was pathetic. I think that he may have been using the wrong word. Apollo was probably attempting to translate the word '*Varonos*', which means Baron – a title of honour. Either way, he was trying to tell me that the drug-dealing ring in Korydallos Prison was very organised, and that he was at the top of the hierarchy.

He used a plastic pre-paid telephone card to rack up a small line, then put a segment of a plastic straw up his nose and snorted it. I didn't even know that heroin could be snorted. 'You see this,' he said, unravelling the bigger tin-foil ball, 'this is *Depon*' – a brand of effervescent paracetamol. 'When you burn it, it looks just like *prezza*. I cut this 70/30,' he said, holding his nose and taking a deep sniff.

I didn't say anything. I lit another cigarette and stared at the little TV in the corner of the room. A Greek game show with general knowledge questions was on. I tried to phonetically read the question that was written on the screen aloud, but couldn't understand it. 'What does it mean?' I asked him, changing the subject.

He squinted at the screen. 'Which *mosquweetoes* bite people, male, female or both?' he said, mispronouncing the word 'mosquitoes'.

'I didn't know there was a difference, did you?' I asked.

He ignored me and grabbed the plastic card to rack up another line. I shifted my attention back to the TV. The answer had been revealed. 'What's the answer? I can't read it.'

Apollo glanced at the TV again, his eyes starting to look glazed and dopey. 'Females,' he said, before racking up another line of heroin.

'Maybe you were right then,' I said.

'Yeah? Right about what?'

'Maybe they *are* all fucking whores then!' I tried to joke. I didn't believe a word I was saying – I was just scared and nervous.

He smiled. 'Of course I'm right. *Reh Andrea, auto einai diko sou* – Andreas, man, this one's yours.'

I looked at the line of heroin in front of him; it was smaller than the one he'd just snorted. It was a little taster for beginners. 'No *prezza reh*, oxygen is my drug,' I said – plagiarising my cellmate Vasilis's expression.

'OK,' Apollo said. He pushed the line back into the pile of heroin and grabbed a plastic card to cut it with the bigger pile of paracetamol. '*Eisai roufianos?* – Are you a rat?'

I tutted.

'*Eisai kalo paidi* – you're a good kid; I can tell I can trust you. Now can you leave me? I have some business I need to deal with,' he said, brushing me off.

29

AN EASY TARGET

Journal extract – Day 147 – 14 December 2009

Teresa bought me a Bible, so I've decided that I'm going to read it. Not as a Christian, but just to educate myself. I've heard so much about this book, but who has actually read it? It's bloody long.

Today was the pakali *(grocery) and for some reason they didn't have the document with my money, so I couldn't get my things and have to wait until Thursday. It's Monday today. I had only three €4 telephone cards, I rang the parents for an hour and saved €2 on the card for next time, only I was pick-pocketed and lost it. So it means that I lost an hour on the telephone, which I needed because I'm not getting more cards until Thursday now. It's only €2, but it's stressful how something so small can bring me down.*

Riya is flying to Greece tomorrow, but I doubt I will get to see her until Thursday because she lands too late and visiting is at 3 p.m. It's all just pushing it too fine. The social worker here says she hasn't even been accepted yet for a visit … and in Avlona when we planned her trip she was allowed three open visits – her flights were based around that! It's stressful but I need to see the positives; if I can't see her tomorrow at least I can call her and it will be a lot cheaper. I miss her so much and I'm so disheartened that we don't get an open visit, but it's better than nothing.

So, what's been going on the past few days? Waking up around 9 a.m., going for a walk outside, 11 a.m. taking the food, which is chaos. At first I didn't want to push through people to get to the front, but I realised everyone was pushing in front of me. So I've started to join in and hope someone doesn't want to punch me.

At the front of the wing, on the right, was a staircase that led down to the communal shower area. Other than being absolutely disgusting, having a shower in Korydallos Prison was a bit like listening to the Middle Eastern version of *The X Factor*. There were usually inmates singing in there, very badly, in different languages. It wasn't an open shower room that all inmates shared; there were five or six shower cubicles that were separated by a concrete structure. There were no cubical doors, so most of us would hang a sheet over the doorframe for privacy. It was better that way, considering privacy is almost non-existent when behind bars.

Inside the cubical, I would take off my clothes and hang them over the concrete frame, above the sheet where the cubical door should have been. It made it easy for inmates to steal clothes. Luckily it happened to me only once – just a pair of boxers. I always wore flip-flops and made sure that I never touched the shower walls because they were always covered with semen. On a positive note, the water was lukewarm, a lot warmer than the water in Avlona (the *Archi Fylakas* there was right in that sense). I would turn it on and let the water run first, which poured out of a rusting tap. The only downside was that (occasionally) the water would stop running. There would be a clogging sound, then the tap would spit out a spray of brown liquid and I'd have to quickly move my body to the side so that it wouldn't cover me.

Each cubical shared the same drainage system: an open gutter on the floor that channelled the dirty water from each cubical to a drain on the left side of the room. Unfortunately, inmates would use the showers as a toilet, probably because they couldn't afford toilet paper. When I showered, lumps of shit would often flow past through the gutter that ran on the floor, against the wall. Sometimes the faeces would be so big that they would get stuck in my cubicle. The smell was unbearable! I would fill up both my hands with water and try to splash the crap away – back into the ever-flowing stream of piss and spunk. Ashmul used to shower with no flip-flops and no sheet – butt naked for everyone to see. He didn't seem to care about what he was standing in barefoot.

If I took a while showering, the inmate waiting to use it would start shouting and force me to hurry up. The queue of inmates in the shower room was always long because the wing was far too overpopulated. I would rush, having to put my clothes back on when I was still wet. Sometimes I would drop them, which would upset me because they were now covered in different bodily fluids. I would walk back through the chilly wing back to cell forty-nine, which was more often than not full of Stelios's friends. If I then needed to use the toilet, I would have to ask everyone if they could leave the cell for a few minutes. We all did it for each other – it was a rule that we could use the toilet only to urinate when we were locked up.

On one occasion, when I got back to my cell after a shower, a man with a perfectly hooked nose and hunched back was lying on my bunk with his back against my pillow. On the chair next to Stelios's bunk sat Thoma, a man with long oily hair I'd previously met, who was smoking a cigarette. He didn't talk very much and seemed always to be in his own world. Vasilis told me that he had recently moved to Gamma from the psychiatric wing. Staring into space, he looked like a broken man.

The three of them were in the middle of a conversation, but stopped as I walked into the cell.

'*Peirazei?* – Do you mind?' asked the man lying on my bunk, referring to whether he should move.

'*Katse fileh mou* – Sit my friend,' I replied, brushing a cockroach off the end of my bunk with my palm. The truth was that it did matter – I wanted him to leave. It was so frustrating not having my own space; all I wanted was a bit of privacy and space to change into some warm clothes. I sat down on the end of my bunk and began to dry my feet with a towel before sliding on a clean pair of socks.

The hunchbacked man was called Nicos, but Stelios had nicknamed him 'methadone man'. Methadone was the substitute drug for heroin that the prison doctors would give the addicts to wean them off without going 'cold turkey'. While on a course of prescribed methadone, 'methadone man' was still buying heroin from Apollo's guys and taking it regularly. On top of that, he was taking any pill he could get his hands on. Stelios handed him a pill; I had no idea what it was. Methadone man crushed it up on the table using a plastic pre-paid telephone card, racked it into a line and snorted it using a segment of a plastic straw.

'What's he snorting?' I asked Vasilis, who was lying on his top bunk.

'Andrew, I don't know; he's a very stupid man. He snorts everything, even painkillers.'

Thoma and methadone man would be in our cell every day, sometimes for hours on end.

Journal extract – Day 153 – 20 December 2009

Every day I spend here I'm realising what it's really like – there are so many heroin addicts. Stelios and methadone man were smoking it in our cell the other day, the second time I've seen it done in front of me. They used the metallic seal from a coffee can, put a lump of heroin on it, put a lighter underneath and sucked the smoke through a straw. It has a distinct smell. They were stoned afterwards, but not as stoned as you would think – probably because I witnessed Apollo cut it with 70 per cent paracetamol! Good if they had a headache I guess.

Also, I've read Genesis, Exodus and Leviticus from the Bible and am going to start Numbers soon. I'm learning so much.

┼┼┼┼

I'd waited for three days to see Marios (the social worker) and I desperately needed to speak to him. Riya was flying to Greece and I still didn't know if she'd been accepted as a visitor yet. In Korydallos Prison, only outsiders who share an inmate's surname are allowed to visit them without a previous application made to the social worker. To book an appointment with Marios, an inmate had to write his name on a piece of paper and post it into a box at the front of the wing – this procedure could take weeks. On the day that Riya had arrived in Athens, I noticed Marios walking into the Gamma wing office. There was no point in asking the *ypallilos* if I could see Marios briefly – I would have been forced to book an appointment again. Instead, I caught the attention of the *ypallilos* and shouted '*farmaca!* – medication!' He buzzed me through, thinking that I needed to take my medicine. Rather than going to the doctor's office, I quickly knocked on Marios's door when the *ypallilos* wasn't looking.

I pleaded with Marios that he allow Riya to visit, but not only for one visit, for as many as possible! At first he was sceptical, but told me that he would try his hardest. When I suggested an open visit he said, 'Now you're pushing it!' Nevertheless, my little stunt managed to have Riya approved for visiting, and he allowed her to come and visit me three times.

I remember my heart thumping as I walked into the visiting room and I saw her face behind the dirty pane of glass. She was a foot away from me, but between us was a clouded force field, stopping me from holding her in my arms again. A Skype video call would probably have offered a better-quality image, but nevertheless, seeing her in front of me was amazing – and I'm sure the feeling was mutual. I was filled with happiness. We spent our visits talking about anything other than prison, as though I wasn't even in prison at all. She told me that I looked really different, probably because of the unshaven stubble and rugged hair.

When she wasn't visiting me, or seeing many of Athens' beautiful sights, I would call her hotel for a tenth of the cost of a call to England. I was over the moon for the entire week she was there. I didn't care about sleeping with cockroaches, I didn't care about shit in the showers, I didn't care about living with criminals and I didn't care about being wrongly accused of murder any more – all I cared about was knowing that when I woke up, I would see her face. The week ended, she flew back to the UK and everything turned to shit again. I was the most depressed I'd ever been.

Journal extract – Day 153 – 20 December 2009

I had a really bad dream last night. My body was deteriorating, my skin and muscles were all falling off my body, my teeth were falling out. My skin cracked like an eggshell. My dad was there, in shock, holding my heart and trying to put it back into my body. I was screaming – 'I'm dying, I'm dying!' Scary shit! The other night I had a fucked-up dream too – I can only remember one bit. There was a little girl sitting on the floor, then I realised she was holding a knife and cutting off her own foot.

I seem to be having dreams of people chopping off their own limbs and bodies falling apart. It's fucked up, why would my mind do this to me?

Journal extract – Day 157 – 24 December 2009

Today I have been a waste of space. I haven't wanted to do anything. Not lie down, not sit up, not stand up, not walk, not read, not watch television. I just want to be unconscious.

Yesterday the guards called my name through the speaker and I received a document, which I thought said my court date was 15 January. It would have been amazing, but it is just a 'symvoulio' – a judicial council review that all inmates have after six months of imprisonment. It could get me out of prison, but I'm trying not to bank on it. I was excited when I thought it was a court date, now I feel a bit let down. It's that feeling again, every time it gets worse and worse, my heart sinks. I can't help how my body feels.

I just need closure. For the truth to come out and justice to prevail. Justice will never truly prevail though. The dodgy 'cops' who got me here in the first place will just get away with it. No one will stop them.

For the first time since my arrest, the fear of being found guilty started to gnaw at my mind. I was already a murderer in the eyes of the Greek authorities – what if witnesses in court were to tell lies? What if Jonathan Hiles's friends were to claim that it was me who killed their friend? Would their South Wales Police statements be accepted in a Greek court? Or would their false words (along with those of the Zante police) absolutely destroy my life? I had no control over their actions and it was eating me alive. I was facing twenty years' imprisonment for a crime that someone else had committed. What would be the point of living? I would be institutionalised and branded a murderer, I would have a criminal record and I would be in my forties with no work experience or degree. What would be the point? Riya would move on and marry somebody else, my friends would settle down with wives and kids, my family would move back to north London and carry on as normal. If I were to be found guilty, my life would be over. The constant battle between positive and negative thoughts had become too exhausting and I started to realise that being found guilty was a possibility. It was the first time that I'd imagined a scenario of the trial verdict – sitting in the courtroom and discovering that I'd been wrongfully found guilty. How would I feel? Just thinking about it devastated me in ways that I couldn't even describe. In the twenty-first century, how could anything so unjust even be a possibility?

╫╫

Journal extract – Day 158 – 25 December 2009

> *We wish you a shitty Christmas, we wish you a shitty Christmas, we wish you a shitty Christmas and a crappy New Year. Shit lamb meat we bring ... for you and your cellmates ... we wish you a shitty Christmas and a crappy New Yeaaaaaar. Actually, I take back the crappy New Year bit. I'm hoping 2010 will be a lot better.*

On Christmas Day the guards left the doors open for a bit longer in the evening, so all of the prisoners could celebrate together. The prison guards gave each prisoner a can of beer, which is the stupidest thing that they could have done. The inmates with no money (which is a hell of a lot) would sell their beer to inmates with money, so there were several drunk inmates roaming the wing and causing trouble. A number of them were probably stoned on heroin too. Up until that point, I'd never seen so many fights in one evening.

Journal extract – Day 162 – 29 December 2009

Today is Michael's birthday; he would have been twenty-three. Felt a bit weird today but I asked Riya if maybe she could go to his grave and put some flowers down for me. I'm sure she did, I'll call her tomorrow.

I finished Deuteronomy in the Bible and started Joshua. Moses died, it was a huge shame, but Joshua seems to be handling things OK. The Old Testament is crazy: if you work on a Sunday you shall be put to death, or if a girl has sex before marriage she shall be stoned at the door of her father's house! If those rules applied these days we would run out of stones and women would be extinct. It would be a world with no humans or stones. Actually that's not true, you could always use the stones more than once! Anyway, it's a bit crazy. After the Jews were led by Moses out of Egypt – cut a long story short – they basically went around to different towns after trekking through the desert for forty bloody years, and killing everyone and taking over. I don't understand. What happened to 'thou shall not kill'?

I always saw Leonarde the Romanian guy walking around Gamma, but he started to ignore me after a while. I don't know why. He seemed to be the kind of guy who stuck to his own kind, and he'd made it pretty clear on my first day that he was only walking with me so that others knew I wasn't alone. After a while he'd talk to me only when he wanted something, like a packet of cigarettes or some coffee. The day before New Year's Eve, he came into my cell with a large water bottle filled with alcohol and tried to sell it to me – or swap it for a multipack of 200 cigarettes. He referred to it as the spirit 'Raki', but it was probably prison-brewed in a similar way to how we brewed alcohol in Avlona. Vasilis told me that half of it was probably water. Either way, I didn't want it, so I declined the offer.

I hadn't seen Apollo in about three weeks and I hoped that he'd been moved to a different wing. His clique usually hung around next to the bench in the far right-hand corner of the courtyard, but they'd been there without him for quite a while. All of a sudden, Apollo popped up again in the hallway when I was walking back to my cell one day.

'*Reh Andrea*, they caught me for dealing drugs and put me in solitary for a week. When are you coming for coffee?'

'Maybe later. I have *episkeptirio* – a visit.'

'*Meta* – After,' he insisted.

I didn't have a visit that day; I went back to my cell to sit with Stelios and methadone man. When I later went to collect the food, Apollo saw me and pressured me to go into his cell again. One of his cellmates was cooking some sort of stew using a miniature, portable electric hob, and he insisted that I stayed to eat with them.

'No, it's OK. You eat, I'm eating later,' I said.

He frowned. 'You eat this shit they give? It is full of *salio*.'

My face told him that I didn't understand.

He turned to his cellmate. '*Pavlo, poia einai i lexi yia to "salio" sta Anglika?* – Pavlos, what's the word for "*salio*" in English?'

'*Saleeveh*,' Pavlos answered.

'Saliva. Yeh, I could've guessed that,' I said. 'All right, cool.' I sat on his bottom bunk while he played *tavli* with Pavlos. Apollo's eyes were distant and he kept closing them as though he was constantly falling asleep. His reactions were sluggish; it took him a few moments to throw the dice into the backgammon board and move the pieces. At one stage he made a mistake and started to move Pavlos's pieces by accident. Apollo forced his eyes open, took a breath and gave himself a few little slaps on his cheeks to sober himself up.

'*Thelis frappe Andrea?* – You want a *frappe*, Andreas?' he blurted, grabbing his nose and taking a big sniff.

'Yeah, OK.'

'*Pavlo, fiaxe tou filou mas tou Andreas ena cafe!* – Pavlos, make our friend Andrew a coffee!' he demanded to his cellmate. Pavlos stopped playing and acted immediately upon the request.

'*Reh Andrea*, I am very sick from drugs,' Apollo said. I didn't think that he meant actual 'sickness', he was probably trying to tell me that he was as high as a kite. The guy was swaying like a tree in the wind; if I pushed him slightly he probably would have fallen off his chair. Pavlos handed me the *frappe* and they continued to play.

'*Min pareis ta zaria grygora* – Don't pick up the dice quickly,' Apollo said to Pavlos calmly. Pavlos was picking up the dice before Apollo had the chance to see the numbers; his reactions seemed to be very delayed from the drugs. Apollo threw the dice for his next turn and Pavlos picked up the dice too quickly again. Apollo stood up and slammed the backgammon board shut.

'*Ti sou eipa reh malaka!* – What did I tell you, wanker!' he thundered. He slid the backgammon board off the table so violently that it smashed against the wall and I flinched. Apollo's heroin-fuelled outburst left him stumbling forward – catching his balance before he knocked the coffees off the table in front of him.

'*Siga reh!* – Take it easy, man!' said Pavlos, who threw his hands up to surrender.

'*Siga?* – Take it easy?' asked Apollo.

I stood up and tried to slide out of the cell before a fight kicked off.

'*Katse esi!* – You sit!' roared Apollo while pointing at me with his index finger; his puffy eyes were filled with fire. 'It's time to eat,' he said. Pavlos picked up the backgammon board from the floor and filled it with the plastic pieces. Then we sat around the table and tension resonated in the cell. Three of us sat on the bottom bunks while Apollo 'the king' sat on his plastic throne. Their other cellmate served up the chicken and rice stew into four plastic bowls and one was placed in front of me. They had salt, pepper and lemon, Coca-Colas and other fizzy drinks. It was the best meal I'd eaten in half a year. For dessert they snorted long lines of heroin, and again, Apollo tried to persuade me to take some. The only reason he was being nice to me was because he saw me as a young guy in prison, probably with money, going through a tough time. In his eyes, I was a very easy target to become a heroin addict. I was pressured into being there; it wasn't out of choice. But there was still a part of me that felt like he would protect me if I needed him. I needed to keep him close, but not too close. I was playing with fire.

9 January 2010, BBC News

PROTEST STAGED OVER BRITISH STUDENT IN GREEK JAIL

Supporters of a British student held in Greece on manslaughter charges have protested at London's Greek embassy.

Andrew Symeou, 21, is accused of killing Jonathan Hiles, 18, of Cardiff, by punching him in a nightclub on the isle of Zante in 2007.

Mr Symeou, of Enfield, north London, is in Korydallos Prison in Athens, a jail condemned by Amnesty International.

His sister Sophie, who led supporters in the protest, said the case against him was 'riddled with contradictions'.

About 100 protesters chanted 'enough is enough' and 'justice for Andrew' outside the embassy in west London.

They called for an end to his detention, a trial date to be set and an inquiry into allegations of police misconduct.

Sophie Symeou said, 'The case against my brother is riddled with contradictions and inconsistencies suggestive of manipulation and in places fabrication of evidence by police officers.

'Andrew has been held in a Greek prison without a trial for nearly six months and has been refused bail twice.

'My brother has suffered for too long and this cannot continue – we are protesting outside the Greek embassy to say enough is enough.'

Mr Hiles, who was in Britain's roller-hockey team, died in July 2007 two days after falling off a dance podium in a nightclub.

Bournemouth University student Mr Symeou has denied killing him, saying that he was not in the club at the time.

Fair Trials International has said Mr Symeou's friends claim they were 'beaten, punched, slapped and threatened' by police officers in Greece until they gave statements implicating him.

He was extradited to Greece in July after losing a High Court battle.

Mr Symeou was held at a detention centre for young people north of Athens until he was transferred to Korydallos Prison.

Fair Trials International chief executive Jago Russell said, 'Andrew has already been held for months in a Greek jail without any opportunity to clear his name.

'We are urging Greece to bring this family's unjustified ordeal to an end, to release Andrew on bail and to investigate the serious allegations of police misconduct.'

Human rights group Amnesty International and the European Committee for the Prevention of Torture have repeatedly expressed concern about Korydallos Prison.

30

WAITING FOR EXAM RESULTS

Journal extract – Day 176 – 12 January 2010

It's a new year now, 2010. I was arrested in 2008 … it's all taking so long. What a waste of my life. Anyway, things are going to change now, I can feel it. I'm still in prison after six months and it's painful. I just have to live with the cockroaches a little longer. My 'symvoulio', which is like a bail hearing, is on the 15th. I'm praying I get out of here because I can't take much more. It hasn't only been 177 days since my extradition, this burden has been eating me alive for over a year and a half – the prison is just a way for them to torture my mind when I'm already dealing with so much. Bastards. I find myself more and more depressed every day. I just want to be an object, have no feeling or emotion without becoming a heroin addict. I can see it's not hard to fall down that path in prison.

A lot has happened since I last wrote in my journal. For start-ers, Vasilis has left. Suddenly the judicial council decided that he could wait for his trial outside – they changed their minds about him being dangerous after eleven months of being in prison. He's out and I'm so happy for the guy. It's given me some hope that I may be free next week. I'm trying not to depend on it and just

*forget about it, but it's easier said than done. What can I say ...
I'm prone to bad news now. I just don't want to feel that pain
again when I hear the words I shouldn't be hearing. It's the unknown that is the most stressful thing. I will feel better next week
regardless of the result. I think I will still be here, but I have hope.*

*Anyway, Vasilis is gone and Stelios asked the guards if they
could put his friend Thoma into our cell. He is OK, very quiet.
He seems like a broken man. I think he used to be an alcoholic
because on Christmas when the guards gave us beer he couldn't
drink it. Anyway, this is the first time I've been in a cell with
no one who speaks English. It's hard, but good for me to further
improve my Greek.*

*There's been shitloads of fights lately, for example the other day
Apollo the hitman/pimp/drug dealer and his mates beat the crap
out of a gypsy and then they all whipped him with rubber hoses.
It doesn't sound like it would hurt much ... but the guy being
whipped was covered in blood, dripping from head to toe. He was
screaming and screaming. Apollo later told me it was because he
owed €500 worth of heroin. It's obviously not good to get into
debt with these people. Luckily I've had no trouble with them so
far and it's been a month and a half in Gamma. It would be good
to keep Apollo thinking that there is a possibility I could end up
one of his top customers for a while, just in case I need his help if
anyone starts trouble with me. The worst thing I could do is start
to piss him off, then the only guys I would have in prison who
are on my side are Stelios, who is a skinny pussy, Thoma, who is
broken, and Ashmul , who is ... well he's just a Moushmoullo.*

*I'm on the book of Samuel II in the Bible, about a third of
the way through. David is now the king – what a guy. Tonight
I don't really want to read. I just can't wait to be unconscious,
but dread waking up here again to the same day.*

Oh yeh, I forgot, there was a protest in London outside the

Greek embassy the other day; 140 people turned up – how good is that? It is making me emotional just knowing that so many people back home are fighting for my release. I couldn't be more grateful. It is so difficult to describe the feeling – when you're in here you forget that the outside world still exists; the world is still spinning. I wouldn't have expected that many people. Hopefully it is all helping and makes a difference, but it seems like it's normal in this country to be in prison for a year, even if you are found innocent in the end.

Journal extract – Day 177 – 13 January ~~2009~~ 2010

I'm not used to writing 2010 yet! To me it still feels like 2008. Time hasn't moved since I was 19!

I couldn't fall asleep last night; cockroaches kept falling on me and I was just stressing out. Again I woke up HERE! I need to stop stressing out and just remember that I will be reading this in twenty years' time and thinking 'I have achieved' – not wishing I could go back to change things ... have no regrets.

They really should let me out of here, it is the correct choice to make. I just want the judicial council hearing on Friday to come and go, hear the words and just carry on regardless of the result.

I'm still fat and I still smoke. I've decided I don't give a shit any more. I've started being lazy and haven't done press-ups in a week. It's because of the Xanax; they have started giving them to me during the day now, whereas before it was at night. They make me so lazy.

Journal extract – Day 178 – 14 January 2010

The hearing is tomorrow. I'm trying not to think about it too much. But how the fuck do you 'not think about something'?

Attempting to not think about it is technically thinking about it. I probably won't hear a result for a while anyway. The longer the better; it means they are really contemplating it. It's stressful because I know I'm going to receive a document in Greek saying either I'm free or not and I won't understand it. I'm expecting to stay here until trial. Which is OK, I can do it – I'm not a pussy.

Journal extract – Day 179 – 15 January ~~200~~ 2010

I still can't write '2010' without thinking! Anyway, George Pyromallis (my lawyer) said the hearing went as well as it could today. So in a week, maybe two, I will get a document through saying YES or NO! It's stressful so I'm just going to assume it's a NO … but I can't stop the little bit of hope inside of me saying 'it has to be a yes'. So I'm in a bit of a muddle. I'm not going to cry if it's a no at least. Whatever happens is meant to be. George said that the judges were asking for fifty grand bail! What the fuck? Do they think we shit money? Anyway, I don't know what's going to happen, but he said they listened to everything and were well aware of the publicity. Imagine if I make bail. Happiness for the first time in almost two years – being a part of my family again. Well I still am a part of them, but just not physically, apart from Tuesdays and Thursdays for half a fucking hour behind a bloody piece of filthy glass. Bullshit. I reckon the odds for freedom are 50/50. Please God, give me a break, I'm a good guy. I'm looking forward to having my life, I can feel it is close.

Also, Joan Ryan our MP brought up my case yesterday in Parliament defending me, which is very good.

Joan Ryan explained the ins and outs of the case in the House of Commons. She even stated: 'There has been a serious abuse of process in the gathering of evidence and the production of written statements, and at worst that evidence has been manipulated and sometimes fabricated to incriminate Andrew falsely.' She explained that key witnesses contradicted statements that they had signed in Greece, and that there were allegations of police brutality:

> More worrying, though, is that even though the public prosecutor [in Greece] is aware of the allegations, she has so far refused to acknowledge that anything of the sort could possibly have ever happened. In her proposal to the judicial counsel of Zante, without even bothering to have investigated the allegations, which all of us would agree are serious in their own right and clearly relevant to the case against Andrew, she dismisses the allegations out of hand as 'trite' and claims that nothing of the kind had occurred ... All that he [Andrew] and his family have ever sought is a fair hearing. Andrew has never sought to avoid the opportunity to clear his name; nor has he tried to avoid justice. He has made it clear on countless occasions that he is willing to cooperate with the police. Indeed, his legal team have contacted Scotland Yard and South Wales Police and urged them to investigate. Those are not the actions of someone who is trying to avoid justice ... When the rights of one of our citizens are threatened the government has a duty to step in ... Today, we reflect not only on the detention of Andrew Symeou, but on the tragic and untimely death of Jonathan Hiles and the suffering that it has brought to his family and friends. Jonathan cannot face a jury; his life was cut short in an act of mindless and senseless violence, but his memory deserves justice, as do his friends and family. They deserve better than this shoddy investigation that is so obviously marred by inconsistencies and anomalies. Another injustice will bring them no comfort. It is in the interest of everyone, Andrew, the family and friends of

Jonathan Hiles and the Greek judicial system itself, for this case to be fully and openly investigated. But that will not be possible unless and until the British Government make representations in the clearest possible terms to the Greek authorities to prevent a miscarriage of justice. One young man has lost his life, and I urge the Minister to do everything he can to ensure that we do not ruin the life of another.

Chris Bryant, the minister of state for Europe, stated that the British government is not able to interfere in the judicial process, but can provide welfare and support via consular staff and take up justified complaints when the treatment of British citizens is not in line with international standards. I gathered that to mean that representatives from the British consulate in Greece would continue to bring me books to read. On a more positive note, he agreed to meet with my family and raise the case with his Greek counterpart – Dimitrios Droutsas.

Journal extract – Day 180 – 16 January 2010

I tried ringing the mobile number Vasilis gave to me, but it was turned off. Stelios has his house number so will try that soon. Would be good to chat to him considering we never got to say a proper goodbye. Also, I received a letter from Arnas, so I need to write a letter back; I think that will be my job tomorrow.

This hope of potential freedom is strange. I was telling Riya today on the phone that it's like waiting for exam results, only if you fail you have to stay in prison.

31

A TRANQUIL MISHMASH

After a few slow and monotonous weeks I'd discovered that the judicial council's decision was to leave me in prison. According to them, I was still 'dangerous' and they were afraid that I might 're-offend'. I hadn't even been questioned by police in the investigation, let alone found guilty in a court of law. As much as I'd convinced myself that I was prepared to remain locked up, I couldn't even bring myself to leave my bunk for two days. Ashmul agreed to collect my food from downstairs for a packet of cigarettes. I didn't want to walk into the hallway any more; then again, I didn't want to be in the cell either. Everything was torturing me – the repetition; the violence; the screaming, shouting and wolf-whistling; the lack of privacy; the lack of hygiene; the cockroaches and mice; listening to Stelios moan about the same shit every day; having to constantly keep my guard up – it was exhausting and doing my head in. My depression was getting worse and it felt like I'd been in Korydallos for far longer than it had actually been. The hardest thing was having no idea how long it would be before I could leave – it could've been another month, six months, or even a year; who was to know? Even before returning home I'd be sitting in the dock of a high-profile homicide trial in what could quite possibly be one of the most corrupt countries in Europe. Maybe my life was over? There were too many unknowns and my 21-year-old mind couldn't deal with them. The word 'depressed' isn't powerful enough to describe how I felt.

I finally forced myself to go for a walk on the ground floor of the wing. I remember feeling light-headed and weak because I hadn't moved a muscle in days. Pavlos told me that Apollo needed a favour – I didn't care about keeping him at arm's length any more, nothing mattered. The worst thing that could have happened is that someone beat the crap out of me or killed me. In a time of such depression, when it feels like the world is crushing in on you, you don't think logically and an eternity of nothing-ness doesn't even seem that bad any more. I walked in, sat down and sparked up a cigarette. I didn't even say hello – I remember feeling dazed and in my own world. He showed me a few hits of heroin that were individually wrapped in little bits of folded paper and suggested that I deliver them for him to other cells for a cut of the profit. I told him to deliver them himself, or get someone who needs the money to do it – then I stood up to leave.

He threw his hands in the air, as though he was surrendering. 'I was thinking you might need a job! I'm asking all my friends. You don't want it? OK,' he said.

'Fuck this,' I said, and walked out. I couldn't take it any more. My eyes swelled.

He followed me into the hallway. '*Reh Andrea* come and tell me what's wrong. You look fucked up, let's have a coffee.' He put his arm around me and walked me back into cell thirty-three.

I was given no choice but to sit down again. 'It's my *Symvoulio* – I'm not getting out of prison for a long time. The police told lies; I might even go down for twenty years and I don't need people like you trying to turn me into a fucking drug dealer.'

'You're right, I just see a young guy like you in here … you don't know it but you have balls … and I trust you,' he said with his hand on my shoulder. 'I won't make you do it, there are many others who would.' He sat down and racked up two lines of heroin on the table.

'Cool,' I said. 'Anyway, I can ask my friends *Stelios* and *Thoma* if you want.'

'I don't know them, I don't trust them.' He snorted the line closest to him and handed me the segment of a plastic straw. I took it in my hand and looked at the line of heroin in front of me. Two inches long; a mixture of fine brown powder and a few crystallised clumps. In prison – in that moment – I wasn't myself. I'd allowed my environment to slowly consume who I was. It wasn't me; it's as though I'd forgotten my own identity and I was just another prisoner. I don't take heroin; why would I ever take heroin? At what point in my life would I have been associated with people who took heroin? My life was fine; I had a lovely girlfriend and good friends. I was happy, then it turned to shit and I was forced to leave my home and live in Korydallos prison instead. The world was fucked up and my life was on the verge of ruin. I'd been dealing with the wrongful accusation for a year and a half and it was all too much to endure. I put the straw up my right nostril, held my left nostril closed, pressed the end of the straw against the tip of the line, took a big sniff and followed it to the other end. It burnt the inside of my nose like fire and the tang of chemicals drizzled down the back of my throat. I swallowed; it tasted like bile. I put another cigarette between my lips. Apollo lit it for me.

'You play *tavli*?' he asked.

I could feel myself welling up. I hid it well. 'Nah, I'm gonna go.'

'Any time, you know this,' he said.

I walked back to cell forty-nine – a pathetic walk of shame that was becoming heavier with each step. Thoma and Stelios

were asleep, but Ashmul was nowhere to be seen; he was probably with his Bangladeshi friends in one of the cells upstairs.
I sat on my bunk. My head felt dazed from my racing heart. I
told myself to forget about it and smoked a cigarette. My eyes
started to stream because of what I'd just done – I was ashamed
of myself. Everything became weighty, as though time itself had
been diluted. I collapsed backwards with my feet still on the floor.
I sunk deeper and deeper into the mattress and my body was
overwhelmed with a warm chemical bliss. My mind and body
separated – my body was sedated while my mind was lost at the
edge of consciousness, a tranquil mishmash of lucid dreams and
clouded thoughts.

I don't know how many hours had passed. I woke up to a song
on Stelios's radio that would play every evening called 'Opa Opa'. I
 stumbled over to the toilet, but couldn't urinate even though
I needed to. Instead I vomited; it was mainly liquid because I
hadn't eaten.

'*Ipiate?* – Did you drink/snort?' asked Stelios.

'*Ohi* – No,' I lied.

Journal extract – Day 187 – 22 January 2010

*Yesterday was a bad day, but today I'm feeling better. I was a
dick. Now I'm just trying to think positively. Everything may
happen for a reason. Maybe not making bail means this whole
fucked-up ordeal will end sooner, even if it means staying in
prison. It's all cool, you are OK, Andrew. Things could be so
much worse. Imagine if all the evidence implicated you and
you had no way of discrediting it … or no way of proving your
innocence. You can … and you will. You had a bit of a slump
but it's time to pick yourself back up. You just have to carry on.*

OK, it's only been one hour since I wrote that last paragraph.

I was happily eating my soggy pasta and suddenly there was a lot of shouting outside in the hall. We all went outside to see what was going on. It was the biggest fight/war I've ever seen in my life. About 100 prisoners were beating the crap out of each other; one African guy was on the ground getting very badly beaten. They whipped him with hoses and beat him with what looked like some kind of poles. He was screaming and there was blood everywhere. The guards couldn't do anything, it was too hectic. Oh my God, that wasn't the end. It started to die down a bit, and then suddenly someone threw a huge bin full of rubbish from the third floor to the ground floor. Again, herds of prisoners were shouting, screaming and suddenly everyone was throwing pots, pans, chairs, tables and bins from all floors. One guy even managed to rip a telephone off the wall on the third floor and threw it down to the ground floor. I'm still in shock. I think it was an Albanian/African war. Crazy … They just locked us back up early because it was getting way out of hand. The floor was covered in blood. When one Albanian gets into a fight, they all fight. When one African gets into a fight, all the Africans fight. It is all about race. Today wasn't just a series of fights, it was a war and I don't think it's over. I'm going to speak to the social worker and try to be moved to a better section of the prison. This is too crazy.

Journal extract – Day 188 – 23 January 2010

It's been exactly six months since the day I was extradited, and what a day it's been. We've been locked up all day because of the riots. They only opened the doors for food, but had locked off all the gates, segregating all the floors. I went down at 11 a.m. to collect food and the war started again on the middle floor. At least twenty of the Albanians on the ground floor were rioting behind

the bars that led to the stairs – kicking and smashing the bars
with wooden table and chair legs. They were screaming 'Anixe
tin porta! – Open the door!' They were screaming and shouting.
Another riot was happening right above me. About ten guards
ran upstairs to stop it. A man was thrown down the stairs to
my left and looked like he could even have been dead. He landed
in front of my feet covered with blood from head to toe. I was
still standing in shock with my Tupperware container and food
coupon in hand, when one of the big bins came flying from the
top floor, covering all the Albanian men on the ground floor with
rubbish and hitting one on the head. Two guards carried the
prisoner who was drenched in blood out of Gamma wing.

The main Albanian guy who was screaming and bashing the bars
was a friend of my cellmate Stelios. I have no idea why he was
in prison, but he would often come to our cell for a cigarette and
coffee. The man was absolutely huge, at least six and a half feet
tall. He was hefty but muscular, and it seemed as though he could
have crushed my head with his bare hands. Regardless of his intimidating size, he had a non-threatening face that would normally
remind me of Winnie-the-Pooh. I'd say he was probably about
thirty years old and had light brown hair that looked almost ginger
from certain angles. He'd nicknamed me '*Hondroulli*', which could
be used to mean 'chubby'. But he was chubby too, so I'd say '*Ego*
eimai "Hondroulli Ena" kai esi eisai "Hondroulli Dyo"– I'm "Chubby
One" and you're "Chubby Two".' He would chuckle and high-five
me, so I was very surprised when I saw him act so violently. It was
like watching the smiley Disney character become a monster.

The man who'd just been badly beaten and covered from head
to toe in blood must have been a close friend of his (or maybe
even a relative). Along with an army of prisoners, he screamed
with passion behind the bars and continued to strike them

fiercely with wooden table legs. '*ANIXE!* – OPEN!' he screeched in a high-pitched, erratic panic. His sweat-drenched face was plastered with fury while he attempted to break open the lock of the barred gate. God knows what would have happened if he'd succeeded; it would have been a stampede!

I couldn't go back up to my floor because there was a crazy riot going on. All I could do was stand at the front of the ground floor and watch in horror. A guard ran over to the bars (from the outside, where I was standing) and it seemed like he had no idea what to do because he was on his own. He tried to calm down Chubby Two and spoke to him through the bars in a way that was stern but gentle at the same time. '*Siga, siga* – Slow down/ take it easy,' he said.

Chubby Two was too overwhelmed to even acknowledge him. The hoarde of inmates continued to hit the bars ferociously and scream at the top of their voices in distress.

'*Siga!* – Take it easy!' the *ypallilos* yelled.

Chubby Two gave the bars one last strike and then relaxed for a split second to take a breath. The *ypallilos* must have seen it as a sudden moment of vulnerability, because he fed his arms through the bars and held Chubby's reddened face in both of his palms. It was brave of him, as he was risking his hands being hit by one of the many wooden table legs. 'It's OK,' the guard said, softly, but loud enough for it to be heard over the chaotic cries of other prisoners on the ground floor. '*Siga* – Take it easy.'

He tried to pull the guard's hands away from his face, but the guard held onto his cheeks. '*Anixe tin porta!* – Open the door!' said Chubby Two, but he choked up a bit as the words came out. His body relaxed but the army of inmates behind him continued to fill the wing with deep, protesting screams. Then he dropped the wooden table leg, as if giving up. He gripped onto the prison guard's arms like a scared child holding onto a parent. He let out a loud, hysterical wail that resonated in a way that was almost operatic. Tears streamed down his cheeks and dripped onto the guard's hands, which still held his face.

'See, it's OK, it's OK,' the *ypallilos* said.

It all happened so fast and there was little time for me to acknowledge how it made me feel as an observer. It's an image that's stayed in my mind, perhaps more vividly than other memories of prison. In hindsight, it may be because I'd never seen a prisoner reveal any sign of emotion up until that point, and in the same moment, it was the first time that I'd ever witnessed an act of compassion from a prison *ypallilos*. They were two men from opposite ends of the spectrum: one – an Albanian inmate; the other – a Greek prison guard. In that moment, their roles in the social context of prison were almost diminished and they were just two men; one emotionally distraught; the other empathetic and courageous. It's hard to believe that such a stressful and violent picture could also be so human and meaningful.

Journal extract – Day 188 – 24 January 2010

So, they opened the door for one hour this morning. I tried to call my mum but all the phones were turned off. Now they have locked us up again and said they aren't opening the doors. So I can't call Riya or my mum, and my mum is on her own. She is going to be thinking, why hasn't he called? And Riya is going to be worried that something is wrong because I told her that I would call her yesterday. This is reminding me of the bad memory in Patras, locked up in the small cell for four bloody days.

Ahhh, the guard just opened the door to give me my medicine and confirmed that there will be no telephones today because the whole of Gamma is in detention. He is a cool guy, he speaks English well. When he first saw me he said, 'So you're the Cypriot Londoner? My girlfriend read about your case and told me. The system is fucked up, man, just be patient and you will be fine.'

Journal extract – Day 189 – 25 January 2010

Still locked in the cell. Today has been slow. I started reading Kings 1 in the Bible. King David died and his son Solomon took over – also a very cool guy. They made a temple in the name of God and they describe every little dimension and detail. It was long, and I actually read it all because I'm so bored in here. I feel like I could build the temple if I had the equipment. Overall the Bible isn't really what I thought it would be so far. Anyway, I don't want to get into a debate about religion with myself at the moment so I will change the subject.

It's friggin' cold! The cell is like a fridge and it stinks like shit. It's been a crap day and apparently we are going to have this detention all week.

Journal extract – Day 190 – 26 January 2010

So, still locked up. I woke up, pulled my bag from under the bunk to change my clothes and there was a stray cat relaxing on it. He must have sneaked in and been sleeping here all night. He's just chilling with us now. Stelios seems to be quite fond of him and has called him Marco. He has been letting Marco on his bed when he clearly has fleas. But Stelios doesn't care, he only showers once a week, not even that.

This morning a guard opened the door and took me to see Marios the social worker to make an application to move to Alpha wing. I hope it's accepted now because Gamma is too much to handle.

32

DAYS OF THE WEEK

The nights were still freezing and the blanket that I'd been sleeping with was too thin to keep me warm. My dad had bought me a thick, furry blanket, which the guards allowed me to have – so sleeping thereafter was a lot less shivery. When I received it I noticed that they'd ripped off all the edges, just in case there were drugs sewn into the finishing seam. I ended up with two blankets, so I gave Ashmul my old one because he slept with only a bed sheet. Gamma was in 'detention' for over a week, but on the fourth day we were allowed a few minutes in the hallway to make phone calls. I thought Ashmul was grateful that I offered him a blanket, but as soon as the cell door was unlocked, he took the blanket to his friend's cell and swapped it for a packet of cigarettes.

Having to live in a small, cockroach-infested cell without being allowed to leave for more than ten minutes a day was a form of slow torture – especially with Stelios moaning all the time. By the end of the week I'd learned to drown out the sound of his irritating voice and replace it with my own rambling thoughts. His constant jabbering became a mellow frequency of sound in the background. On the other hand, Stelios was entertaining sometimes, especially when he slept. He would still have his Tourette-style outbursts in his sleep; he would be snoring …

then he'd fart, then mumble; '*moushmoullo!*' or sing a short burst of random Greek songs. He was a very odd character, but had a good heart. For example, he owned a lighter case made out of kebab skewers that one of the Chinese inmates had made. It looked professionally finished, but when the lid was taken off you could see that it was really made of thin wooden sticks. The initials 'A. S.' were painted on one side, so he gave it to me as a gift. The only problem was that it said 'ABDUL' on the other side. So, whoever Abdul was – I still have his lighter case.

During the week's detention, the guards brought the food to our cells and we couldn't even go for short walks or a shower. The only positive is that it gave me some more time to read and write. I'd read quite a lot of the Bible and had already finished both of Nelson Mandela's autobiographies. I'd started to write him a letter, expressing how inspired I was by his story. I told him that the basis of my story was quite simply summarised with a Latin quote that he'd mentioned in his books, which was: '*Quis custodiet ipsos custodes?* – Who will guard the guardians themselves?' I don't know what my motivation was behind writing to Nelson Mandela; a response would have been incredible. I felt as though I had a better understanding of the injustice that he faced because we were both wronged by our own governments that should have protected us. I am no Mandela, of course, and my time in prison can't compare to the twenty-seven years of his life that he spent locked up! Nevertheless, I was certainly inspired by him.

Journal Entry – Day 192 – 28 January 2010

So, yesterday they randomly called my name on the speaker and told me to pack all my things. I said goodbye to Stelios and Thoma. It was odd saying goodbye to Stelios after two months; I guess it was because we got along, even though we could hardly

communicate ... and when we did it was the same conversa-
tion every day. I managed to pack all of my stuff as compactly
as possible and left, forgetting my coffee shaker, my plastic food
container, and even Michael's wooden cross and the religious
icon that Maria gave to me. I don't get it, it means too much to
me, why would I forget it? My mind was elsewhere. It's OK
though, I got it all back.

I'm now living on the ground floor of Alpha in cell four with
a Chinese man called Weng and two Greek men – Dimitris
and Georgios (of course ... what other names would they
have?). Anyway, will catch up with you tomorrow.

Love from Andrew xxx.

PS. There are no cockroaches in this cell, thank God.

Weng was tall and thin. His fringe was so long that it covered
half of his face and I couldn't see his eyes. One of the first things
I asked him was, 'Can you see?'

'I can see,' he said calmly. He told me that he was on remand
waiting for a trial regarding a stolen credit card. He briefly explained the story to me – something about coming to Greece,
meeting a guy who gave him a copy of a card ... but the guy
stole all of the money and Weng ended up being blamed. It all
sounded pretty dodgy.

Journal Entry – Day 193 – 29 January 2010

My other cellmate Dimitris is actually quite a funny guy and
speaks perfect English. He's here for a drug crime from 1999,
which was forgotten about. Now, in 2010, he's been caught by
police for doing wheelies on his motorbike and they realised that
he was wanted for a crime from over ten years ago. What a
stupid, stupid, lazy system they have over here. Georgios seems

like an OK guy so far. He doesn't speak any English, but told me that he's an ex-heroin addict … injecting and everything. I'm assuming he's here for drugs then!

Journal Entry – Day 206 – 11 February 2010

At the moment everything here is OK. Weng and Dimitris speak English and Georgios is a chilled-out guy. They are all relatively new inmates. We have a TV and no one comes into our cell during the day, unlike in Gamma forty-nine where Thoma and methadone man would play tavli all day and sit on my bed. I started to feel like I had nowhere to go. I'm a lot happier here, I need to be thankful that it's all working out and I am OK. I just have to hope that it stays this way. I'm going to have down days, but once I know my court date hopefully that will happen less.

I don't know why, but the majority of the Chinese inmates in Korydallos loved to make things and sell them. Weng didn't build backgammon boards and lighter cases out of wooden skewers like the inmates in Gamma wing; he would plait together strands of thin nylon thread and tiny plastic beads to make ornaments, Christian crosses and little bracelets. When Weng was out of the cell, Georgios would take one of Weng's unfinished pieces and floss his teeth with the nylon thread that Weng was yet to plait. Weng had no idea what Georgios was up to. Granted it was a little disrespectful and immature, but I found it kind of funny at the same time. The way Georgios just didn't give a crap made me laugh a bit. I wasn't going to open my mouth and tell Weng – it was nothing to do with me. My eyes and ears were always closed in prison, and that code of silence had always served me well.

‡‡‡

A chilly winter gradually phased into a sunny spring and Dimitris was eventually released. Over the previous two months, he and I had had a series of arguments over my snoring, which was loud and deep because of the Xanax I was taking. He couldn't sleep, so he demanded that I make a request to be moved to a different cell. It was he who had a problem with living in cell four, so it was fair for me to suggest that he request to move to another cell instead. Plus, I'd been in prison for eight months and he'd been in prison for eight weeks. Everyone knew that inmates who'd been in prison the longest always had priority; it was an unwritten rule. I wasn't prepared to leave cell four, especially upon the request of a relatively new inmate who had no other friends in prison. Dimitris refused; I refused; so every time I fell asleep he would shout '*Xypna malaka!* – Wake up, wanker!' I'd wake up, and start to purposely snore even louder to piss him off. Neither of us slept; we were both too stubborn for our own good. It caused tension in the cell for almost a week and one day I sarcastically asked him, 'Did you have a good sleep, mate?' He squared up to me and pushed me. I lost my temper and pushed him back. He clenched his fist – Georgios stopped him before anything happened. Dimitris was a good guy; we usually got along quite well and I'd enticed him to become angry on this occasion. We were under a lot of stress and it was unbearable to live in a cramped cell with no sleep. In the end, he gave up and decided to live with my snoring. When he was eventually released we shook hands and he wished me all the luck in the world. I'd watched him come and go, but I was still there – rotting.

There were silly disagreements between Weng and Georgios too. Weng had made dumbbells out of coffee cans filled with sand from the courtyard and other items that he'd found lying around. Georgios lent them to his friend in another cell and Weng kept on asking him where they were. 'Could you ask Georgios where my dumbbells are?' Weng asked of me.

I acted as the translator. '*Reh Georgio, pou einai ta pragmata tou* – Georgios, man, where are his things?' I lifted invisible dumbbells with my right arm because I didn't know the Greek word for them.

'*Pes tou, oti porei na roufa ta archidia mou* – Tell him, he can suck my balls,' Georgios replied while walking out of the cell door.

'I think you're gonna have to wait a while for them, mate,' I said. Weng never saw the dumbbells again and had requested to be moved to a different cell.

With two spare bunks in our cell, Georgios asked the guards if they could move his friends into our cell; Zafeiris from Lesbos and Costas from Athens – probably the biggest, heroin-addicted, thieving fiends on earth. Suddenly, the 'safe' cell that I'd been put into was no longer safe. On a positive note, the dumbbells were back.

Zafeiris was thin and bald, but he always had a bit of unshaven facial hair. If I had to compare him to an animal – it would be a meerkat. He had a little mouth and a pointy nose, which made him look harmless at times, but possibly conniving. Zafeiris claimed that he'd 'done many big' criminal jobs before, but was only in prison for armed robbery. He held up a shop with a gun and forced the girl behind the counter to fill up a bag with money and the boxes of cigarettes on display. He was forty-four years old and had spent six years in Patras Prison before Korydallos. He had no kids, no girlfriend and was addicted to heroin. He told me that he loved to go clubbing and take ecstasy, even at the age of forty-four. As for Costas (who just looked like your average forty-year-old Greek guy), I still have no idea why he was there. I didn't even ask, but he was getting into fights over drugs on almost a weekly basis.

Journal Entry – Day 239 – 15 March 2010

My lawyer went to Patras and finally found out my court date.

4 June. About two and a half more months before I get my life back. I feel relieved that I know now, so that's good. It is quite a long time but I was expecting a lot longer to be honest. So now I have a date to focus on and don't need to keep stressing about being here for another year. I think they will transfer me to another prison in Patras. Zafeiris was there for six years, so I will ask him how that was...

Zafeiris told me that Patras Prison is a lot more relaxed than Korydallos, but when it kicks off … it kicks off. He advised me that I should tell the guards that I'm Greek and to put me in their Alpha wing. 'You don't wanna live in Gamma there; it's very bad, like Gamma in Korydallos,' he said. It made me think of the riots and cockroaches that I'd had to put up with for so long. I'd survived it, but I didn't want to ever have to experience anything like it again. I wasn't looking forward to the transfer, but I knew that it was something that I had to do to fight for my life back. At least knowing the court date was a massive lift. It was like I'd been running a marathon for months and I could suddenly see the finish line – just another stretch.

卌

Minutes turned into hours, hours turned into days, and days turned into weeks. Months passed slowly and our cell had become a hangout for heroin addicts. I knew that I had to deal with it for only a little while longer. I'd watched Georgios, an ex-heroin addict who was clean for three years, get sucked back into the downward spiral of snorting the stuff on a daily basis. His personality had noticeably changed; he was no longer a quiet, cool guy. He'd even begun to hold himself in a manner that was more sluggish, like he'd stopped caring about anything other than drugs. He was easily aggravated and was often getting into fights and arguments with other inmates. It was exactly as my friend Vasilis in Gamma forty-nine had said: it starts off as a little thing with your friends, then it starts to be every week … then every few days … then every day. It made me think about how dangerous it could have been if my mistake in Gamma (with Apollo) had turned into a habit, and then an addiction. I'm happy that I was mentally strong enough for that not to have happened.

The four of us got along quite well sometimes, regardless of their drug habits. We would sit in the cell, smoking, drinking *frappes* and chatting some days. My Greek had really improved and I remember one day I told them a joke in Greek that my auntie Georgina had told me years before: Two doctors watched a fat man running for a bus. His right arm was sticking out and curved downwards, like a teapot handle. The doctors looked at his deformed arm; one of them argued that the man was born with the abnormality – the other argued that it was the result of an accident. They followed the man onto the bus and asked him why his arm was deformed; was it the result of an accident or was it something that he was born with? The fat man stretched out his perfectly functioning arm and responded, 'Oh shit! *Epese to karpouzi mou!* – My watermelon fell!' My cellmates all seemed to find it hilarious. Maybe it was a 'had to be there' kind of moment, which needs actions and facial expressions to make the joke funny.

'Who told you this joke? Was it from *Gougli?*' Zafeiris asked, chuckling.

'Who's *Gougli?*'

'*Xerete ti einai gougli reh* – You know what *gougli* is, man,' he said.

'I have no idea what you're talking about.'

'You know: *youtubes, facebooks* – and *gougli!*'

'Google! Not *gougli.*'

Zafeiris chuckled and put his arm around me. 'Gougli …

Gougle ... whatever. You know, *Mesa sti fylaki eimai o pateras sou* – Inside prison, I'm your father.'

Zafeiris wasn't my 'father' in prison. My dad was a good man who would do absolutely anything for his family. Zafeiris was a piece of shit; he used to steal from me for drugs. If he was my real dad I'd probably never see him, or even want to see him. A typical day would consist of my cellmates and their friends using my books to snort heroin off – one day I'd even caught them snorting off my copy of the Bible that my auntie Teresa had bought me. It offended me, but I didn't make a deal of it because I didn't need the stress.

The guy who they would buy the drugs from would knock on our cell door and enter. '*Ti egine manges?* – What's happening lads?' He was Albanian and I knew him from Avlona's Parartima – short, skinny and bald with a big head. He told me that he was on remand for drugs, but Georgios from Crete in Avlona told me that he was lying and that his real crime was very different. I can't say that it was 100 per cent true, but Georgios told me that the guy's girlfriend had been cheating on him; she'd become pregnant and there was a possibility that another man was the father. Apparently, he pretended not to know about the other man, and during an intimate moment with his girlfriend, he went down to perform oral sex on her. According to Georgios, he grabbed a gun that he had planted under the bed, forced the barrel into her vagina and shot her internally.

He was twenty-one years old and had been transferred to Korydallos not long after me. Within a week of his transfer he was involved in the drug-dealing scene in Alpha with the 'king' of the Albanians. He would come into our cell. '*Koita* – look.' He would unravel a pile of heroin wrapped in a piece of newspaper. My three cellmates' eyes would gleam at the sight and they were probably salivating like hungry dogs. They would start to bombard the young drug dealer with propositions like 'If you give me the drugs now, I'll give you a card and a big can of coffee' or 'If you give me the drugs now, I'll give you two cards next week AND a packet of cigarettes.' The drug-dealing kid would smile and refuse – knowing that he had them all wrapped around his little finger. My cellmates would roam the wing looking for people to pickpocket and would come back hours later with bruises. The Albanian kid would return. My cellmates would offer him less than what his 'king' had instructed. The drug dealer would accept the offer and wait a few days for the rest of the payment. Other inmates would enter our cell throughout the day and ask for the phone cards or cigarettes that they were already owed from the previous week. '*Deftera* – Monday,' '*Triti* – Tuesday,' '*Tetarti!* – Wednesday!' The answers my cellmates would give were merely random, meaningless days of the week. They were in heaps of debt to drug dealers with links to Albanian mafia – they were morons because it was how riots would start. I didn't feel the need to warn them; it was something that they already knew. It didn't stop them – they were addicts and they just couldn't help themselves.

I went for a walk in the courtyard one day and the Albanian drug-dealing kid approached me. We walked up and down for a bit; I tried to forget about what he may have been in prison for and just treated him like any other person. His English was very broken, but he ended up explaining a few things to me. What he couldn't say in English I could understand in Greek: heroin addicts that had money caused no trouble; it was simply a way for them to medicate themselves. They would have a friend on the outside who would transfer money to the drug supplier through Western Union. The drug supplier would phone their friends on the outside, who would let him know whether the money had been transferred or not. Customers like this would receive heroin after a very small cut with paracetamol. Inmates like my cellmates

were junkies who couldn't afford to take drugs. They would resort
to thieving and get into debt. It was junkies like these who would
get themselves into trouble – and you really wouldn't want to be
in trouble with these guys. Some junkies would even prostitute
themselves for phone cards or a hit of heroin – one man even offered me a blowjob for a telephone card. I declined the offer and
couldn't believe my ears.

The Albanian kid trusted me for some reason; I don't know
why, maybe it was because he knew me as the barber in Avlona
– or maybe it was because he was young and had yet to learn to
keep his mouth shut. He told me that the junkies are sold heavily
cut drugs because they are less likely to make money from them.
Costas, Zafeiris and Georgios were snorting paracetamol with
heroin scraps in it.

One morning I lost my temper because two telephone cards
that I'd hidden under my mattress were gone – €20 worth. I
used to lie on my bunk and daydream about speaking to Riya
or my sister Sophie on the phone – or calling up my mum and
dad to find out what was happening on the outside. At the
beginning of the week I would strategically plan the days and
times that I would call them. It would break up the day and
I would feel like my life had some sort of structure – something
that I may have taken for granted in my youth, but now craved.
If I'd finished reading a book, or felt that my Greek had improved, I would reward myself with a spontaneous phone call to
anyone of my choice because my mum had given me a list of all
of my friends' phone numbers back at home. I would replay the
conversations in my head and do absolutely anything psychologically possible to escape from the four walls around me. It is
far too easy in prison to completely forget that the world is still
spinning on the outside of the prison walls. My telephone calls
were a huge escape, and on this particular day, my only escape

was about to go up my cellmates' noses. 'Where are my cards?' I asked them.

They all responded one by one. '*Den xero* – I don't know.'

'Are you all *thick*? We're in a fucking cell. The door's locked.' I could feel myself losing my temper and started calling them a bunch of thieving pricks. I called them all *gyftous* – gypsies and junkies. Although I appreciate that addiction is an illness, I was filled with anger and frustration. Costas went crazy; he stood up and pushed me. I grabbed his fist and smashed it against my face. 'Go on you little cunt, do it!' Zafeiris jumped down from his bunk and stood between us – he was my 'dad' after all. '*Gami sou!* – Fuck you!' I roared to Costas.

'*I mana sou* – Your mum,' he blurted back.

Zafeiris pushed him. '*Ohi manes, entaxi?* – No mums, okay?'

Costas fell backward onto his bottom bunk. '*Gamo ton! Dolofonos einai!* – Fuck him! He's a murderer!' he cried.

'Look at the state of you *Costa*, you're a fucking junkie. You're covered in bruises – with your black eyes. Why're you covered in bruises? Why do you think you have black eyes *Costa*!?'

An *ypallilos* unlocked the cell door and we became silent – he must have been walking past and heard the shouting. He strolled in and stared us all up and down. '*Kalimera kyries* – Morning ladies,' he said. I sat down and filled a cigarette paper with tobacco, then rolled it and licked the sticky edge while allowing my pounding heart to return to a normal pace.

'*Kalimera*.'

'*Kalimera*…' I mumbled.

'*Ehoume ena provlima?* – Do we have a problem?'

Costas stayed silent. Georgios tutted. '*Ohi* – No.'

'*Teliosata na paizete malakia o enas ston allon?* – So you've finished wanking each other off then?' he asked sarcastically with a subtle snigger.

Costas tutted. Zafeiris smirked and Georgios half smiled.

The guard grinned. '*Nai kalo, etsi nomiza* – Yeah good, that's what I thought.'

He walked back outside and locked us in. I lay down and took a deep drag of the roll-up cigarette, reminding myself that I had to stay cool. In control. I'd come so far; I couldn't ruin it now.

33

FED UP

Alpha wing was meant to be quieter than Gamma but it was just as loud. Whenever there was a football match on TV, hundreds of prisoners would bang on the cell doors screaming with joy. If the cell doors happened to be unlocked, football fans would run into the hallway celebrating. I met a number of inmates who told me that they were in prison for football hooliganism – especially *Panathinaikos* fans. Fights would start and it would inevitably result in an early lock-in for the evening.

Every few nights at around 10 p.m. an *ypallilos* would unlock the cell door and walk into our cell with a large mallet. He would step onto my bottom bunk, lean over Zafeiris's top bunk and repeatedly strike the iron prison bars that were mounted in the outside wall. The prison staff would check all of the cells in the wing, and all we could hear were loud bangs for hours when we were trying to sleep. Ever since the Korydallos inmate Vassilis Paleokostas had escaped with a rented helicopter a year earlier, the guards would be extra careful for potential prison break attempts. Apparently, he'd rented a helicopter to come and pick him up from the courtyard. They'd dangled a rope ladder, which he'd grabbed onto and then was flown away into the distance. In prison, Paleokostas was a god! It seemed that almost every inmate idolised him. But what is the point of life if you're constantly on the run? My ex-cellmate Vasilis told me that when it happened, almost every inmate was chanting out their cell windows and watching in amazement. Apparently, some had even set fire to their bed sheets and dangled them out of their windows out of excitement because someone was rebelling against the system. That must have been quite an eventful day in Korydallos Prison.

╫╫

It was evening and I'd just collected my food; the process of distributing it to the inmates had gone quite smoothly. I remember that it was a Sunday, because on Sundays the food in Korydallos was just cold, boiled, white rice on its own with either a pot of plain yoghurt or a banana on the side. On this particular evening they were serving bananas and there were a few left over. Inmates began to fight their way to the front to grab one and it turned into a mini riot. I watched a group of inmates roll around on the floor, kicking and punching each other. A Greek man in his sixties was standing next to me; his grey, bearded jaw had dropped and was quivering slightly at the sight.

'They're like a bunch of monkeys,' I said to him.

The man nodded in agreement. 'Son, these people haven't been brought up; they've been dragged up,' he said. His name was Stefanos and I would see him outside in the courtyard on most days. We had a spot at the back of the courtyard where we'd sit for hours with an American Greek/Venezuelan called Tom and a new inmate called Mahmood who was Iranian. I remember it so vividly – I would spin my *pegleri* and fill my lungs with cigarette smoke. The warm sun shone on my face and I would squint my eyes. 'Rich in vitamin D,' Stefanos would say, as though it would counteract the effects of what we were breathing. We'd pass the time with idle conversation; they would tell me stories about their lives – I would tell them about my life in north London.

Stefanos was Greek, but told me that he'd lived in several different countries. At one stage he'd lived in Golders Green in London
for a while and had worked for the company IBM for decades.
He said that he'd started off washing their windows when he was
a teenager and ended up running a department years later. I can't
remember exactly why he was on remand in Korydallos; it was for
some sort of white-collar crime to do with a property.

The external wall of Alpha's courtyard was the only thing sep-
arating us from the outside world. Looking over the barbed wire
we could see blocks of flats with balconies where civilians would
be sitting. 'We're 10 feet away from freedom,' Stefanos said.

'Yep, and they're 10 feet away from prison! They don't exactly
have a sea-view,' I replied.

'One step out of line and they'll be right here with us!' he said.

Mahmood overheard our conversation and joined in. 'Man,
they don't even have to do anything! If the police pick you out
for no reason, they will be right here with us!' he said. Mahmood
looked a bit like my cousin Andrew Demetriou – one of the 'Bum
Squad' members who'd worked towards the Justice for Symeou
campaign almost two years earlier. Mahmood stood accused of
human trafficking, but claimed that he was the one being smuggled into the EU. Apparently he'd had to flee Iran illegally to run
away from dodgy policemen who wanted him dead. He'd caught
them on video doing something illegal and sent it to CNN, and
then was threatened by the officers because he'd exposed them.
When making it into Greece, the police had caught both him and
the other illegal immigrants. He had a passport, lots of cash
and nice clothes. It made no sense to the Greek police; a man
with a passport who could afford to enter the country legally
would never need to be smuggled into the country. They accused
him of being the smuggler and he faced life imprisonment.

Tom was from Chicago, and was on holiday in Greece when

he was arrested. I used to call him 'big man' because he was absolutely huge – not fat, just very broad and tall. He told me that his name was *Athanasios*, but people called him *Sakis* – short for *Athanasakis* – but went by 'Tom'.

'How many names do you have?' I joked. It was the first time we'd met in the courtyard.

'Only three! What's your name buddy,' he asked, putting his hand out to shake mine.

My hand met his. 'Andrew, but people call me Dave; you can call me Ben,' I kidded.

'Nice to meet'cha, Ben.'

I chuckled. 'I'm joking with you, man, it's Andrew.'

He seemed like a nice guy, but he would often say very odd things. For example, one day he said, 'I think I need a haircut.' Other than five flimsy hairs that he'd combed over – his head was as bald as a bowling ball.

'Ha, good one.'

'What d'you mean?' he asked – his face was straight.

'You said you need a haircut, you were joking – it was funny.'

'I do need a haircut, my hair's getting a bit too long,' he said as the reflection of the sun bounced off his bald head. 'But the sides and back of your head are completely shaved,' I said.

'Yeah, I use a razor for that.'

'So you don't need a haircut,' I suggested.

'I was talking about the top of my head, dude.'

I couldn't help myself. 'But you're completely bald,' I said.

He became defensive. 'No, I'm not.'

'Why do you leave those little strands of hair? Why don't you just shave them off?' I asked him.

'There's something about a bald head that I don't like,' he said.

Tom told me that he was in prison because a woman had accused him of threatening her with a knife and stealing her purse – he claimed that he was totally innocent. A few days later he casually brought up his case again, only the story had changed; suddenly he was being wrongly accused of threatening a man with a gun. It didn't really matter to me if he was innocent or not, but he could at least stick to the same story.

The four of us (Stefanos, Tom, Mahmood and I) were acquainted with a number of weird inmates who would often sit with us in the courtyard, which was different from Gamma's. There was a small patch of grass and a tree, and inmates had created their own gym equipment out of water bottles that they'd filled with rocky sand and wrapped in bed sheets. The rest of the courtyard was a huge rectangle, and, like Gamma, it was just made of grey rocks and gravel that cats would use as a litter tray.

There was one day in particular, when a funny-looking, short Albanian guy sat with us – he reminded me of 'Dr Nick' from *The Simpsons*. He started complaining that there are no virgin girls left in the world because they all have sex so young these days. He said that when he was released, he would lock up a ten-year-old girl and wait for her to grow up so that he could marry her.

'Yeah, she's gonna love you for that, mate. You'll make a great husband,' I said.

'Man, I'm serious,' he insisted. 'How else will I find a virgin? I don't want my wife to be ruined!'

Mahmood let out an irritated breath and shook his head. 'You're a very sick man you know.'

There was also an eccentric Greek guy called Kyriacos who had thinning hair and a lazy eye. He was brought up in Germany so he spoke with a strange muddle of the two accents. Every few days he would sit next to me and say, 'Hey, man, you need to give me your email address.' He would constantly propose that I fly to Munich when we were released and go to Oktoberfest together, like best mates. One day he brought a piece of paper and a pen into the courtyard to take my email address. I was put on the spot, and didn't want him to email me. At the same time, I couldn't refuse to give it to him. I wrote *andrewsemailaddress@hotmail.com.* 'Thanks, man, I'll email you. I can't wait … hey, I was just thinking, you want to go do some *prezza* – heroin?'

'No no, I'm OK my friend,' I said.

I tried to spend as much time out of the cell as possible because it had become a drug den – but the courtyard was also full of nutters. Tom and I started to play the card game UNO on the middle floor hallway. Normal playing cards weren't allowed in prison because it encouraged gambling – even though backgammon, chess, dominos, UNO and any other game under the sun was perfectly acceptable. Several other inmates started to notice us playing and would join in on the game. Before I knew it, a friendly game between the two of us had become a game with eight players who would gamble for quite a lot of money. It had stopped being fun because things would get heated. Arguments would happen and fights would start – they would try to involve Tom and me because we'd started the game. One guy even turned to me and said, '*Den mou edose ta tsigara mou akoma!* – He hasn't given me my cigarettes yet!'

'*Kai einai to provlima mou?* – And that's my problem?' I asked him. He seemed to think that I was the high commissioner of the game, like a croupier in a casino. Tom and I stopped playing with them, and even weeks later it was still going on without us.

Journal extract – Day 260 – 6 April 2010

I thought I would write a little bit in here, it's been a while. I haven't been thinking about the trial too much and I'm glad it's now less than two months away. The days are passing and I'm OK. I just miss everyone too much, I really do. It's been a long time and being held captive makes it feel as though it's been

twice as long. Sometimes I forget that everyone is still living
their lives out there, it's a crazy feeling. I was speaking with
Mahmood and he said 'pretend you have just got into prison,
forget the past nine months'. It's funny, I actually say that to
myself sometimes.

I received a letter from Arnas yesterday. He didn't reply for
ages because he went to court in Rhodes. He said that they gave
him twelve years. I feel so sorry for the guy.

Things in my cell started to become worse than they already were.
Costas, Zafeiris and Georgios were hiding half a kilo of heroin in
our cell that belonged to somebody else. I thought it was ridiculous; what moron would give that amount of drugs to three addicts? It was like throwing a rump steak into a room full of stray
dogs and asking them to keep it safe. Every day I would watch
them take out the heroin that didn't belong to them and snort
lines of the stuff. Costas managed to get hold of some *Depon* (effervescent paracetamol), which they burnt and cut the drugs with.
The person who owned the drugs couldn't have been that stupid,
and my cellmates weren't exactly using scales to measure whether
the drugs had the same weight after cutting them! Their plan was
destined to backfire, but yet again, they couldn't help themselves.
It was a time bomb waiting to explode. To say that the situation
made me uncomfortable would be an understatement.

'You won't say a thing!' Zafeiris exclaimed.

'Say a thing about what?' I asked. However much I didn't like
the situation, my eyes and ears were shut in prison – as always.

Zafeiris struck my left cheek with his right palm and I let out
a surprised wail as it stung on impact. 'You think this is funny!?
I see you talking with the Albanian. Don't think we haven't seen
you,' he shouted.

The three of them had surrounded me. I'd been living with

these guys for months now; they didn't intimidate me at all. They were losers. 'You're stealing this guy's drugs! I'm not gonna say shit, but he'll figure it out himself. You know that, right!?'

One night, when they were asleep, my heart began to race and I was plagued with insomnia. I didn't know if I was being paranoid or not, but they were acting in a way that led me to believe that they would let me take the blame if they were to get caught with the drugs. I heard things that I couldn't translate, but I was sure that they had it planned. During the days I would notice subtle smiles and looks between them. There were three of them and one of me; it would be three against one. I felt vulnerable, exposed and alone. I couldn't tell any of my family because they were already stressed out enough. I wanted to move cell but I had no excuse to. I couldn't tell the guards the truth because I wasn't a rat. Mahmood, Stefanos and Tom were in cells that were full. If I requested to be moved, I could have been lumbered with murderers and rapists who were even worse than these guys! Sometimes they were cool, and we'd sit down in the cell laughing and joking. It was all so confusing. After a week of my pillow absorbing my tears, I'd decided that the best thing to do was wait until I was transferred to Patras. I just had to live with it for a little while longer.

Journal extract – Day 299 – 15 May 2010

My chest is full of anxiety, I need to relax. I don't want to be here any more, I want to go home. I want to go home I want to go home I want to go home I want to go home. But guess what, I can't, so I'm going to have to stop being a dick and just accept it.

I can't believe it's been 300 days tomorrow. I'm fed up of not being free. I'm fed up of it all. I'm fed up of Tupperware containers and plastic cutlery. I'm fed up of food coupons and squatting to shit at specific times. I'm fed up of living in a cell with heroin-addicted thieves. I'm fed up of living out of a sports bag. I'm fed up of having no privacy. I'm fed up of dirty showers. I'm fed up of phone cards. I'm fed up of seeing my family through a dirty window for half an hour. I'm fed up with hearing Greek. I'm fed up of Greece. I'm fed up of being locked up. I'm fed up of eating shit prison food full of spit and bogeys. I'm fed up of sleeping on a one-inch-thick mattress. I'm fed up of being wrongly accused of killing someone. I'm fed up of not being happy. I'm fed up of having a headache. I'm fed up of having to write in this stupid fucking journal like a twelve-year-old girl. I'm fed up of reading. I'm fed up of stressing out. I'm fed up of being depressed. I'm fed up of having anxiety. I'm fed up of everything.

OK I think I've established that I'm fed up. I feel so frickin' weak because I can never let my guard down; it's exhausting. I'm tired; I want to be free again. I don't deserve this shit.

34

TO FLY OR TO FALL?

It was ridiculous: my family was expected to pay for all of the defence witnesses to fly to Greece *and* for their accommodation. If a person in a similar situation to me couldn't afford to do so, the trial would be completely one-sided. I spoke to Sophie on the phone – she told me that she'd decided to fund-raise for the trial. She organised an event in north London with singers and food, where many people turned up to support our cause. I'm lucky to have an older sister who would go to so much effort. I'd always looked up to her growing up – and I still did. She raised thousands of pounds. To be in a foreign prison with so much support back home was overwhelming.

Journal extract – Day 307 – 23 May 2010

Today I went outside and had a walk with American Tom. He always says things that make me feel like shit, like, 'Wow, dude, aren't you nervous? This is it, innocent or guilty!'

I always try to stop myself from justifying my case, but would end up saying something like, 'I'll prove my innocence, the evidence speaks for itself.'

Then he would say, 'Yeh but … dude … come on! This is

Greece! What if something fucked up happens and they find you guilty?'

Why is this prick trying to stress me out? Is there a possibility that he's right? Could I be found guilty for this crime I didn't commit? It's the question that brings on my anxiety, and he was just tapping at it and trying to fuck with my head – like poking a bear.

Journal extract – Day 308 – 24 May 2010

Last night I had a massive argument with Costas because he said that Zafeiris wanted to sleep on my bottom bunk and I sleep on the top. I asked him why, and he said that it was something to do with Zafeiris's head being injured. I said, 'No, he steals from me, why would I let him sleep on my bed?' We got into a huge argument about it and he called me a murderer again. Zafeiris is being cold with me now but I don't care because he's a tosser. Today he said to me, 'I'm going to kill you and cut you into small pieces.' I said, 'Cool, you can make souvlakia [kebabs].' You just don't know who these people are. I'm living with strangers who are criminals.

Journal extract – Day 314 – 30 May 2010

I've finished Jeremiah in the Bible, and after I've finished writing in here I'm going to start the next book. Going to try to have the Old Testament finished before Friday so that I can start the New Testament in Patras. It hasn't made me feel religious in any way, it's just interesting to read and learn.

I'm worrying about Patras now … but what will be will be. I just need to visualise what will happen, remember what Arnas said – it doesn't matter how long it takes to happen, all that matters is that it will. Visualise the future: I leave prison with no handcuffs and I hug everybody. We go back to the hotel, or wherever they are staying. We sit down and talk for ages. I have an amazing shower. We go to a restaurant and have a delicious meal. We have a few drinks and a great sleep that night on a real bed. Wow, this is making me happy and emotional. OK, skip a little while. I'm on the plane. I'm very excited. We land in London, I get off the plane and smell the fresh British air. We see all our family and friends at the airport waiting and we all hug. I see Riya there and I give her the biggest hug, I pick her up off the ground. This is really making me feel good because I know it's going to happen. I just need to keep thinking about it. I've gone through the hardest parts, now it's just about getting over the final hurdle. I'm so close. I am proud of myself for getting through this.

Now ... I can get through this last stage. I don't fear prison any more. If anyone in Patras gives me grief I know how to deal with it. I don't think anyone will. Be a man. You can do it. Just remember to think these phrases and keep repeating them:

I can do this.

I am a man.

I am innocent.

I am strong.

I don't give a fuck.

━━━

On 31 May I was transferred to Patras Prison and it was one of the worst transfers that I'd experienced. It was early morning and I heard my name being called out over the speaker. I shivered. *This is it*, I thought. I packed all of my things and said goodbye to my junkie cellmates. 'How will I know what happened to you?' Zafeiris asked.

'Just have a look on *Gougli!*' I said.

He laughed. After everything that the three of them had put me through, they all stood up, shook my hand and kissed me on both cheeks – it was the Greek tradition when someone left prison.

The guards left me in a holding cell with about twelve other inmates for two hours before dumping me on the same transfer vehicle that I'd been transferred in almost a year earlier. Yet again, four prisoners were squeezed into a cage that was just about big enough to fit two people. It was scorching hot and the journey took over four hours. Every now and then I would poke my eye through the little hole so that I could see Greece. The world was still out there; I couldn't give up hope that I'd be out there soon.

Journal extract – Day 316 – 1 June 2010

I don't know where my mind was for those few hours. I just blanked out into a trance – I had to. At some points I found myself complaining in my mind, then I realised that it doesn't help and only makes it more difficult to endure.

When we got to Patras we were mixed with some other prisoners and they dumped about twenty of us in another holding cell. Every half an hour they would take out two people at a time to be strip searched and have all their bags checked – it's a very stressful process. Finally they called me to go through; I was the last one. I started unpacking my bag and all my clothes were thrown all over the floor. They were shouting 'Pame pame – Hurry hurry'.

I remember a few weeks ago Zafeiris told me that Gamma wing in Patras Prison is the worst and to tell them to put me in Alpha because I'm Greek. I also remember what Yiannis Economou told me – the old man who I first saw in the police

van as soon as I landed in Athens a year ago – 'they're going to
fuck you in Patras'.

I was drenched in sweat. It was 5 p.m. and I hadn't eaten or drunk any water for the entire day. I stood butt naked in the hallway of Patras Prison with several staff members walking past. It was the most stressful thing that I'd experienced and I was overwhelmed with humiliation. The *ypallilos* was allocating prisoners to the different prison wings. '*Symeou – Gamma,*' he said.

I grinded my teeth when I heard the words; I couldn't bear to be put in the worst wing of the prison.

'*Yiati Gamma? Eimai Ellinas!* – Why Gamma? I'm Greek!' I cried.

'*Ohi, den eisai Ellinas. Eisai Romanos* – No, you're not Greek, you're Romanian.'

I picked up a fresh pair of boxers from the floor and started to put them on. 'In all seriousness, I'm actually not Romanian. I don't have a clue where you got that from, but I'm a Greek Cypriot from the UK. Listen to my accent, have you ever heard a Romanian talk like this?'

He tutted. '*Romanos.*'

'Please, can't you just put me in *Alpha?*'

He made no eye contact and tutted again. '*Ohi, fiye* – No, leave.'

I was drenched with fear and sent to find Gamma on my own. I didn't feel the need to protest any more; I knew that it would be a waste of the little energy I had left.

I was allocated to cell six on the top floor and I made my way up the stairs. Patras Prison was laid out in a completely different way from Korydallos. The main hallway was a square shape and eight large cells ran off a thin corridor that led to a courtyard. I was emotionally drained, but my heart pounded as I entered my cell. As soon as I walked in my new cellmates helped me with my bags and prepared my bed for me. The cell was a large square with bunk beds in each corner and there was a separate room with a toilet and sink for some privacy. The windows were tall and wide, leaving the cell airy and cool. There were eight of us in there, and I noticed that one of them was an Albanian guy who used to serve the food in Korydallos.

'*Pineis?* – Do you drink/snort?' the biggest guy asked me.

'No.'

'Good, because if you did I would make you leave this cell.'

'I'm glad you've said that.'

'Yeah, no one does drugs here. I've been here since you were … maybe ten years old. The junkies … all they do is steal and make life difficult.'

It was at that moment when I realised that Zafeiris's view of Patras Prison's Gamma wing was based purely on racism. Zafeiris himself was one of the junkies that my new cellmate was talking about. Zafeiris would have preferred to share a cell with a group of Greek junkies than respectful Albanians or Africans. I should have known better than to listen to him. My new cellmates were kind and offered to help me in any way that they could. Everyone in the cell was quiet and had respect for each other's privacy and belongings. After fearing what Patras Prison would be like, it was an absolute sigh of relief. The majority of them were doing life sentences, some of them for drug crimes as minor as cannabis. I'd been suffering in prison for almost a year now, and hopefully this was the last hurdle.

━━━━

It was the morning of 4 June, the day that I'd been waiting two years for. My legs were like jelly but I was excited to finally clear my name. My dad had brought me a suit to wear and I was dressed and ready to leave. It felt strange – it was the summer and

I'd been wearing T-shirts and shorts in the baking sun. I hadn't worn a suit since my High Court appeal in London!

I walked down the stairs onto the ground floor and I stood in the hallway of a new prison wearing a full suit. It made me feel uncomfortable because I looked ridiculous and out of place. I had a glance at the time – it was getting late and they still hadn't called my name. '*Eho dikastirio symera!* – I have court today!' I said to the *ypallilos* at the front of the wing.

'*Ohi, den eheis* – No, you don't,' he said.

There was a lawyers' strike on that day. My lawyer George Pyromallis had managed to get dispensation from it, so the trial was still set to go ahead. The prison had made the assumption that my trial must have been adjourned because of it.

'*Fere mou ta hartia sou yia na deite* – Go and get me your papers for me to see,' he said.

I ran back up to cell six on the top floor as fast as I could. Sweat was dripping through my suit in the summer heat. One of my cellmates asked, 'How did it go?'

'I haven't gone yet,' I mumbled, nervously hunting for the papers in my blue Nike sports bag.

'*Akoma!?* – Still!?' At least an hour had passed and I hadn't left yet. The document was in the bottom of my bag. *Phew*, I thought. I ran downstairs and showed it to the *ypallilos*. He started to argue with his colleagues in Greek and I couldn't really follow the conversation. I understood key bits like 'but he has court!' and 'but how is he going to get there!?' They ended up taking me in a van that was packed with old men who were going to hospital from the prison. I had to stand because there were no seats. One of the old men looked me up and down. '*Tha pas sto nosokomeio?* – You're going to hospital?' His facial expression reflected his confusion.

I opened my mouth, about to answer him when another old

inmate butted in. '*Vevaia den einai, to paidi foraei ena kostoumi re vlaka!* – Of course he's not, the kid's wearing a suit, you idiot!'

I was dropped off outside of the court, where a group of police officers were waiting for me. My heart began to race as they forced my wrists into handcuffs and escorted me into the building. I'd been guided through a back entrance and I was suddenly inside the courtroom. It had a distinctive smell of old wood and was laid out like a church. There were several rows of long, wooden seats facing a towering, wooden bench where three female judges sat below a large icon of Jesus Christ. I looked to my left as I walked in and could see my family; my dad offered me his 'thumbs up' gesture that he always did. My gran, who'd flown over from Cyprus, was there. I also saw my uncle Theo, my uncle George, my godfather Lef and my aunties Georgina and Teresa. In my peripheral vision I could see Chris and Charlie on the right side of the courtroom. The victim's father was sitting just behind them. He'd travelled almost 2,000 miles overseas to watch the wrong man being tried for the murder of his son.

I sat down. *Breathe*, I told myself. I looked to my right; George Pyromallis acknowledged me and nodded – his assistant Vanessa offered a sympathetic smile.

The court assigned the jury, which took at least an hour. After this process there was the public prosecutor to the left, two jurors, three judges, and another two jurors to the right. They loomed above me and examined my every facial expression and movement. Their close scrutiny made me feel like I'd done something wrong, to the point where I almost had to remind myself that I was an innocent man.

It turned out that the court had failed to summon any witnesses. It was a joke. All they'd had to do was send the relevant witnesses letters via post. Shock was written all over the judges' faces when they realised that Chris Kyriacou and Charlie Klitou were present. We knew that they hadn't been summoned and they were only there because we'd told them to come. We feared that the court had failed to summon Jonathan Hiles's friends too, so the charity Fair Trials International had sent them letters on our behalf. They were informed that the trial was set for 4 June and that they may not receive a summons. Mr Hiles was present, but his son's five friends didn't attend. It was in the interest of justice that the friends of the victim were there. I refused to continue with the trial unless all the witnesses were present, and George Pyromallis made that very clear to the judges.

I took the stand. It was a wooden lectern that faced the bench with an old copy of the Bible resting on the top – a book that I'd almost finished reading. I looked up at them. They towered over me like three powerful queens. Through a young, female translator, I pleaded with them that they grant me bail. I explained how difficult it is being the youngest foreign person in a maximum-security prison. After almost a year behind bars I couldn't bear it any longer. I told the judges that I was unwilling to continue the trial without the prosecution witnesses and that it wasn't my fault that they were absent. I wanted justice! I wanted every witness present for a full trial because I had nothing to hide – I wanted to clear my name!

They asked me if I would be able to financially support myself if let out of prison.

I replied, 'Yes, my family are financially stable.'

'*Den ehei lefta!* – They have no money!' the translator blurted.

'No…' I said.

'Ooh, sorry. *EHEI lefta!* – they DO have money!' I had to stop myself from shaking my head in disbelief. What if I hadn't understood a word of Greek? The judge's decision to grant me bail would probably have been clouded by the assumption that I couldn't afford to live.

George Pyromallis stood up to speak. 'In my entire *seventeen years* as a criminal lawyer, I have never experienced a *defendant* request the summoning of *prosecution* witnesses!' he bellowed in Greek. There was a deep tone to his voice that made it powerful, even when he was speaking softly. He demanded that the judges grant me bail and explained that I had a residence in Greece where I could live.

There was a recess. We were suspended in mid-air, waiting to either fly or fall. I was about to discover whether I'd have to go through the painful transfer back to Korydallos and live with the junkies or be with my family. I couldn't bear the thought of going back there – it was like a nightmare. This time, they needed to make the right choice.

My gran asked a young police officer if he could kindly take me out of handcuffs. '*Einai ena kalo paidi* – He's a good kid,' the officer said, releasing them from my wrists. For the first time I was able to hug my family and it felt incredible. After months and months, to be with them all again in the flesh almost made me forget that I was about to discover something huge. Lef called Riya on his mobile and it was amazing hearing her voice. 'If I make bail we'll put you on the first plane out here,' I told her. I didn't want to raise my hopes, but I could feel my heart rate increasing as I heard the words escape my lips.

George Pyromallis had re-entered the courtroom after going for his cigarette break. 'What do you think the likelihood of bail is?' I asked him.

He always remained impartial when it came to these things. 'It could go either way, Andrew. Let's see.'

An hour had quickly passed and all those present in the court were asked to rise. The judges and jurors walked in and took their seats at the bench. Everyone was asked to sit and the main judge began to reveal the bail decision.

They had no idea what I'd been through; nobody did, not even my family. Even those reading this memoir will never truly understand. There's only so much of a story you can tell on paper. The subtleties of prison life are difficult to put into words, as some of the most important things (which are almost too insignificant to mention) make my experience difficult to recreate. The smell of the prison air; the faces I would see every day; the Greek prison culture. I was the only one who lived it in there. I was the only one who saw it; who felt it; who smelled it – if I think hard enough I still can. Being in prison for something that I knew I hadn't done was a rollercoaster of emotions: fear, sadness, frustration. But the cruellest test of all was patience; a test of how much I could take. My entire time in prison flashed before me in my mind. It seemed like years ago – landing in Athens and being dragged into the police van with toothless Yiannis Economou; the transfer jail; Patras and Zakynthos police stations with 'Sean Penn' and 'Mel Gibson'; Avlona – Arnas; Fivos; Christos electrocuting himself and piercing his own tongue; prison school. Korydallos – Leonarde smiling on that first day; Stelios, Ashmul and Vasilis; the cockroaches; Apollo; heroin; the crazy riots. Alpha wing – the junkies; *'Fuck him, he's a murderer.'* It had all changed my life so much. It was like prison had chewed me up and spat me back out a different person. It had been a journey that I couldn't have imagined ever happening. It was my experience – and it was over. My eyes began to stream as the translator informed me that I'd be released on bail for €30,000, but was not allowed to leave Greece.

I could hear my family sobbing behind me – it was a surreal feeling. I was bursting with happiness because I didn't have to go back to Korydallos, but furious because my bail should have been granted a year earlier. I rotted in a series of Greek prisons for almost a year; how was I supposed to feel? Did they not understand how that can affect a young person's life? Was I supposed to thank them now? Was I supposed to feel grateful that they'd let me go free? Fuck them – I shouldn't have been there in the first place. At the time it reminded me of the line from the Oasis song 'Half the world away': 'You can't give me the dreams that were mine anyway.'

When I left the court in the custody of the police officers, the young officer high-fived me before the handcuffs went back on. 'Amazing, man! You are free! Now you can go party in Mykonos! Yeah baby!' he said.

'I don't think so,' I replied – still overwhelmed with shock. The news was yet to sink in.

I could see that there were journalists with cameras outside of the court waiting for me to exit. 'Here, do this,' the officer said while putting my suit jacket over my head to cover my face like I was Josef Fritzl.

'No!' I said. 'What do I have to hide?'

'OK, whatever you want, my friend!' he replied before we walked out. My head was held high.

It took a week for the bail money to be transferred to the court and for the prison to let me go. On the day of my release, one of the inmates in my cell helped me pack my things and wished me luck. He shook my hand. 'You remind me of myself when I was your age. Don't waste your life,' he said.

After four hours of being held in a holding cell on my own, a couple of police officers entered the prison and handcuffed me. 'Why are you handcuffing me!? I'm a free man!' I said while they escorted me to their unmarked police car and sat me in the back seat.

They sat in the front and turned on the engine. 'Because you are a foreigner, we have to take you to the police station and you will sign some papers first.'

'Then I'll be free?' I asked.

I could tell from the back of the driver's head that he was smiling. 'Yes. What will you do tonight?' one of them asked.

'Tonight, I'll be spending time with my family.'

I recalled the morning of the day I was extradited – almost a year had passed since then. I remembered the journey from Belgravia Police Station to Heathrow Airport. 'I can't tell you what's going to happen in Greece, but I won't be handcuffing you', was what one of the Scotland Yard officers said. I could still hear the sound of his deep voice in my mind. It felt like an eternity ago, and I couldn't believe how much had happened since.

For the entire hour's drive to Patras town centre, I stared out of the window in amazement. The view was very different from that of a city. Everything travels so fast when watching central London from a moving car; shops and buildings fly by and it blurs into a shade of concrete grey. This view stayed the same for almost the entire journey, and it was as though I was staring at a beautiful painted canvas. After almost a year of being locked up, I watched a sparkling blue sea with a soaring mountain in the distance. It was carpeted with hundreds of trees that reflected a leafy, green glow, and the mountain was mirrored on the surface of the wavy sea beneath it. The peak of the mountain was right in front of me, and it was the closest to it that I'd ever been so far. I couldn't believe my eyes. It was the most stunning thing that I'd ever seen.

PART IV

There is a higher court than courts of justice and that is the court of conscience. It supersedes all other courts.
– Mahatma Gandhi

4 June 2010, BBC News

ANDREW SYMEOU GRANTED BAIL OVER DEATH ON GREEK ISLAND

A student held in a Greek jail on suspicion of killing an 18-year-old Welsh roller-hockey player on holiday has been granted bail.

Andrew Symeou, from Middlesex, is accused of the manslaughter of Jonathan Hiles, from Cardiff, in an incident at a Zakynthos nightclub in July 2007.

Mr Symeou, 21, who denies being in the nightclub at the time, has been held since his extradition in July 2009.

Fair Trials International called for his trial to begin as soon as possible.

Mr Hiles, who was in Britain's roller-hockey team, fell off a dance podium after losing consciousness when he was punched hard in the face, it is alleged.

He suffered a severe brain injury and died two days later.

Mr Symeou, a Bournemouth University student, is accused of manslaughter and his trial was scheduled to begin on Friday at Patras on the west coast of the Greek mainland.

However, due to the absence of key prosecution witnesses, the public prosecutor requested an adjournment.

A new date for the trial will be set by the Court of Appeal in Patras in due course.

Fair Trials International, a human rights charity which is backing Mr Symeou, said the Greek authorities had accepted that the latest delays in his trial were their fault and granted him bail.

Jago Russell, the charity's chief executive, said, 'After a long legal battle, we are delighted that he is finally going to be released on bail.'

Right to liberty

'We hope that the Greek authorities now do everything within their power to ensure his trial goes ahead as soon as possible.'

Mr Symeou will remain in custody until the bail conditions are met, said the charity.

Fair Trials International said it had challenged previous refusals by the Greek courts to grant Mr Symeou bail in the European Court of Human Rights.

It argued that it had been discriminatory, a violation of Andrew's right to liberty and contrary to the principle that Andrew should be presumed innocent until proven guilty.

In a statement the Foreign and Commonwealth Office (FCO) said, 'It is our understanding that as result of today's court hearing, Andrew is due to be released on bail.'

The statement said consular staff in Greece had offered assistance to both the families of Andrew Symeou and Jonathan Hiles.

DOES IT HAVE TO BE A PAIR OF SOCKS?

Rumbling motor scooters filled the streets in Patras town centre. They emitted the warm smell of combusting petrol – a familiar scent that I've always loved. The front windows of the car were open, so the fumes lingered in my nostrils as we approached the police station.

It was so strange seeing cars driving past and pedestrians living their everyday lives, some doing their daily shop, or standing on the edge of the pavement and sticking an arm out to flag down dark purple-coloured taxi-cabs. Suddenly, I could see my uncle George standing just behind a parked van, then I could see my dad, then the rest of the family! They'd all been waiting for me, probably for hours and hours. Words can't describe how great it felt. After everything that I'd gone through I was about to be with my family again. No more prison cells, no more handcuffs, a real bed and an amazing meal!

'*Ade! Kane to "beep beep!*" – Come on! Do the "beep beep!"' I said to the officers in the front seat.

The officer who was driving used the bottom of his palm to slam the middle of the steering wheel – I could tell from the back of his head that he was smiling again. He held down the horn for a few prolonged seconds, which grabbed the attention of my family across the street. They looked over to the police car and could see me through the window, sitting in the back seat. Their sombre faces became beaming smiles and I was welcomed with waving hands. My mum threw both of her arms up in the air and I waved back with both of my cuffed hands.

The officer parked and opened the car door for me. He helped me out and I was instantly suffocated with hugs as soon as I stepped out.

'Handcuffs!?' my mum yelled.

'Don't worry, they're coming off!' I reassured her.

Within ten minutes I was walking the streets of Patras. I watched my feet stepping on the pavement in amazement. It didn't feel real. At the time I believed that I'd stroll out of prison and feel exactly the same as how I always had in the outside world. Surprisingly, my surroundings were more difficult to digest than I'd thought. Small things, which I normally wouldn't notice, stood out because they were so different from what I'd become used to in prison. The stone slabs on the ground made a zig-zag pattern and fitted together perfectly. It was a strange thing to acknowledge, but it was such a drastic change from the endless concrete flooring.

I was shocked because the world seemed to be *absolutely huge*. I'd become content with being in very small spaces for long periods of time, and the largest outdoor area was a courtyard surrounded by tall, barbed-wired walls. In comparison, the high street seemed as though it was never ending. Everything was buzzing and loud, and it was great to see lots of women walking the streets – I'd been surrounded by other males for far too long!

Such 'normal' things seemed so strange to me. I wasn't an alien exploring a newfound world; I'd seen cars and smelled burning petrol from motor scooters before – I'd seen pavements and high streets. I'd definitely seen women before.

'This is so weird!' I said to my sister Sophie. She clung onto my arm as we walked towards the hotel, practically skipping.

'I bet!' she said.

'It's only been eleven months!' I added. In that moment, I was reminded that the case wasn't over. This was only a little taste of freedom – a tease. I wasn't allowed to go home, so I technically wasn't free at all. *Forget it*, I thought. I was with my family again and that was all that mattered in that moment. It was definitely a lot better than where I'd woken up that morning anyway.

The walk to the hotel was probably about fifteen minutes, and I went straight up to the room and lay on the bed. I told everyone how amazingly comfortable and soft I thought the beds were.

'What? These beds?' my uncle George questioned. 'These beds are shit!'

He was right, they were hard and lumpy, but any bed would have felt incredible in comparison to the thin mattresses that I'd been sleeping on for the past year.

I was given some time to myself, and I had (what I believed to be) the best shower ever. There were no inmates singing or rushing me, no faeces floating near my feet, no spunk covering the walls, and no splatters of brown liquid. I didn't even have to wear flip-flops. It was just warm water and soap that smelled amazing. I felt so privileged, especially as I could use the toilet without having to squat. On my first night out of prison, I felt like a king – and the toilet was my throne.

That evening we headed to a lovely Greek restaurant for my first meal out. I sat at the head of a long table, which was outdoors in the fresh air. The pedestrianised road was packed with rows of tall, beautiful trees. Their thin branches were lush with thick, green leaves and they cradled juicy oranges the size of grapefruits.

We ordered some drinks and (of course) we stood for a toast. 'To Andrew,' said my dad.

'To Andrew!'

'To me!' I said before we lost ourselves in joyful conversation that had been a long time coming.

When the food came I couldn't believe my nose – *souvlaki kebabs* cooked to perfection, mouth-watering lamb chops and *kalamari* rings drenched in lemon that melted on the tongue. The waiters brought over traditional Greek salads – with feta cheese, black olives and tomatoes that were redder than any I'd ever seen; then they brought bowls of rice and thickly cut chips. The metal cutlery felt cold and heavy in my hands because I'd been using plastic cutlery for so long. I stabbed a piece of chargrilled pork and put it to my mouth. I noticed that I'd got into the habit of biting the fork too hard with my two front teeth, which isn't noticeable when using softer, plastic cutlery. Even the way that I'd been eating had changed and I couldn't help but wonder how I might I have changed in other ways. I chewed and tasted the herby flavours and meaty juices. It was *pretty damn good*.

—|||—

The next day, my grandma, uncles and aunties left early for the airport. I didn't want them to leave Greece because I was so happy to see them. I knew that they couldn't hang around forever, as some of them had been there for weeks already. Unfortunately for me, they had lives to get back to. I, on the other hand, couldn't get back to my life just yet. My family had almost dropped their lives in London completely, so we took a coach to Athens to live in an apartment owned by my great-uncle Andreas.

Getting used to life outside of prison didn't happen overnight. I'd still sit for hours a day, thinking, drinking *frappes*, smoking cigarettes and spinning my *pegleri* between my fingers while feeling the raging sun heating up my face. *Rich in vitamin D*, I'd think – remembering the words of Stefanos from Korydallos. It's funny how one little phrase would act as a cue for a string of memories and thoughts about prison. Suddenly I'd be reminiscing about the riots: people covered from head to toe in blood and beaten half to death. I was out – so why did I have to think about it? At least now I was on a balcony overlooking an urban Athens road – not the most beautiful view, but definitely safer than a courtyard full of prisoners. I was a step closer to freedom, and I remembered what Arnas had told me when I was abruptly made to leave Avlona's Parartima: 'It doesn't matter how long it takes to happen, all that matters is that it will.'

I still had some habits that I'd acquired on the inside. For example, when I used to have dinner, I'd finish eating and then wash my plate – but only my plate – nobody else's. When having dinner at home we would always take it in turns to do the washing up, which would never happen in prison. I even found myself pushing in front of people in supermarket queues, as though I needed to reach the checkout before someone would steal the items from my plastic basket. It was a completely unacceptable way to act!

As time passed, the bad prison habits tended to lessen, as did the special treatment from my mum. I was hoping that she would feel sorry for me after everything that I'd been through – hopefully she'd want to spoil me and let me relax. That lasted about two days, then I had to clean, cook, shop and help in any way that I could. I loved it though – just being with my family made me very happy.

They'd bought a USB internet stick, so for the next few weeks I was constantly using Skype to talk to Riya and my friends. We all had so much to catch up on. I told them stories of how 'this crazy guy' pierced his own tongue with a wire, and how the Avlona school opened my eyes to how important education is.

I tended to tell them of the light-hearted memories that I have from my time in Avlona, as opposed to the heroin scene and 'mad prison riots' that I'd witnessed in Korydallos. I did tell people about them (to some extent) but I made them out to be nutty stories that weren't a big deal at all. The honest truth was that I couldn't get the bad memories out of my mind, and I still couldn't sleep because of it. I tended to put a very positive twist on the things that I'd tell people, because I found it so difficult to explain how I truly felt.

Now that I was out of prison we needed a bigger apartment, so my parents rented one in another part of Athens called 'Neos Kosmos'. It was a five-minute walk from a *Sklavenitis* supermarket, which is comparable to a Sainsbury's. A corner shop was right downstairs, which sold *Sklavenitis's* own-brand food for double the price! There was a tram stop down the road, which took us straight to central Athens in one direction, and to the beach in the other – ten minutes each way.

Having been uprooted and transported from cell to cell, wing to wing or prison to prison for the past year, I felt like I could settle in absolutely anywhere. The apartment was perfect, and it had become home.

My dad was in the UK for a lot of the time, fighting for work and trying to keep his interior architecture firm going. Things weren't going too well for the business, not only because of the case, but because they'd been hit pretty hard by the recession. I was out of prison, so at least he was able to focus more on building it up again. On the other hand, my mum was in Athens a lot more and she'd started to volunteer at the church's food programme. She would go to Omonia Square a few times a week and serve meal packs to the needy. I was asked if I'd like to volunteer, which I wanted to do because I had so much time on my hands. In prison I'd witnessed the poverty that some people were facing, and I wanted to give back to the community. But to be honest, the thought of bumping into people from prison worried me. Jamal would have been released from Avlona and I knew for a fact that he and his friends used to sell drugs in Omonia Square. My mum had probably served him food without even knowing who he was. I didn't want to risk seeing him – or anyone else from prison who'd recognise me.

The delay before the actual trial was disgraceful; it had been months and I had a life to get back to! How long did the Greek authorities want me to sit around and wait?

Back home, the coalition government came into power and our new Tory MP Nick de Bois was very supportive. He raised the profile of my case in Parliament and managed to call for a meeting with the new Deputy Prime Minister, Nick Clegg. My dad and Sophie met with him, lobbying the DPM to push for a speedy trial date or bail to the UK.

Slow weeks became even slower months, but nothing seemed to come of the meeting. I'd already been in Greece for way over a year and we still hadn't heard anything of a new court date. At least there had been quite a bit of coverage in the UK media about the controversies of the European Arrest Warrant. My case highlighted a severe flaw in the legislation, so a short documentary about me had been shown on a programme called *Inside Out*. The BBC's *The One Show* followed up the report, so they came to Athens to interview me. When the piece was aired, Riya recorded it and sent it to me over the internet. It exposed the inconsistencies of the Greek investigation, and expressed that what was happening to me was gravely unjust. In a nutshell, it proved my innocence in a ten-minute television piece! If only it would be that quick to prove my innocence in the eyes of Greek law. It was all taking so long, and it left our emotions fluctuating. The way we were living wasn't normal. I was living the life of a loser:

I was twenty-two years old, I had no job, I lived with my mum and I hardly left the apartment. Sometimes I wouldn't leave for two weeks at a time, and when I did, it would be a short walk to the supermarket.

My mum and I would pass the time watching films and series box sets on DVD. The one that we loved the most was *The Sopranos*, which is (in my opinion) the greatest television show of all time. It's about the life of a New Jersey mobster battling depression and balancing his gangster life with his pseudo upper-middle-class, suburban family life. The main character, Tony Soprano, has some great quotes that I absolutely loved, like: 'I'm like King Midas in reverse, everything I touch turns to shit!' and (my favourite) 'Every day is a gift, just ... does it have to be a pair of socks?' It was exactly how I felt; I appreciated that every day was a gift because I was so happy to be out of prison, but at the same time a dark cloud still loomed over me. I was in limbo. My mum and I watched all eighty-six hours of *The Sopranos*, almost back-to-back, because we didn't have very much else to do. It was *frickin' amazing*.

Of course I'd made an effort to witness all the beauty that Athens had to offer. Riya flew over to stay with me and we walked up to the Acropolis and took a day trip to Poseidon's Temple (which was very similar to the Parthenon, only it was miles away from Athens and took *hours* to get there and back). I've always been intrigued by ancient Greek civilisation, and the temple ruins exuded history and culture.

It was amazing for us to be together again. I remember the day she'd landed in Athens; I'd taken a bus to the airport to meet her. I don't know why, but I was filled with nerves and had to take a Xanax to relax. My nerves turned into joy when I finally held her in my arms again, then we spent the entire bus ride to the apartment laughing and joking. It was as though we hadn't been apart at all. We just fitted back together again, like two pieces of a puzzle.

We took a boat trip to a Saronic island called Aegina – only 17 miles off the coast of Athens. We stayed there for a few nights and it was such an incredible feeling. Sunbathing on a mountain cliff with my girlfriend next to me, and watching the shimmering, blue sea was like being in heaven in comparison to prison. At times I couldn't even believe that it was real. The trip eventually came to an end and she had to go back to north London. I travelled with her to the airport and walked her to the departures gate. Our eyes began to stream because I had to let her go – all over again.

┼┼┼

My bail conditions stated that I had to sign in at the police station every month, which was a ridiculous task. I'd travel to my assigned police station on the Metro, but when I'd arrive there the documentation would be lost and the officers wouldn't know what to do! The officers would supposedly call up another police station and tell me that I'd have to go there – so I'd travel across Athens and be told exactly the same thing. It was so frustrating, and the very first time I was even given a blank sheet of paper to sign. There wasn't any information written on the document whatsoever, and it was probably going to get lost or thrown straight into the bin. Why did I have to waste entire days to complete a pointless task that should have been so easy to achieve? The months were passing slowly and, regardless of the frustration I'd face, I'd still turn up at the police station on the days when I was supposed to. I didn't want to give the authorities anything at all to use against me in court. I jumped through every hoop that they asked of me – however exhausting it was.

I had no clue as to when my next court date would be set. It was assumed that it would only be a few months, but five had passed and I still didn't know when I could clear my name and return home.

We ended up waiting nine months for the trial to start – and what a trial it was.

36

OR SOMETHING LIKE THAT

The trial was set to begin in Patras on 4 March 2011, so we found two studio apartments online to rent for the duration. I overheard my mum sitting at her computer and choking up with emotion. The landlord, Eugenia Siozos, had emailed us saying that she'd read about my case online. She thought it was so unjust that she offered us the studio apartments free of charge. It was the nicest, most selfless thing that anyone had ever done for my family and me. My dad was losing his business and my parents' life savings were being spent on legal fees – to then be offered something so generous was overwhelming. My mum couldn't thank her enough, but insisted that we pay. Eugenia refused to accept any money! My parents reluctantly accepted (but had already planned to give the Siozos family a monetary 'gift' at some stage).

Eugenia and her husband, Dimitris, were the nicest people you could possibly imagine. They didn't even know us but invited my family to dinner, and I spent quite a bit of time playing video games with their son Vasilis on a few occasions.

Before I met the Siozos family, I'd started thinking cynically about humanity. But these complete strangers had been so kind to us. They did more than offer us somewhere to live:

they reminded us that there is beauty and goodness in the world after all.

╫╫

4 March 2011, Patras, Greece

I splashed my face with water then heaved over the toilet. There was a churning feeling of sickness in my stomach; it was the day that I'd been anticipating for almost three years. I got changed into my suit, meticulously; I had to look as perfect as possible. I fastened and unfastened my tie repeatedly until I was almost late. My mobile phone rang: 'Hurry up!' I heard my sister's voice screeching.

'All right, all right. Relax!'

It was a top-floor apartment so I took the lift down to the ground floor. The entire back wall of the lift was a mirror and I looked at my reflection as the lift descended. I was such a *big* guy; I'd really let myself go, and I felt like my appearance didn't reflect my true nature. There were dark, grey circles around my eyes – almost like a panda's. I looked drained, unhealthy and bloated.

The lift door opened and I saw my family standing before me. My dad threw his arms around my shoulders and patted me on the back. 'Ready?'

'Yeah.' I replied. 'The beginning of the end.'

'The beginning of your life,' my mum added.

My grandma grabbed onto my arm as we made our way to the courthouse. The apartment was only a few blocks away so we could walk there in a few minutes. It was a lovely day – early – so the air was cool. The sky burst with sunshine, which was a warning that I'd be sweating through my suit later.

Entering the court with my family was a completely different feeling from going to court in handcuffs. When I'd been taken to court directly from prison I'd actually felt far less anxious and sick because I saw it as my chance to be released from prison. My family gave me great strength, but now – nine months later – I was facing going *back* to prison, and for a very long time. I was confident that I would clear my name, but judging from the previous three years, I knew that absolutely anything could happen. Prison for twenty years was something that I couldn't even bear to imagine. This trial was the most important thing that would ever happen to me – it was a fight for my life.

I approached the court and a journalist pointed a camera in my face and followed me. 'Andrew! Did you urinate on Jonathan?'

'No.'

'Did you punch Jonathan, Andrew?' he asked excitedly.

'No.' It was so frustrating because I was caught by surprise. I didn't want to say anything else – I was far too nervous and it wouldn't have come out properly. All I wanted was for the trial to finally start so that the truth could unfold.

I sat down on the defendant's bench towards the front of the courtroom. It faced where the counsel panel would sit, but the judges and jurors were yet to walk into the room through a side door. Right above where they would sit was a large, slightly wonky icon of Jesus Christ on the back wall. A figure that represents 'divine justice' for so many people around the world was crooked. It made me feel uneasy; 'crooked justice'. I wanted someone to climb up there and straighten it!

I could feel the presence of the victim's family metres behind me. I forced myself to focus on the portrait and held my friend Michael's cross in my hands for good luck; it had been with me throughout my time in prison too.

The counsel panel walked in and everyone present in the room stood up. My heart fluttered – the president judge asked everyone to sit and began to fill the room with the echoing projection of her voice. She read out the prosecution witness register. For the first time, Chris Kyriacou, Charlie Klitou and all five of Jonathan Hiles's friends were present in the courtroom.

The Hiles family had decided to appoint a lawyer, who needed some time to review the case. It was, of course, their right to have legal representation, especially in a foreign land where they didn't understand the system. A Greek criminal trial is conducted in a completely different way from one in the UK; the public prosecutor sits next to the counsel bench and asks questions along with the judges and jurors.

The Hiles family's lawyer asked for an adjournment so that he could review the case – but it didn't worry me in the slightest. I wanted a fair trial, and I didn't want there to be any reason for people to think that it wasn't. The fact that they'd hired a lawyer was a good thing; I was hoping that they'd *finally* take a look at the shoddy investigation into their son's death. Surely they would acknowledge the serious flaws in it, which my family had tried to show them three years earlier.

The first day in court lasted only an hour and it was adjourned for a further six days – to 10 March.

We returned on 10 March, but the trial ended after forty-five minutes because the translator appointed by the court could hardly speak English. Her English was nowhere near strong enough to translate an entire homicide trial.

I sat on the defendant's bench with the translator sitting to my left. The clerk read out the charge, which I'd already read in English several times. The translator then leaned forward to listen with a confused expression etched across her face. Imagine the mum from the movie *My Big Fat Greek Wedding*: a heavy-set woman with puffy hair who looked like she'd come straight from the hairdressers. She raised her hand towards my face to stop me from making any distracting noises and then began to whisper in my ear in her thick Greek accent. 'You was very high up and something happened. Then you hits a boy on his head, and he falls, and then he dies … or something like that.'

I couldn't believe what I was hearing; I was on trial for my life and the woman couldn't even translate the charge! Seventy-five per cent of the vital information had been left out of her translation and it wasn't at all what the document said. She seemed like a very nice lady, but I had no choice but to raise my hand and tell the judges that the translation wasn't good enough. I felt bad because the woman was sitting right next to me, but the translation had to be completely flawless. The judge asked me a question and the translator whispered into my ear, 'You would like a new translator?'

'Yes,' I said. 'Sorry.'

She smiled. 'It's OK *agapi mou* – my love.'

The court staff faffed around; they used their mobile phones to contact translators who may have been available on the day. In the end they brought in a lawyer from another courtroom to translate for a little while; they may as well have run around the courthouse screaming, '*Does anybody speak English!? Somebody!? Anybody!?*' No official translators were immediately available, so the trial was adjourned until 17 March (seven days later) and on 17 March there was a lawyers' strike, so it was further pushed back to 22 March. Almost three weeks had passed and the long-awaited trial hadn't even started yet.

37

ONE HUNDRED PER CENT

According to the trial transcript, the British embassy had recommended a translator called Theo Buchelos. He could speak seven languages, which flew through his lips as though each of them were his mother tongue. Theo could hear one language and almost simultaneously translate it with hardly any thought process – it was very impressive. The court appointed him and the trial finally commenced on 22 March 2011.

Mark O'Gorman (the only eyewitness to the alleged attack) was the first of the victim's friends to testify. I'd often been lying on my prison cell bunk, thinking about what he'd already said to the South Wales Police. He made it very clear that a punch was thrown, but that he was not 100 per cent sure of the attacker's identity. I was looking forward to his cross-examination.

He strolled past me on my left and then stood at the wooden lectern facing the counsel panel. Mark was slightly chubby, with scruffy brown hair and glasses.

Before starting his testimony, he took a sip of drinking water and placed the half-finished bottle at his feet.

His description of the hours building up to the incident was consistent with the detailed statement that he'd made to the South Wales Police in 2007: it was his first night in Zante – he and his immediate group of friends had a few drinks in the hotel bar. Mark headed to the main 'strip' of bars and nightclubs with his friends Jason Mordecai, Robert Hares and Christopher Paglionico at around 11.15 p.m. They sat outside the Rescue club, where Jonathan Hiles and Lee Burgess met them some time later. The group of six boys entered the dance area of the nightclub.

Mark explained that at around 1.00 or 1.30 a.m., he and his friends were dancing on a podium, which stood at around 5 feet. Mark said that he 'felt something wet' on him and thought that it may have been a drink that someone had spilt. 'I turned and saw Andrew Symeou urinating on the stage,' Mark said.

I was absolutely outraged and had to grind my teeth to stop myself from a hysterical outburst. I couldn't believe my ears! The moment I heard him say my name in his testimony, I realised why they'd flown almost 2,000 miles from Cardiff to Greece. They weren't in court to discover whether I was the attacker or not; it seemed like they were there for a guilty verdict. I wanted to jump out of my seat and call him every derogatory name under the sun – but that wouldn't have helped me at all. With each word he spoke, I became more and more furious.

'Andrew then punched Jonathan with his right hand, hitting Jonathan on his left cheek.'

After everything that I'd gone through and everything that we'd fought for, hearing my name being slandered in a court of law was devastating and shocking. I knew that it was a possibility – but I didn't anticipate such a fearless and malicious testimony from a person who had already admitted that he was unsure.

Mark explained that the force of the punch caused Jonathan to stumble back and fall off the stage. 'Andrew' was in the company of two other males and Mark said that he remembered one having light hair.

I could feel myself shaking with anger. My attention quickly transferred to my lawyer George Pyromallis and his assistant Vanessa who were both sitting on the right-hand side of the courtroom. George gave a cynical smile and nodded. 'OK, OK,' he mouthed. George wasn't expecting Mark O'Gorman to implicate me as the attacker, especially with such certainty. It completely contradicted his statement made to the South Wales Police.

My attention switched to the back of Mark O'Gorman, who was still giving evidence. Mark was asked to turn around and look me in the eyes. 'Are you 100 per cent sure this man was the person who attacked your friend?' the prosecuting lawyer asked him.

Mark turned his head to the side and glanced at me behind him. Our eyes met: mine were wide and stared in astonishment; his flicked away after a fraction of a second. 'Yes, I'm sure,' he told the court.

I'm finding it difficult to describe the feeling. A completely random person was trying to destroy my entire life. I'd never felt such rage before; my heart was beating at at least four times a healthy speed. I turned my head to the right and looked behind me where my family and Riya were sitting. Her jaw had dropped and she shook her head in disgust. It seemed as though none of us knew how to digest the sudden turn of events. It was such a devastating shock.

When I was on holiday in Zante, in 2007, I had a thick moustache and beard that was shaped with a razor – my sideburns met at my chin, and my lip and entire chin were covered in facial hair. No witnesses mentioned this distinctive feature in their statements made to South Wales Police, and in the Greek word-for-word identical statements that they had all signed, it stated: 'I wish to point out that the perpetrator had shaved off his goatee on the day of the incident and had left only slightly long sideburns.' Through what we had been exposing in the media, my appearance on the night in question was now common knowledge.

When asked to describe my appearance, Mark O'Gorman told the court that he remembers me having long sideburns – but demonstrated with his hands on his own face that the sideburns met at the chin.

The expression on the president judge's face made it obvious that she was confused. She asked Mark to confirm whether the attacker had sideburns. 'Or was there facial hair covering his chin?' she asked.

'Yes,' he said.

'So he had a full beard? A goatee and a moustache?'

'Yes,' he twitched.

Mark told the court that after Jonathan's death, he and his four friends had sat with a professional photographer in Laganas Police Station. All five of them (together) looked through photographs on a laptop, which were of people partying in the Rescue nightclub – the night before Jonathan was attacked: 'When we were looking at the photographs, my friend Christopher Paglionico said, "There he is [the attacker]", then Jason Mordecai later said, "Let's look at that one again." Everyone recognised him and I have no doubt that it was the man in the photograph.'

Mark also mentioned being shown CCTV of the Rescue nightclub from the time of the incident, where three males were seen running out of the establishment.

George Pyromallis began his cross-examination with the question: 'Are you familiar with the term *perjury?*'

'Yes, I know what it is.'

'In the statement you made to the Greek police you said, "I wish to point out that the perpetrator had shaved off his goatee on the day of the incident and had left only slightly long sideburns" – why is that?' George probed.

We'd been exposing the Greek word-for-word statements as flawed and fabricated for three years. It was a complete surprise, but they were suddenly of some use to us! The fact that they said the guy was clean-shaven must have come from somewhere.

Mark O'Gorman claimed that he hadn't told the Zante police that the perpetrator was clean-shaven. It was lost in translation and he told the Zante police to 'keep an open mind' – 'Andrew may have shaved off his beard after the attack and I told the police that they shouldn't only look out for people with facial hair,' he said.

It was an absurd suggestion to make. It was a known fact to them that I'd already left the island, hence I was not present in the police station, but my two friends were.

He continued, 'I remember mentioning sideburns, but I was tired from being in the hospital with Jonny [Jonathan] when I made that statement and I can't really remember.'

George honed in on the fact that there was no mention of facial hair in his South Wales Police statement either – or any of his friends' statements, all of which were made in 2007. Mark's answer was, 'I didn't say he had facial hair, and I didn't say that he didn't.'

'Why didn't you mention it in the statement?' George asked.

'When I made the statement with the police officer in Wales he mainly asked me about Andrew's clothing. It was question and answer – and he didn't ask the question,' said Mark.

George shook his head. 'In your statement to the police in Wales you gave a description of the male: "He was about five foot nine inches tall with short dark brown hair. He was white but well-tanned. He was wearing a blue polo shirt with collars turned up and I think dark or brown shorts and trainers"– are you telling this court that the police officer asked you each of these specific details and you confirmed them? Are you saying that the officer even asked *you* if the attacker had his *collars turned up!?* Do you not think it's more likely that the officer asked *you* to describe what the person looked like? You gave this detailed description voluntarily, didn't you?'

'I just answered the questions,' he said.

'It's quite a detailed description; you even mentioned that his collars were turned up. You gave *thirteen pages of testimony* and you decided not to mention the most obvious identifying feature!?' George thundered.

'I didn't think it was important,' Mark O'Gorman mumbled.

'But the collars were more important to mention!? The collars were more important than the attacker having distinctive facial hair!?'

After a two-hour testimony, George Pyromallis questioned:

In your statement to the South Wales Police you stated, 'although I'm quite sure it was this male [Andrew who attacked Jonathan] I can't be 100 per cent sure'. So in your original statement, when it was fresh in your mind, you were unsure of the attacker's identity ... and yet *here you are four years later* completely certain! How can that be!?

'I wasn't 100 per cent sure then, but I'm 100 per cent sure now,' he mumbled.

Christopher Paglionico was the next prosecution witness to testify – another schoolfriend of Jonathan Hiles.

A Mediterranean-looking guy approached the lectern; he had a darker tone to his skin and short, dark brown hair. Similarly to Mark O'Gorman's testimony, he looked me in the eye and told the court that he was 100 per cent certain I was the person who had attacked his friend, even though he openly admitted that he didn't see the incident. Christopher stated that he'd seen 'me' drunk and unstable for 'four or five seconds' and was about 6 feet away.

He said, 'It was dark, but there was enough light to recognise his face.' Christopher told the court that he saw 'Andrew' urinating near his party who were dancing on the stage. He went to the nightclub's toilet to clean up; during this period the alleged attack had occurred. Mark later told him that the perpetrator was the man who'd been urinating.

Christopher Paglionico gave very similar reasons to Mark O'Gorman when questioned about the inconsistencies between his statements made to Greek and South Wales Police in 2007. He stated that in Greece, all of his friends mentioned facial hair to the police, but it all must have been lost in translation: 'I said from the very beginning that he had a beard, to both the police in Greece and in Wales. I even told the police officer in Wales that Andrew had an "artistic beard", I don't know why she hadn't written it down.'

Like Mark O'Gorman, Christopher mentioned seeing CCTV of three men running out of the nightclub and was given the 'impression that they were escaping from something'. He later stated that he and his immediate group of friends witnessed a series of photographs on a laptop in the Zante Police Station, but couldn't recall how many:

> When we saw the images on the laptop, we could all see the screen. Firstly, I pointed him [Andrew] out after witnessing about forty or fifty images. Jason Mordecai then confirmed that he [Andrew] was the attacker, I didn't influence him in any way; Jason recognised the male by himself.

╫

Since being released from prison, my anxiety on a day-to-day basis had lessened because I was around people who were constantly remaining positive. But as soon as I discovered what we were up against, the anxiety came flooding back and I indulged in drugs like Xanax. Suddenly we were fighting two battles – not only against the shoddy Greek investigation, but against the victim's friends too.

There was a stressful two-week break between court days, and I was finding it very difficult to cope with the shocking turn of events. How could we possibly take on everyone? I struggled to sleep because I would be thinking about it and tormenting myself – I actually had a better night's sleep in prison surrounded by cockroaches.

The only thing keeping me going was the knowledge that I was an innocent man, and I believed that the judges saw the truth – surely.

The next day in court was 6 April. As soon as the trial continued, George Pyromallis lodged a perjury lawsuit against Mark O'Gorman and Christopher Paglionico. Mr Hiles's lawyer proposed that this was a tactic to intimidate the three remaining friends of Jonathan Hiles, who were all present in the courtroom to hear the announcement. I guess there was some truth to this, because I wanted them to fear the consequences of their empty words. Mark O'Gorman and Christopher Paglionico didn't even hesitate to add distinctive facial hair to the alleged attacker. The details of my defence had been exposed in the media. Photographs of me taken on the holiday had been plastered all over the news and I'd been telling the British judges in my extradition appeal that I had a beard – which the attacker was never described as having. There was evidence that their testimonies had been premeditated in order to ensure a guilty verdict – is that not perjury? It seemed as though they didn't want the truth; they wanted the person accused to pay.

Prosecution witness Jason Mordecai took an oath – agreeing to tell the truth and nothing but the truth. He started his testimony by telling the court how close he and Jonathan were; they'd been friends from the age of eight. I could relate to that; I'd known Michael my entire life and was distraught when we lost him. It was the same year that Jonathan had died and I couldn't imagine being in a courtroom, five years later, having to revisit such a tragic event in my life.

Jason continued his testimony:

We came to Zante on holiday and on our first night we went to Rescue club. Andrew Symeou was urinating on the stage where we were dancing. Some of it landed on me, so I went to the toilets to clean myself up. He was with another tall blond male; we didn't talk, but I think he was with Andrew. I didn't see the punch because I was in the toilet.

The accusation that I'd urinated in the middle of a nightclub was disgusting, and is something that I'd never even consider doing – even if I had been drinking! I kept on hearing about this blond person; where was he!? All of my friends on the holiday were Greek Cypriot – other than Aron who's black!

Jason Mordecai was challenged about his statement made to the police in Greece, where he had stated that the blond male was the attacker.

'I never once said that the person who hit my friend was blond! I mentioned him in the statement because I thought that he was Andrew's friend! Mark [O'Gorman] said that Andrew punched Jonny,' said Jason. In court, he described the attacker as having brown hair and thin sideburns that met with his goatee beard. Then he said that the attacker had eyes that he would 'never forget'. 'There was no doubt in my mind, or any of my friends' minds, that it was Andrew Symeou who urinated and punched Jonny.'

I was more prepared to hear my name being defamed than the previous day in court, so it wasn't a complete surprise. Nevertheless, my blood was still boiling and I felt like a volcano on the brink of erupting. These people had no idea who I was and no idea whether I'd killed their friend or not! If they had convinced themselves to believe it, they were very wrong. I'd spent eleven months coping in a series of Greek prisons, but composing myself that day in court was far more difficult.

When questioned about his statement to the Greek police, which stated: 'I wish to point out that the perpetrator had shaved off his goatee on the day of the incident and had left only slightly long sideburns', Jason's reason was the same as Mark O'Gorman's and Christopher Paglionico's: that he and his friends told the Greek police that the attacker may have shaved later and to keep an open mind when searching for him.

He was then questioned about the description he gave of the attacker in his South Wales Police statement. Jason stated, 'I didn't mention his facial hair to the police in Wales because it was question and answer; he didn't ask the question so I thought that he already knew.'

A recess was called and the council panel left through the side door. Jason's two-hour-long testimony had finished and we made eye contact for a few seconds as he walked towards the public benches. I'd never looked at anyone with such fire in my eyes. 'You're a fucking liar,' I mouthed.

'You killed my best mate!' Jason blurted, even though he wasn't a witness to the alleged attack.

I started to breathe heavily – I was about to lose it. I couldn't bear to hear my name being slandered any more – I wanted to explode. They were sitting on the left side of the courtroom and I couldn't stop myself from staring in disgust. 'You're all liars and I'm going to sue you!' I screamed.

'Sue away! You're a murderer!' I heard an older woman say.

'Look, he's showing his true colours now,' cried another older man.

It brought back flashbacks of prison: '*Skotoses enan anthropo, kai rotas yiati?* – You killed a man, and you ask why?', '*Gamo ton! Dolofonos einai!* – Fuck him! He's a murderer!' I couldn't bear any of it any more.

It was almost impossible to control myself – the volcano was erupting. My dad grabbed me and pulled me to the side. 'Calm down, you're doing so well! Do you really want to fuck this all up now!?'

He was right; I had to treat it in the same way as I always had and control my emotions. I stormed into the hallway and took a puff of my uncle George's cigarette, even though I'd stopped smoking six months earlier.

Robert Hares was the fourth prosecution witness to testify. He was quite a handsome guy – tall, thin and blond. He stood confidently and told the court that he was in the Rescue club at the time of the attack. Robert said that someone was urinating on the stage where they were dancing. He went to the toilet and when he returned – according to Mark O'Gorman – the person urinating had hit Jonathan. Robert described the man as 'slightly beefy' and wearing a blue polo shirt; he had short dark hair and an 'artistic beard and moustache'. 'I didn't see Jonathan being hit, but I saw the man urinating – and that man was Andrew Symeou.'

Robert gave the same reasons for the inconsistencies between statements, and why there was never any mention of facial hair at all; in Greece it was lost in translation – and in Wales the police officer asked only about the perpetrator's hair and clothes.

The prosecuting lawyer stood up. 'Can you look at the defendant?' he said.

Robert turned around and looked me in the eyes.

'Can you look this man in the eyes and tell the court that you are 100 per cent sure that this is the man who attacked your friend?'

'Yes, 100 per cent.' There was a fierce look in his eyes as he said the words and I was blasted with a numbing shudder.

George Pyromallis cross-examined Robert.

According to your statement made to Greek police at the time, the attacker was drunk, clean-shaven and wearing a blue polo shirt. There are several photographs of the defendant taken from different cameras throughout the time of the incident. These show that the defendant was in a different nightclub, wearing a yellow T-shirt with thick facial hair. How can you explain this?

'Well … I didn't mention the beard because I wasn't asked about a beard – I can't tell you about his clothing; maybe he changed his clothes?'

George began to circle the witness, forcing an animated, confused face. 'So you're suggesting to this court that the defendant was wearing a blue polo shirt – he attacked your friend – then ran back to his hotel, changed his clothes, sobered up and shaved his beard within a few minutes!?'

'If someone commits a crime, they may want to change their appearance. He could have changed his clothes,' Robert answered.

George nudged Theo, the translator. '*Vlepis para poly tileorasi pes tou* – Tell him he watches too much television.' Then George began to quote Robert's South Wales Police statement:

I can describe this male [the attacker] as being white but well-tanned, he was five foot ten inches tall with a bulky build, quite stocky, I thought he appeared to have something of a foreign appearance due to his facial features but I can't really describe why. He had black spiky hair, which stood up about one-two inches. He was wearing a blue polo shirt with the collars turned up and blue or dark-coloured jeans.

'Why didn't you mention the facial hair?' George asked.

'The officer didn't ask the question.'

George looked like he was about to lose his temper. 'But look at what you said here: "something of a foreign appearance due to his facial features"!' George turned to the judges. 'Look! He even says the words "facial features" and he doesn't mention the facial hair!?' His attention flicked back to Robert. 'What did the police officer ask you then? Tell us, what was the question!?'

'I can't remember, it was a long time ago.'

Lee Burgess was the last of the five to testify – a lanky brown-haired guy who openly admitted that he was very drunk at the time of the attack. He told the court that once seeing my picture, he had a 'feeling' that he'd seen me before and had a 'feeling' that the attacker had a beard. He said that he can't be 100 per cent sure because he did not see the incident, but believes his friends. Later in his testimony he was 100 per cent sure that the attacker was me. 'He had features that I can't forget. Mainly his beard and eyes.'

I was hearing the same bullshit over and over. Lee Burgess's testimony was so ridiculous that it must have completely shattered the credibility of all five of them – if they even had a scrap of credibility to begin with.

38

A CLEAN-SHAVEN MALE

During the break before the next day in court, our solicitors in London had contacted the South Wales Police officers who had taken statements from Mark O'Gorman, Christopher Paglionico, Jason Mordecai, Robert Hares and Lee Burgess for the coroner's inquest in Wales. The two officers agreed to make written testimonies for the trial in Greece and answer a few questions that we had.

On 8 April, George Pyromallis submitted these two statements to the court. One of the officers had stated:

In relation to the statements [of Jonathan Hiles's friends in Wales], I can confirm that the witnesses were spoken to individually at their home addresses, with the exception of Lee BURGESS who was spoken to at his place of work, and their own accounts of the incident were discussed and then recorded in written statement format. This would have covered points of what they had seen, what they had heard, their actions before, during and after the incident and also antecedent knowledge of their friend Jonathan. This included descriptive details of the male responsible. In this case, I can only say that if there is no record of the suspect having facial hair then it was not mentioned by the witness. I would normally ask this question when talking about descriptions. Following completion of their statements they would have been read back to the witness and following their agreement as to the content of the statements they were signed as being a true and accurate statement.

The police officer who took Christopher Paglionico's statement said:

Generally, in obtaining a statement, I would ask the witness to give a full detailed account of what took place. I would then make notes and on completion of the witness's first account question further to expand on any issues that I judged as being relevant to the enquiry. When obtaining descriptive details from the witness of any person or persons that they mentioned, I would ask the witness to describe in detail the person from head to toe and I would ask them to describe their facial details. Due to the passage of time, I am unable to say if on this occasion I specifically asked about facial hair; however I would have expected this to be covered when asked about any distinctive features. Finally, I would have either read the statement back to Christopher or asked him to read it himself prior to signing it as an accurate account of his evidence.

We lodged perjury suits against Jason Mordecai, Robert Hares and Lee Burgess.

Chris Kyriacou was called to testify by the public prosecutor, but was there to defend my innocence. He explained to the court that he was with me on the night of the incident in Zante. At the time of the attack we were in a completely different nightclub over 200 metres away, and told the court that our party spent the night out with two different groups of girls: Toni Martelli and her three friends – and Christina Christou and her two friends.

I'd left the island on 22 July. Chris gave a detailed account of how the police were showing my photograph, and that of another blond male, at the hotel on 24 July. They then took he and Charlie to the police station and didn't tell him that someone had died. While questioning him in a darkened room over a period of eight hours, police officers also slapped and punched him. He said that a female translator was present and bore witness to some of the violence. She looked at Chris sympathetically, but the police officers sent her out after some time. Chris said that there were probably around fifteen police officers in the police station at the time. One of them had seized his passport from the hotel; they then violently intimidated him and forced him to sign a document in Greek that he didn't understand. Chris told the court that he'd made a complaint to the British embassy as soon as he left the police station. Someone from the British consulate came to see him and Charlie in their hotel room – but was thrown out by the manager for trespassing.

The prosecuting lawyer made a request to the judges: 'The testimony of the translator, Electra, who was present in the interrogation of Chris Kyriacou is necessary to submit. Her testimony may discredit the witness!'

'I have no objection to that,' George Pyromallis thundered. 'But if we summon Electra, I request that we summon the translator, Jake, who was present in the questioning of Jonathan Hiles's five friends. With his testimony, these five witnesses could be further discredited!'

The judges didn't summon any of the translators and Chris continued his testimony:

When we got back to England we went through photographs of the night, which were taken by different people. They built a picture of the night and it wasn't long after the holiday, so I could remember at the time. Andrew's family hired a solicitor and we all made statements. If it wasn't for that, I probably wouldn't remember that night now.

'Is there anything else you would like to add?' asked the main judge.

What I signed in Greece was retracted. When I saw Andrew's family, I told them that I was so sorry for what happened and that I would do whatever I could to help. We remained friends for a while, but once he was arrested he didn't want to speak to me. I've come to court to testify because I know Andrew didn't do this. I've known him since we were kids, he isn't a violent person – he isn't capable of doing this. He has good manners; he's polite; his family are good people – he's had a good upbringing. I've never seen him involved in a fight. It breaks my heart to see him in this position because of a statement that I was forced to sign.

Charlie Klitou was next to testify; he too gave a full description of what happened on the night of the attack. He was with me in a different bar called Bad Boys, which he too could remember because it was documented with a solicitor in 2007. He stated that after the incident in the police station he attended hospital after being punched in the jaw by a police officer – he couldn't eat. He said that he later saw a psychiatrist, who diagnosed him as having post-traumatic stress from the incident in the police station.

'How many police officers would you say were in the police station?' asked the prosecuting lawyer.

'Erm … maybe seven or eight?'

'Lies! How can you explain that your friend Chris Kyriacou saw fifteen policemen in the police station!? It couldn't have been that traumatic if you can't even remember how many there were.'

'If that's what Chris said, that's what he thinks! I would say there were about seven or eight, I didn't count them!' Charlie said.

††††

Patras is home to the Basilica of St Andrew, which is ironic because I am his namesake. Apparently, the apostle was crucified in Patras in the late first century, and the cathedral there is one where his relics are now kept.

I would go there every few days to unwind. The scent of burnt candle wax and incense lingered in the airy space and I could almost hear the echo of my own breath. Soaring walls were covered in biblical artwork, each of which burst with colour and told a different story. A broad, domed ceiling displayed a huge mural of Jesus Christ, whose eyes were wide and mesmerising. Sometimes I felt like I could have stayed in there forever, like how I used to sit at Michael's grave years earlier. I didn't really pray very much; it was more therapeutic just to sit and let my mind wander. When I was there, I would feel sheltered from the chaos back at the apartment. I'd leave the cathedral and take a stroll by the sea in the early-summer Greek sun. I would sit and listen to the waves slap the rocky coastline – they would break into white splatter and I would feel a cool spray of salty seawater on my face.

My cousin (and 'Bum Squad' member) Andrew Demetriou flew out to Greece to surprise me, as did my friend Kristianna Paraskeva and godfather Lef. My aunties Teresa and Georgina were coming back and forth – and even my uncle Spyros and auntie Nikki came for part of the trial. It was amazing to see them all, but difficult to fully enjoy their company with the thought of the trial in the back of my mind.

Between court days we'd spend most of our time in a local café. I absolutely loved it there because the café owned every board game that I could possibly imagine. I would meet my grandma and uncle George there most mornings and we'd play *tavli* for a while. The others would meet us later and we would all play a Greek card game, which was similar to Rummy. I remember one afternoon we all played Greek Monopoly. Sometimes we played games for hours – it passed the time and kept our minds busy. I never would have spent so much time with my family back at home; this was probably the only positive thing I could say about my time in Patras in 2011.

We appeared in court again after an eleven-day break to hear the testimonies of the Rescue nightclub owner, the photographer, a Rescue nightclub member of staff, a security guard and one of the investigating Greek police officers. None of them saw the incident or a person urinating.

A member of staff from the nightclub testified, claiming that there were no raised stages in the establishment. The prosecuting lawyer submitted a photograph to the court, which showed people dancing on an elevated stage with no safety barriers. 'How can you explain that these people are raised then!?' he asked.

'I don't know,' said the witness – denying all knowledge.

Of course there were raised stages in the nightclub! It wasn't an opinion; it was a fact. Anyone could have gone there and seen for themselves. The president judge just rolled her eyes.

A security guard who worked at the entrance of the nightclub gave his testimony: 'I thought someone may have fainted, but I was told that a boy was hit. One of the boy's friends came with me to look for the guy who punched him, but we couldn't find him. I can't speak English, so I don't know who they were looking for!'

One of the nightclub's owners, Anastasios Zades, told the court that he wasn't in the establishment at the time of the incident, but was told about it three days later. He briefly explained how the nightclub is laid out, saying that there are some stairs leading up to balconies. 'The dance floor is flat, not elevated,' he claimed. Anastasios stated that there were no CCTV cameras installed in the nightclub until 2009 – two years after the incident. He wanted the judges to know that he could prove this with receipts – and I'm not sure why he was so intent on making this point.

The president judge pulled him up on this, reminding him that CCTV had been mentioned in the investigation. Anastasios Zades denied all knowledge and said that any images or video that were included in the investigation must have been from the photographer – James Gibson.

James Gibson testified in court next, explaining that he wasn't in the nightclub on the night in question. He was taking promotional photographs there on the night before the incident (the night I was there) and he couldn't remember taking any video. The photographs that he'd taken the night before the attack were used in the investigation at Laganas Police Station in Zante. James Gibson told the court that he was present when the photos were shown to Jonathan Hiles's five friends.

> I stayed at the police station for about three hours with my laptop. The boys looked at the photos together. They picked out someone from the photos, but there was definitely some doubt. One boy said, 'maybe it was him', then another said, 'no, well ... maybe,' then they began to convince each other. It was a difficult and stressful process. I'm not sure who they picked out. The police wanted them to find the perpetrator and the boys were tired and pressured.

One of the investigating police officers, Angelos Polizos, later gave his testimony. He was born in 1987, so must have been only nineteen or twenty years old when the incident had occurred. As a witness for a serious homicide trial, he represented the entire Laganas police force, wearing jeans, trainers and a hoodie.

Angelos stated that there was no CCTV in the nightclub at the time. When asked why CCTV had been referenced in the investigation, Angelos claimed that they meant a 'DVD with photographs saved on it'.

Why were the police hiding such vital evidence? It would have instantly exonerated me as the attacker! The CCTV would have shown me entering the Rescue nightclub at around 4 a.m., staying near the front bar and then leaving. It would not have shown me entering or leaving the nightclub at any earlier time – but it had mysteriously vanished.

Angelos continued his testimony:

> We showed the photographs to the victim's friends, which were taken on the previous night. They looked at these individually and they all identified one as the perpetrator. We zoomed in on the photo and sent it to all the police stations, airports, ports and to Interpol. From the information we received back, the alleged offender was staying at the Mariana Hotel in Laganas. When we showed the photograph to the manager of the hotel, he told us that the suspect had departed back to England. His two friends admitted that this male was Andrew Symeou.

The young officer made it clear that there was no reason to violently intimidate Chris Kyriacou and Charlie Klitou because they'd volunteered the information. He also stated that he wasn't present during the majority of the interrogations: 'There was no reason to force the witnesses to tell us things that they didn't know about; the statements were taken by an interpreter and we tried to tie the case up.'

Angelos Polizos was grilled about the word-for-word identical statements signed by Mark O'Gorman, Christopher Paglionico, Jason Mordecai, Robert Hares and Lee Burgess: 'I don't know why the statements of Jonathan Hiles's friends are the same; in no event did we copy one statement to another. They all said the same thing.'

The young officer described the perpetrator as '1.65 to 1.70 metres tall, a tanned complexion, with regular short hair and a beard'.

In George Pyromallis's cross-examination, Angelos was shown a photograph of me in the Rescue club, taken by James Gibson on the night before the incident. My beard was clearly visible and my eyes were closed – it was a picture of a crowded dance floor, which was taken from afar and zoomed in. 'Is this the photograph of Andrew Symeou which was used in the investigation and identified him as the attacker?' asked George.

'Yes.'

'So the description you're giving now … is it the description that the friends of the victim gave? Or are you just telling us what you see in the photograph?' he asked.

'Yes, I'm describing the photograph.'

'Right, because in your investigation the victim's friends stated that the attacker was clean-shaven.'

'Yes, I don't remember them mentioning a beard. I remember them saying that the attacker must have shaved his beard and left long sideburns.'

George took a deep breath and raised his voice, 'Are *you* telling this court … that the suspect who you – and the victim's friends – were looking for at the time of Jonathan's death was *a clean-shaven* male!?' he roared.

'Yes,' Angelos nodded.

The trial continued the next day – 20 April 2011. The DJ who was working in the nightclub on the night in question gave his testimony to the court – he didn't see the attack, but said that he had alerted the security staff with a laser when he saw that a person had fallen. One of the bar staff gave evidence just after; he told the court only that the nightclub had no raised stages and that there were no CCTV cameras.

A second nightclub security guard testified to the court:

I was alerted that someone was hurt, so I entered the nightclub and saw a man lying down. I asked what had happened; one person said he was hit with a bottle – another said that he was punched. The man was unconscious and his friends were very nervous. We carried the victim outside with my colleague and the victim's friends, then an ambulance came. I went back into the nightclub with one of the man's friends – I can't remember his name – we were looking for the man responsible, but found nothing. He described the man as dark-haired and stocky, but there was also mention of a blond male too. There were a lot of people in the place by this time; it was difficult to get past people because no one stopped dancing. The lighting was low and disco lights were flashing – the victim's friends couldn't recognise anyone.

The witness made it clear that at no stage was distinctive facial hair mentioned to him. 'None of them told me that the man responsible had a beard. They told me that the man was stocky, not with words, but with gestures. They didn't gesture that the guy had a beard.'

The prosecution was complete.

39

ANY BLONDE WILL DO

My defence was simple – I wasn't even in the nightclub at the time of the attack. We submitted photographs that were taken by my friend Andrew Christophides and female friends of ours called Toni Martelli and Christina Christou. All the photographs were taken throughout the night of the attack and had been up-loaded to Facebook not long after they'd all returned from the holiday in 2007. Toni and Christina were from separate parties and didn't know each other – they happened to be in Zante at the same time as us.

A forensic photography expert tested the original digital image files that were taken on all three of the cameras. His report came back saying that the original images had not been altered and that the date of the digital image files must have been the date that the cameras had been set to at the time. The dates on all three of the cameras must all have been the same – 19 July (before midnight) and 20 July (thereafter). Everyone wore the same clothing in all of the pictures, further suggesting that it was the same night. Moreover, there were pictures on the same cameras from a night earlier, and I was wearing the same cloth-ing as in photographs taken by James Gibson (the professional photographer), who was present only on that one night. The photographs were clearly legitimate and undoubtedly strengthened my defence.

One of the photographs (which was taken on the night of the incident) was of a group of me and friends in a different nightclub. You could zoom in on my watch, which clearly showed the time as being 1.20 (a.m.) – the same time as the digital information on the image file (11.20 p.m., set to British time) and around the time of the alleged attack in the Rescue nightclub.

The prosecuting lawyer stood up and objected to the submission of the photographs. 'These images must be fake!' he yelled.

'You haven't even looked at the pictures! You're just saying that they're fake because you don't like what they show!' George Pyromallis cried.

> If you're making the accusation that these photographs are fake, you're not only accusing the defendant of fabricating evidence, but you're accusing *me* of submitting false evidence *and* the forensic company for producing a false document! If you're serious about this accusation I suggest you lodge a criminal suit against all three of us!

The prosecuting lawyer sat back down and didn't make an official complaint, as it had absolutely no basis in truth.

To counter the forensic report for the photographs, the opposition scanned low-resolution hard copies of the photographs and had them forensically tested for lighting and gamma. I'm surprised that the company had even accepted digital scans of copies. The report, which they later submitted, stated that the datestamps on the photographs had been superimposed onto the image – which all cameras do. Their report also stated that the face of my watch could have been 'crudely cut and pasted'. I was furious because the report was based on low-resolution scans of the original images after being printed on normal printing paper. Our forensic report was based on the original digital image files – their report was not. At no stage were any photographs tampered with, which the court had already accepted.

Even if the court were to disregard the forensic report of the original images, George Pyromallis provided evidence that the photographs had been uploaded to Facebook around 24 July 2007. For the images to be altered, the people who had taken them would have had to alter them before uploading them to the social networking site, and I wasn't even a suspect at that time. The accusation of the photographs being fake was ridiculous.

My friends Andrew Christophides, George Georgiou, Alex Kalli, Jason Demetriou, Aron Rouse, Toni Martelli and Christina Christou gave evidence over the next few court days – as did one of the holiday reps, Georgina Clay. My friends reiterated the statements that they had given to my lawyer in 2007 – all of us were together in a different nightclub over 200 metres away. If it wasn't for the statements made not long after the holiday, it would have been extremely difficult for any of them to remember – so it's lucky that we took that precaution.

The prosecuting lawyer challenged them on all having the same story (we'd been to the same series of nightclubs together, so their statements were very similar). They were all accused of conjuring up a fake alibi to protect me. I doubt that the court took the accusation seriously. We were on holiday together, so we went out together!

One of my best friends, Andrew Christophides, was the first defence witness to testify. The prosecuting lawyer wanted to know if any members of our group on the holiday were blonde, or whether we'd spent time with any blonde people. The alleged perpetrator had been described as being in the company of a blond male.

Andrew told the court that our group of friends were all British Greek Cypriots, apart from Aron, who's black. The prosecuting lawyer showed the court a photograph that had been uploaded to Facebook. The BBC had used the photograph for a news piece on my case; it was a picture of Andrew Christophides, Chris Kyriacou, Charlie Klitou and me with a tall, blond male. The Hiles family had seen it and had probably been told that the blond guy was the alleged accomplice.

'Who is this blond male in the middle of the photograph?' asked the lawyer.

'He was one of the holiday reps … his name was James, I think. He came out on special event nights, but he was working,' Andrew said.

The prosecuting lawyer changed the subject and didn't submit the photograph. It must have shocked him, because he'd probably been told that this blond male was the same person as the blond male from the Greek investigation. Jonathan Hiles's friends – yet again – had wrongly identified someone from a photograph.

Georgina Clay (the holiday rep) testified in court after Andrew. George Pyromallis asked the prosecuting lawyer if he could see the photograph that was submitted earlier, 'the photograph with the blond member of staff from the travel company,' George elaborated.

'I didn't submit that photograph,' the prosecuting lawyer said.

'No, but I'd like to submit it!'

The prosecuting lawyer handed the photograph to George, who showed it to the judges then placed it on the lectern in front of Georgina. 'Do you know this male, the blond one?' he asked softly.

'Yes, he's one of my best friends – James.'

'And you worked together?'

'Yeah, it was my second year working in Zante. I'd worked

there the year before and I asked him if he wanted to come and work with me the next year.'

'In your statement made to the South Wales Police in 2007, you spoke about the Greek police coming to the hotel where the defendant and his friends had been staying – the Mariana Hotel.'

'Yes…' she agreed.

'But at this stage, the defendant had gone back to London. This was the time when the Greek police took Chris Kyriacou and Charlie Klitou to the police station after recognising the defendant's picture. You said the police had two photographs: one photo was of the defendant and the other photo was of a blond male.'

'I remember the pictures, yes,' Georgina nodded.

George picked her South Wales Police statement out of a wad of papers on his desk and walked towards her. 'You said in your statement: "I was at the Hotel Mariana, even though it was my day off, when the Greek police turned up. I was called over by two other staff members and I was asked by the police to identify the photographs." Do you remember this?'

'Yes, that's what happened,' Georgina confirmed.

'You mention that "two other staff members" called you over; would one of those staff members happen to be this blond male – James?'

'Yes.'

'So the police saw James?'

'Yes.'

'And the police showed James the two photographs, one of which was the photograph of the blond male who had been identified as the friend of the attacker?'

'Yes.'

'Did the police ask James if he recognised the blond male in the photograph?'

'Well … yeah. The police asked all of us.'

'And the police had no reason to arrest James? They weren't showing James a picture of *himself* were they? That would be absurd! He *wasn't* the blond male that the victim's friends had identified, was he!?'

'No, the picture was of a Scottish man called Gordon,' she said. 'He stayed in the hotel.'

'And Gordon and James are different people?'

'Of course,' she smiled.

'And do they look alike?'

'Erm ... I'd need to see a picture of Gordon again but I'd say no. Not really.'

'So, would you say that a picture of the defendant and his holiday rep is totally irrelevant to this case?'

'Erm ... I guess so.'

'So this blond male ... Gordon ... was he friends with the defendant?' asked George.

'I never saw Gordon socialising with the Cypriot boys. I couldn't be 100 per cent sure because I wasn't there the whole time ... but in this job you do get to know who becomes friends! I'm 99 per cent sure that they hadn't even spoken.'

Georgina later testified that she was present in the police station when the police interrogated Chris and Charlie. Before being forced to leave she could see Charlie through a door that was ajar and mouthed, 'Are you OK?' Charlie shook his head and mouthed, 'No.' Georgina confirmed that Chris and Charlie instantly made a complaint about the Greek investigating officers' violent behaviour, and that they had forced them to sign documents that they didn't understand. She also told the court that Charlie's face was noticeably swollen and bruised as a result of the beating.

40

THUMBS UP, THUMBS DOWN!

On 16 June I gave my testimony to the court. The night before, I met George Pyromallis in a café with his assistant Vanessa. 'Don't shout, don't get too emotional, just stay calm and tell them the truth. Even if you stand there and say, "it wasn't me", it's fine. Your job is very easy!'

I'd read the Bible, and there was a Psalm that I said I'd wanted to tell the court in my testimony because it was so relevant to the case.

'Don't quote the Bible, Andrew, they think people who quote the Bible are crazy!' he said.

My heart thumped before I stood to testify, but I was as ready as I could ever be. I stood at the wooden lectern and looked up at the public prosecutor, four jurors and three judges. They looked down at me with curious eyes – who could have known what was going through their minds? They had the power to change the course of the rest of my life. I was nervous, but reminded myself how simple my job was: *just tell the truth*. It was a far easier testimony to make than that of some of the prosecution witnesses.

I'd been waiting three years for this moment. I put my hand on the Bible and took the oath:

'I had no involvement in the tragic death of Jonathan Hiles,

I wasn't there and the accusations are false. It's taken three years of suffering to clear my name; one of those years was in a foreign prison.'

After everything that I'd gone through, I became overwhelmed with frustration and anger. 'I was twenty years old when I was extradited here!' I cried.

> Twenty! You can't imagine how difficult it is being the youngest person in a foreign maximum-security prison! I have stories that you wouldn't believe. Sometimes I wish that I could erase them from my memory. I was locked up for someone else's crime and this whole case has been based on a lie! ... I've sat here and witnessed this entire trial – and it has become some sort of sick war. It's clear that the friends of the victim were not describing the attacker, but were describing how I looked in the photograph of me at the time. I know this is the case ... Jonathan Hiles's friends know this is the case ... Mr Hiles knows this is the case – quite frankly, I think that everyone who's sitting in this room knows that this is the case!

Then I said exactly what George Pyromallis had told me not to.

> Psalm 64:2! They sharpen their tongues like swords and aim their words like deadly arrows! They shoot from ambush at the innocent man, they shoot at him suddenly without fear! ... But God will shoot them with their arrows! Suddenly they will be struck down. He will turn their own tongues against them and bring them to ruin!

I couldn't help myself.

I told the court that I'd found it extremely difficult being accused of urinating in a public place, indoors.

This is animalistic behaviour and I'm incapable of doing such a thing … I swear on the lives of everyone who I love, I did not commit this crime! I've never been in a fight before, it isn't in my character – I've never even hit anyone! Anyone who knows me would tell you the same thing.

I buried my face in my hands and felt tears.

If I'm found guilty of this crime, my life is over; my girlfriend will have to move on with her life, my friends will settle down and have careers and families. I would be branded a murderer and have to go to prison for something that someone else did! I sympathise with the Hiles family because they lost their son – it is absolutely tragic – but I can't take responsibility for something that I know I didn't cause. Whatever the outcome of this trial is, I still didn't kill Jonathan Hiles … and now my life is in your hands.

After reiterating where my friends and I were on the night of the attack, I sat down. I was too emotional and angry, but it was over – I couldn't go back and change it. Hopefully they didn't think I was crazy because of the Psalm that I'd attempted to recite.

Was the truth obvious or did they doubt me? I couldn't bear it any more – I needed to know their verdict.

It was time for the public prosecutor to make his recommendation. He was more like a judge and sat to the left of the counsel panel. He'd asked a few questions throughout the trial, but hadn't cross-examined witnesses like the Hiles family's lawyer had. The public prosecutor stood up and told the court that he recommended my acquittal.

It was such a relief – a first real sign of hope that I'd been given by the court. It didn't mean that I was found innocent, or mean that I would definitely be acquitted. It meant that the court acknowledged that the case against me was extremely weak. I tried not to keep my hopes up, but hearing the recommendation was still an incredible feeling.

The trial was postponed until the next day, 17 June, and I knew that it was going to be a big one. It had been a long journey and I'd come so far – but it wasn't quite over yet.

✦

It was the last day in court. I'd never felt such nausea before – my stomach wouldn't stop churning and my eyes were puffy. We heard the closing argument of the prosecuting lawyer – of course, he suggested that I be found guilty. He lodged perjury suits against Chris Kyriacou, Charlie Klitou and me to counter the suits that we'd lodged against the victim's friends. Suddenly everyone was suing each other! He suggested that my friends Chris Kyriacou and Charlie Klitou had voluntarily told the truth in the investigation, and that they were not beaten or violently intimidated by police officers in Zante.

'Look, Andrew Symeou himself even said in his statement that Chris Kyriacou was his best friend! They have made up this entire story to protect him!'

The prosecuting lawyer reminded the court that the five friends of Jonathan Hiles had looked me in the eyes and identified me as the killer with complete certainty. For this, the prosecuting lawyer suggested that the jury must find me guilty. He turned his attention to the panel.

You've all seen the programmes on television, the British come over here and involve themselves in binge drinking and violent behaviour. Andrew came on holiday to get drunk and start trouble – now it's resulted in the death of a young man. If you have any doubt of his innocence, you must find him guilty!

(This isn't right – jurors are expected to do the opposite by law. If there is any reasonable doubt, they must acquit.)

My lawyer George Pyromallis walked towards the judges. He held the wad of police statements in his hand and waved them in the air.

There's over *one hundred* pages of testimony here. It outlines exactly what happened on the night that Jonathan Hiles was attacked. *No facial hair* was mentioned in the perpetrator's description. In over *one hundred pages* of witness statements … *not one hair!* Yet they stood here and added the most obvious facial feature to match the defendant's appearance?

George reminded the court of other witness testimonies, which further suggested that no facial hair was ever mentioned. A Rescue nightclub security guard's testimony was revisited – he'd confirmed that on the night in question there was no mention of facial hair when looking for the perpetrator. The investigating police officer, Angelos Polizos, confirmed that the victim's friends were looking for a clean-shaven male in the preliminary investigation. James Gibson's testimony (the photographer) was mentioned again; he was present when the victim's friends were looking through photographs in the police station. He'd said that there was 'definitely some doubt' when they recognised an individual, and that they had started to convince each other.

George continued:

In Mark O'Gorman's statement made to Welsh police, he states '*I can't be 100 per cent sure*' of the attacker's identity. Yet he has come here, four years later, and is suddenly completely certain? *He must be Superman!* He must be the only person in the world whose memory *improves* with time!

George began to raise his voice.

Not only is there not one piece of credible evidence against the defendant, but there is evidence that Andrew Symeou has no connection with the crime at all! He is a random person from a photograph, which was not even taken on the same night as the incident! Two males were involved in this incident, and only one of them has been mentioned throughout this trial – Jonathan Hiles himself!

I was an innocent man and George had done everything that he could to prove it. I was so proud to have him as my lawyer.

There was an hour's recess for the counsel panel to deliberate on the verdict. We walked down the road to a fast food restaurant for lunch, but I doubt anyone could eat. It was strange, but I was suddenly struck by the same feeling I'd had three years earlier when I was arrested in London. Civilians around me were living their everyday lives – they were on their lunch breaks from work, or were shopping for their families. I felt so insignificant; it was one of the biggest days of my life and the world was still spinning. All I wanted was for it to be a completely normal day again.

I couldn't even sit down, let alone have lunch. My parents, my gran and Sophie all had the same drained, pale faces. I walked around anxiously, but was hiding my nerves with smiles and laughs. 'Why do you all look so miserable, we're going home soon! We should be celebrating now!' My friends Aron Rouse and Jason Demetriou were also there; they probably thought that I'd finally snapped and lost the plot. The truth was that I was the most terrified I'd ever been in my life – if I sat down and let one negative thought pass through my mind I would've broken down. I'd never felt that level of suspense before; it was almost too much to bear.

It felt like the longest hour that had ever passed in my life. When we walked back to the courthouse, I managed to have a word with Theo (the translator) in the hallway. 'I won't understand the verdict; it will all be too quick. Please, could you just give me a thumbs up or thumbs down as soon as you know?'

'Of course, Andrew.' He'd translated the entire trial – and from the soft tone of his voice, I could tell that he was expecting positive news.

I sat on the defendant's bench for the last time and waited for the judges and jurors to enter. They were taking far too long – did it mean that they were really thinking about it? Did it mean that they were considering finding me guilty? If they were to find me innocent, surely it would be a quick and easy decision – why was it taking so long? I sank into the seat – I couldn't move. I stared at the crooked portrait of Jesus in front of me – it was blurry; my eyes couldn't even focus. I was empty. Waiting. Every minute that passed felt like an hour of dangling in mid-air. I couldn't bear it for much longer. I was numb. My head felt heavy. I needed it to end, but I couldn't distract myself from the mental image of Theo turning his thumb to the floor. I couldn't bear the thought of being sentenced to my doom; twenty years in prison and branded a murderer. It had to be a thumbs up – it just *had* to be.

Every now and then the side door would open – the door where the judges and jurors would enter the courtroom. My heart would start to palpitate – but it was only the court clerk.

After a two-and-a-half-hour recess, the door opened and the judges and jurors walked into the courtroom.

The president judge began to speak. I don't know what she

said. All I could hear was a ringing in my ears – my head felt like it was about to burst. The court clerk clapped his hands together with a huge grin on his face. The translator made eye contact; I looked down at his hand and started to wonder as he clenched his fingers into his palm.

He shot his thumb up to the sky.

It was a thumbs up.

After a three-year battle for truth and justice, I'd been found innocent. As soon as I saw the hand gesture, my head collapsed forward. My face was lost in my palms – I filled them with tears. It was over. I could hear my family sobbing behind me. It'd been a long road; a road that none of us could ever have imagined.

'Do you have any questions?' the president judge asked.

'No,' I answered – my eyes began to stream.

The judges and jurors walked out – just like that, it was finished. I stood up and turned to my family. I couldn't even bring myself to look at them – our eyes flooded and we held each other in the tightest embrace possible, as though the world around us had stood still. It was a moment that I'll never forget. After everything that we'd been through as a family – the extradition battle, prison visits, living in Athens and fighting for a court date – it was all over. Forever. I was found innocent. My dad held my face in his hands. 'It's over, Andrew. You're going to go to university and get a good job. You have your entire life ahead of you now. Be proud, you did it son!'

41

THE AIRPORT CATERPILLAR

After a three-year battle to clear my name, the court had found me not guilty. According to the president judge's summing up, it was due to the attacker having 'never been described as sporting a beard'.

> Moreover, the evidence shows that the nightclub had low levels of light, and only flashing, colourful disco lights that could have altered the visual appearance of a person's face. This was made more difficult with the lateness of the hour, and degree of alcohol consumed by the victim's friends before the incident, in addition to their young age. Together with the sworn testimonies of all defence witnesses – the identification of the defendant as the person who fatally attacked the deceased is clearly refuted.

These were all things that should have been revealed in a competent investigation.

I walked out of the courtroom into the hallway and the first person I called was Riya. I choked up, but managed to say the words, 'I've just been found innocent.' All I could hear on the other end of the telephone were wailing cries.

I felt as though I should have been happy – of course I was –

but it wasn't how I'd imagined it would feel. We'd been fighting for justice for so long, and we finally had it! I thought that I'd be over the moon because a weight that'd been holding me down for three years was instantly lifted. What bothered me was that the weight should never have been holding me down in the first place. I'd spent almost a year in prison – where was the justice in that? No one could ever make up for it, or even begin to understand how difficult it was for me.

The not-guilty verdict was too little too late, and it left me feeling completely exhausted. All I remember wanting to do at the time was go back to the apartment and lie down.

━━━

According to the trial transcript, three jurors out of a judicial panel of seven had voted guilty. It made no difference to the verdict, but still pissed me off massively. After witnessing what was (in my opinion) a massive sweep under the carpet regarding the police's flawed investigation, I didn't believe that the ratio was true.

There was no way on earth any jurors voted guilty. I couldn't let this frustration go, so a couple of years later I did some investigating. I managed to find one of the jurors on Facebook because all of their names were listed in the transcript. I sent a message, explaining what the transcript had said about the verdict. I then asked about the process of voting and whether the ratio was true.

Luckily the juror spoke some English, and I received a response within an hour:

> I can tell you for sure is that we didn't have any connection with the judges. We gathered as jurors and we make our decision which was a not-guilty verdict. It was a common decision. Really how did you come into the conclusion that the other three voted

against you? Anyway, these are all that I remember and I can tell you for sure. I have no clue how the other procedures done. Andrew, what's done is done. You cannot erase the past but you can go on with your future. Finally the truth came out. Keep that and try to forget all the hard and difficult times that you had and become strong. Bringing all these back to your mind it will not help you to overcome and go on with your life.

It was such a lovely message to receive, and I appreciated it greatly. A criminal complaint had been lodged against the investigating police officers in Zante. The response was that there was no evidence of any wrongdoing, and that their investigation was totally competent. As for the perjury suits in Greece, they seemed to have been completely forgotten about.

╫╫

24 June 2011

The flight from Athens International Airport to London Heathrow was something that I'd been dreaming about since I'd landed in Greece almost two years earlier. It'd finally become reality – I was sitting next to a window on the right-hand side of the cabin. The smell of aeroplane food and recycled oxygen brought back the memory of my extradition. It seemed like an eternity had passed since that day, yet I could remember it so vividly. I travelled back in my mind to how terrified I was, and how oblivious I was to everything that would follow. It could have been a week, a month, or even years before I could clear my name and return home. 'I'll probably only be there for two weeks and I'll make bail back to the UK,' is what I'd said to Riya on the morning that I was extradited. It had been a life-changing two years in Greece. Finally I was going home.

I stared out of the aircraft's window and saw a few fluffy clouds beneath us. As we approached England, the clouds became bigger and greyer. *Ding* – the seat belt sign lit up. I looked out of the window again; I could see the same bright blue sky above us that I'd become accustomed to in Greece, but we were gliding over a dark, whitish bed of fleecy fog. The plane began its descent. The window next to me turned into a grey painting that was drenched in droplets of condensation from the outside. All of a sudden I could see the River Thames, the Houses of Parliament and the London Eye out of the window. It was an incredible sight, and London's rain-clouded sky had never looked so beautiful.

The plane landed in London, and I didn't know how to feel because I'd never been in the situation before – it was a perfect balance of nerves and excitement. My parents and I exited the plane and walked to the terminal. There was an empty maze of queue-divider belts that we had to weave through in order to get to passport control. There was no queue – only one family in front of us with about four or five young kids. The kids were standing in a line, holding on to each other and running through the empty queue dividers and screaming 'We're a caterpillar!' Something about it gave me a happy feeling – probably because it reminded me of primary school. The boys in my class and I would sometimes hold on to each other and run around in a circle until we'd all fall over. The kids in the airport reminded me that my memories weren't all about prisons and courtrooms. The burden of the case had been hanging over me for so long that I'd started to forget how it felt to be 'me'. Something that I hadn't thought about since I was six years old had suddenly come flooding back to me and filled me with joy.

We walked through the arrivals gate and were bombarded with loud cheers and screams – I couldn't stop smiling. Several of my family and friends were there and they all ran towards me and hugged me – some of them jumped on me and I could hardly breathe. It was all too much – my granddad was there – some of my best friends were too. I remember hugging my cousins Andreas, Eleni and Charlotte with my auntie Mary. I was so happy to see that my uncle Theo, Pav, Koulla and Aki were there. Georgina, Teresa, Jenna, Sarah, Luke and even Sophie's friend Danielle was there too. It was emotional hugging everyone, especially my grandma. They were holding banners and balloons saying: 'WELCOME HOME ANDREW'. I held Riya in my arms for the first time in three years as a free man – it was the best feeling in the world.

We stepped out of the terminal. London's air was cool and I felt fine droplets of rain on my face. I still couldn't believe that I was even there – it was so bizarre. It was so strange to see right-hand-drive cars and English registration plates again.

Riya drove me home – my friends George, Kyri and Pani were squashed into the back seat. Music was playing on the radio – I turned the volume up to full blast and we were all dancing in our seats.

When we arrived, there were about fifty of my family and friends on my driveway – cheering with a massive banner that said: 'WELCOME HOME SYMEOU FAMILY!' It was emotional and overwhelming to see everyone there, together, in my house after two years.

I couldn't believe that I was in my house again. It was the strangest feeling in the world. More and more friends and family kept turning up and we partied until the early hours of the morning.

Someone pinned a '21 today' badge on me, because I'd spent my twenty-first birthday in prison. My friends had had T-shirts custom-made with my face on the front, which said 'He's Back!' A group of my best friends put them on and then put one on me and started to sing 'Happy Birthday', 'We Wish You a Merry Christmas' and then did a countdown to 'Happy New Year!' twice in a row because I'd been gone for two years. It was amazing and everyone in my house must have been smiling.

When I was in Greece I always felt like I was missing out on special moments back home. But on my first night back, I felt like I hadn't missed them at all. They were always there – waiting for me to celebrate.

I was given two Christmases, two Easters, two birthdays, and two New Year's Eves rolled into one huge party – it was one of the best nights of my life.

42

THINK MODE

Months passed. I had my life back, but I still couldn't shake the feeling of anxiety for some reason. Prior to my arrest I'd been a positive person who took each day as it came – suddenly I couldn't stop worrying about the future. I knew that I was expected to go to university and then become successful in one of the most competitive cities in the world. I started to doubt myself and felt incapable. Most of my friends seemed to be comfortable in the workplace, some in huge central London firms. The thought of it terrified me; even the thought of university terrified me. It may sound strange, but I would have felt more comfortable in Korydallos Prison. Once I'd become used to the violence, lack of hygiene and drug problems, all I had to do was wake up in the morning, make a *frappe*, spin my *pegleri* between my fingers and stay out of trouble! I'm not saying that I liked Korydallos Prison, or that I would rather go back there than go to work. In prison (or even out on bail) I didn't have to socialise with people on an intellectual level. I didn't have to prove myself to anyone, or work towards anything on a daily basis. In fact, nobody had expected anything of me for the previous three years! All of a sudden I had an entire life to live and I felt like I was too scared to live it.

I knew what I had to do: I had to draw the positives from my experience and realise that I could mould my life into anything that I wanted it to be. This is, of course, far easier said than done – but I gave it a go. In October 2011 I attended Middlesex University to pursue a degree in Psychology with Marketing and worked part time in a local bar. I forced myself to take small steps towards 'normality' and focus on everyday tasks. Life was falling into place, but something still never felt quite right. For months and months, I felt like my mind was always elsewhere. Throughout my experience in Greece I would constantly attempt to escape my environment, and I would do so by losing myself in thought for long periods of time. The nightmare had ended; I had my life back – so why I was still in 'think' mode? If I wasn't reliving things that had happened in prison or elements of the trial, I was worrying about having to find my right path in life. *What if I go down the wrong route and I have regrets? I've wasted too much time, I can't waste any more.* They were pointless thoughts and I felt like I couldn't stop them. I just didn't feel like 'me' any more. I was trying to be fun and happy like my friends, but I couldn't do it. Even when I was relaxing with my girlfriend or we'd be out on the weekends, I would constantly overthink and not live in the moment. We took a trip to Venice, which was lovely, but as I overlooked the stunning city from the top of St Mark's clock tower, it felt as though I couldn't even absorb it. My body was there, but my mind was flowing in and out. I'd started to realise that I felt most comfortable when in my room, concentrating on my university work – alone.

Almost a year had passed and I ended up completely destroying my relationship with Riya. After everything that we'd been through together, it felt like I couldn't even help it. Losing her was so difficult to accept that I don't even want to write about it.

43

NOT WORTH THE PAPER

Over a year had passed since my return and our lives were back on track. My parents were both working again and I'd managed to start putting my experience behind me. I'd lost almost seventy pounds in weight and passed my first year of university with a first grade. One of my lecturers had selected me as a 'student learning assistant' in my second year of university, so I was being paid to help first-year students with their work in seminars, as well as conducting my own group and one-on-one learning sessions. I was technically a member of staff, so I didn't feel like a normal student. After all the years of being made to feel insignificant, I had a sense of importance – and it felt pretty good.

It was November 2012 and I'd just finished helping a first-year group prepare a presentation assessment. It'd been a long day and I made my way home. I stepped into the house and my mum called me from upstairs. She was sitting in our study, holding a letter in her hands. 'How would you feel about testifying in the Coroner's Court for Jonathan Hiles's inquest?' she asked.

I tutted. 'I wasn't there, so what could I have to add!?'

'Well, that's exactly what you'll have to tell them.'

She handed me the document, which was an official summons from the Cardiff coroner.

Things were going so well in my life; I'd put everything that had happened behind me. What did they want from me now!?

'Can't I just make a written statement?'

'It doesn't look like it,' said my mum.

I was legally required to attend, even though I really didn't want to. After the years of moving forward and rebuilding my life, all the stress came flooding back.

┼┼┼

3 April 2013, the Coroner's Court, Cardiff

It was Day 1 of Jonathan Hiles's inquest and I sat on the second row of the public benches. I couldn't believe that I was being dragged into it all over again. My parents had appointed a barrister to defend me from any slanderous comments – other than that I was simply there to tell the coroner that I wasn't present on the night that Jonathan was allegedly attacked.

My parents were sitting to my right, and to my left were two South Wales police officers who were there to testify. The entire left wall of the courtroom was filled with journalists and reporters. I glanced at one of the journalists who held a pen and notebook in her hands. I looked at the blank, white page of her notebook and wondered what she would end up filling it with. I had absolutely no idea what was about to happen.

Chris Kyriacou and Charlie Klitou walked into the court – they'd been summoned too. I could see both of them in my peripheral vision walking past to the left of me, but I didn't make eye contact with them. The last time I'd seen them had been two years earlier, at the trial in Patras. Even then I hadn't spoken to them. I'd never blamed them for what had happened in Zante: they were put in an awful situation and they did what they had to do to get out of it. Although I'd never held anything against them, I felt like I couldn't be a friend to them any more. Not after everything that had happened.

Jonathan Hiles's five friends entered the courtroom just after Chris and Charlie. I didn't make eye contact with them either – looking at them would have brought back too many dark thoughts that were already behind me.

The courtroom began to fill with the family and friends of the victim – it left a silent tension in the room.

I learned that coroner's courts are quite informal; so all witnesses are present throughout the entirety of the inquests.

The inquest ended up being like another full-blown trial! It began with the testimonies of Jonathan Hiles's five friends, who were with him on the night of the attack. They were each called to testify. The coroner pressed each of them on the point that their statements made to South Wales Police and to the Greek authorities were completely different. For example, the first of them to be questioned by her was Lee Burgess:

> Mr Burgess, I want to talk about how the Greek statements could be so wrong. What you've said to me in court does accord with what you said to the South Wales Police in 2007 – I'm not worried about fine detail but I'm worried about the thrust of your evidence. However, it doesn't accord – as we've established – with the evidence that the Greek authorities have sent me. I'd like you to tell me whether you could provide me with any explanation for that?

'I told them the same thing that I've told you,' Lee answered.

It was a stressful and emotional two-day inquest. Mark O'Gorman (the only eyewitness) identified me with complete certainty as the attacker again. Mark and his four friends seemed to hold onto the proposition that they didn't give a full description of the attacker, or male urinating, because they didn't understand the importance of the South Wales Police statements.

The coroner later commented on Mark O'Gorman's testimony:

Mr O'Gorman, having said that I'm not sympathetic to any suggestion that a witness giving a statement to the police shouldn't take that seriously, I've since been assisted by my coroner's officer. The version of your statement from which I'm working is the typed version, because of course it's much easier to read a typed version than a version handwritten by a police officer, even if it's relatively neat writing. But my coroner's officer has in front of her the handwritten version and she has just handed up to me the last page of the handwritten version. There are two matters that I notice about the handwritten version. One is that the final statement in the handwritten version says: 'I'm prepared to attend at any court proceedings and I consent to any person with a genuine interest in this case be given a copy of this statement.' Well, the first thing is that that statement there appears just above your signature. So the last paragraph is … five lines above your signature. That's the first thing that I noticed in terms of what the statement is going to be used for. The second thing I noticed about this handwritten version is that … just looking at the last page, and that's page thirteen, there are three points on this page where crossings out have been made, and you've initialled them … I'd like you to confirm for me, a) that it's your signature at the bottom, and b) that it's your initials on the crossings out in three places.

Mark O'Gorman was handed the original copy of his statement. 'Erm … yeah.'

'Thank you,' said the coroner.

Over two days the coroner heard evidence from a pathologist, the five friends of the victim, Chris Kyriacou, Charlie Klitou, myself and two South Wales police officers. The coroner's ruling was as follows:

> The evidence about what happened to Jonathan on the even-
> ing of 19/20 July 2007 all comes from Mark O'Gorman. Mr
> O'Gorman is the only person who actually saw Jonathan come
> off the stage on which he was dancing and hit his head. If I accept
> Mr O'Gorman's evidence as truthful and accurate – that another
> person punched Jonathan without provocation and caused him
> to fall off the stage, hit his head and die as a consequence – then
> unlawful killing is the appropriate verdict. If I do not accept his
> evidence, then it is not. I've said that Mr O'Gorman's evidence
> is the only evidence … I'm conscious that the evidence of the
> pathologist who conducted the post-mortem examination in
> Cardiff was that – apart from the devastating head injury, there
> was a facial injury. However – that could have been caused by
> a punch, but wasn't necessarily caused by a punch. So on that
> basis – simply on the pathology – Jonathan could have simply
> fallen. I thought very carefully about whether another person
> on this crowded stage, where everyone was dancing and lots of
> people were likely to have been drinking, could have thrown an
> arm out and accidentally caught Jonathan on the side of his face.
> Mr O'Gorman was sure that that wasn't the case. He described
> very clearly the way in which the man faced up to Jonathan
> after having been challenged about urinating on the dance floor,
> then quite deliberately punched him. I remind myself that when
> considering this I must be satisfied beyond reasonable doubt,
> I must not return a verdict that is unsafe. Ultimately, I do accept
> the evidence of Mr O'Gorman … on this point. I find him to
> be truthful in this respect. I accept that he has an accurate recall
> of the events of the evening of 19/20 July 2007. That therefore
> makes a verdict of unlawful killing appropriate.

I completely agreed with the verdict. It had been said from the very beginning that a punch was thrown, which was indeed unlawful.

The coroner continued:

I could stop there … but in this case, I think that would be inappropriate and I would be doing a disservice to all concerned. It is incumbent upon me in this instance, as in every instance, not only to give my decision but to give full reasons for my decision – and in this respect, I think that I must turn to the question of identity.

If I were sitting with a jury and I were leaving the verdict of 'unlawful killing' open to them, I would direct them as to the identity of those people who may potentially be responsible for the unlawful killing. I intend to follow that same path today as I give you reasons for the decision that I make. In a normal course of events I would not be hearing such an inquest, because the matter would have been heard by way of a criminal trial at Crown Court. There was a criminal trial in this instance, but it wasn't in this country. As Jonathan was brought back to my jurisdiction and no trial has taken place in the Crown Court, I have been obliged to hold an inquest – I did not have a choice in this. I am, by law, prohibited from returning a verdict that appears to determine criminal guilt on the part of a named person. However, that does not apply to my summing up – and in this unusual situation – I'm of the view that I must tackle the issue of the person who threw the punch that caused Jonathan to fall off the stage in the early hours of 20 July 2007.

The only person who saw the punch was Mark O'Gorman, and Mr O'Gorman was sure that the person who threw the punch was the same person who was earlier urinating among the dancers. Others in Jonathan's group had seen the person urinating, so there were several witnesses involved in the question of identification because of the linking of the two events. The identification procedure conducted by the Greek police was *not* the same as the identification procedure that would have taken place in this country. It would not have been an acceptable way of conducting matters in this country. Several witnesses looked over photographs together. Once one witness had made what he thought was the identification, the other witnesses all looked at *that* photograph. This, frankly, placed those witnesses in an appalling situation. While I'm satisfied that they were doing their best on that night, the reason why such care is taken over identification procedures in this country is because it is so easy to get it wrong. In this country, I have known loved ones to identify the body of a deceased to the police, only subsequently to discover that the person is not in fact their family member. I know that has happened on more than one occasion. However much those witnesses looked at the photographs in the police station in Zante – in July 2007 – however much they tried to empty their minds of the views of their friends … I think that that was impossible for them to do. After the first person had pointed out the man we now know is Andrew Symeou in the photograph, all of the young men turned their attention to that photograph, rather than having to pick the suspect out with fresh eyes. Identification in such a situation seems to me a wholly unsafe identification to make.

The photograph wasn't the only matter. I turn from that to the descriptions given by the witnesses who were with Jonathan, and who either saw the punch or the man urinating. The best evidence is generally from first witness statements taken close to the events. The witness statements I received from Greece, and had translated, I'm very sorry to say I've found of no assistance at all. I find that they do not represent the substance of the information given by Jonathan's friends. They are not separate statements of individuals, but a mishmash of information, lumped together by police – and they bear almost no resemblance to the individual versions of events as given by the five young men. In terms of the evidence given since, the witnesses have focused in court on the beard of the man who threw the punch – but there has been doubt as to whether he had a moustache. The identification *now* simply cannot measure up to the standard of proof to which I must adhere. Nearly six years have passed since Jonathan died. The witnesses have all seen Andrew Symeou sitting in the dock of a Greek courtroom in the meantime – and with the best will in the world, I simply cannot rely on the evidence that they give now in that respect.

Having decided that this identification evidence is unsafe, I want to tell you that I then went on to consider whether there was evidence the other way. In other words – whether there was evidence that the person who punched Jonathan was not Andrew Symeou. I considered the other evidence that I heard, most particularly from Andrew Symeou and the friends who were with him on the night. Those three young men gave evidence that they were not in the club where Jonathan was punched at the relevant time. Before considering the evidence of the three individuals, from whom I heard on this point, what struck me on the outset was that … if they're lying, because the three of them *were* at the Rescue bar, and Mr Symeou *did* punch Jonathan, then … to concoct a lie to try and deal with that – by giving the story that they *weren't even in* the bar at the relevant time is a very risky strategy. These are young men, they are of a generation used to Facebook, used to the internet in all its forms, used to an environment in which many people – not just young people – have cameras on their mobile phones and there is often CCTV in bars. A lie of that nature might quite easily be disproved. So at the outset, I say that this would be a risky strategy. Of course it's possible, but it's something that I bear in mind.

I turn now to the oral testimony I heard from Christopher Kyriacou, Charles Klitou and Andrew Symeou himself. I say plainly, that I found these witnesses to be utterly truthful, completely accurate and wholly compelling. I find that not only did Andrew Symeou not punch Jonathan Hiles, but he was not even in the bar at the time. I'm aware that Mr Kyriacou and Mr Klitou made statements to the Greek police saying they were there, and they saw Mr Symeou was the perpetrator of this crime. I'm very sorry to say that these statements are simply not worth the paper they are written on. They contain fanciful information about an argument over a young woman, and I find that they were concocted by the Greek police in a very misguided effort to solve this crime. The story I heard from Mr Kyriacou and Mr Klitou, of the way they were treated, I would not have believed unless I had heard it with my own ears. They were not just badly treated, they were not just bullied – they were beaten. They signed the statements put in front of them for one reason, and one reason only: because they were afraid … and with good reason.

Jonathan's death is an absolute tragedy for his family, but they were not the only ones who were hurt here.

For the avoidance of doubt, I'm returning a verdict of unlawful killing. I do not name the perpetrator of the crime – because that would be unlawful. However, the basis upon which I return this verdict is that I do not know who the person was who killed Jonathan, but I know that that person was not Andrew Symeou.

AND IT WILL

I have a profound memory of my grandfather, Andreas Symeou (who I was named after). It was a sunny, spring afternoon in 2006 when the whole family was sitting around my grandparents' dining table. My granddad began to share gripping stories of his childhood in the Cypriot village of Lapathos, and told us of the hardship that he'd faced growing up there. In the summer of 1955, at the age of twenty-two, he'd decided to immigrate to England for a better way of life. He couldn't afford a boat ticket, so he invested in two piglets – he raised them for a year, and then sold them to a butcher for a hefty profit. Upon his arrival in London he was stranded in Victoria Station, homeless, because the person who he'd planned to live with had never turned up. My granddad was overwhelmed with tears when he told us the story, even though fifty years had passed.

I thought I'd share the memory I have of my granddad because (at the time) it made me feel like I'd never have a story to tell. Only two years later, I experienced something far more harrowing than he ever did. It just goes to show that we have absolutely no idea what our futures will hold.

It's been a journey that I couldn't have imagined, and I've learned some very important lessons along the way. One of the

most obvious is to be extremely careful when abroad – especially
if we ever find ourselves in the hands of foreign police. I've never
blamed Chris and Charlie for what happened. Through no fault
of their own they were forced into a terrible situation at the
young age of eighteen. If I were violently intimidated by people
of authority at that age, I probably would have done exactly the
same thing. Now I've learned that if I were to be picked up and
dragged to a police station when overseas, I wouldn't speak unless
a competent interpreter and British consular staff were contacted.
Most importantly, I wouldn't sign *anything* that I was unsure of.
The police officers could lock me up for days and beat me senseless, but after everything that I've gone through, I'd like to believe
that I still wouldn't sign.

As soon as my family discovered that I'd been wrongly implicated as a killer, they did absolutely everything to try to fix
the mess. At no stage did they ever doubt my innocence – not
even for a moment. I'm fortunate enough to have had the emotional and financial backing of a strong family. What would
have happened if a European Arrest Warrant was issued for
someone else's arrest, and that person had absolutely no support
network? They would have been extradited within ten days of
their arrest and dumped in a Greek prison! With no support,
they could have easily fallen into the trap of heroin addiction
or drug dealing in prison – not to mention been involved in
violent riots. When finally making it to trial, there would have
been *no defence witnesses* and the translation would have been
appalling. With no money for a competent lawyer, they might
have been sentenced to *twenty years* in prison – all because of
an incorrect, unsafe identification from a photograph taken on
a different night to the attack. If it could happen to me, it could
happen to anyone.

Once I'd been arrested for the fatal bodily harm of Jonathan

Hiles, we discovered that a British court would have no power to consider my innocence, and I could spend up to a year and a half in prison on remand. My family gained access to the Greek investigation, which we scrutinised and exposed as completely flawed. We campaigned and protested for this to be acknowledged, and for a competent investigation to be conducted. My parents taught me that we should never give up a battle when truth is onside. It was stressful and exhausting because the world was against us, but nothing would have caused us to give up.

Despite our incredible fight for justice, the European Arrest Warrant meant that my extradition was inevitable. I was treated as though I was guilty and ended up in prison on remand having to endure some horrific situations. In the twenty-first century, within the European Union, this shouldn't be allowed to happen. If the British authorities had the power to scrutinise the Greek investigation, I would have been exonerated – eliminating me from the scene of the crime as soon as they were issued with a warrant for my arrest. Not only would I have been able to continue with my life, but there would have been a chance to find the real assailant, who remains at large. As much as I appreciate that the government have acknowledged the flaws in the European Arrest Warrant, the changes they have made aren't strong enough at all. British citizens facing extradition must be completely safeguarded. We must extradite only if there is sufficient evidence of criminal guilt. Even if we were to disregard my imprisonment completely, I still went through the stress of a lengthy criminal trial abroad – and I didn't fit the description of the perpetrator from Day 1.

The night before I was extradited, my uncle Andy told me that there would 'be many ups and downs'. It was difficult to believe that there would be any 'ups' when incarcerated. Surprisingly, my time in prison wasn't all doom and gloom. I'd made a handful of friends, like Arnas and Fivos, so at least I have some positive memories of my time in Avlona. One of the most memorable was sitting around a table in our cell, drinking prison-brewed alcohol and laughing for what felt like the first time in years. We made the most out of our terrible situation, and on that warm summer night – it felt like we were free.

I wish that my positive memories of prison could outweigh the bad, but they can't at all. My uncle Andy had also told me, 'However difficult it is, whatever you have to go through for this to be over, you will find the inner strength.' When he told me this, I found it very difficult to believe him. Now I understand how true his words were. One of the biggest lessons that I've learned is that we can surprise ourselves with how strong we can be, especially when we have no other choice but to face our fears. With positive thinking and support, however difficult it is to achieve, we can get through anything.

It's been a struggle, but my fight for justice was victorious in the end. The years between 2007 and 2013 will be significant to me for the rest of my life. There *were* many ups and downs, and it's tough to know exactly how it's changed me. From my teenage years into my twenties I would have inevitably grown as a person anyway. I don't feel the need to list how it's negatively affected me, because life is far too short for that. I can't change the past, so I'll just have to let go of any feelings of resentment or bitterness, and turn my bad experience around as much as I can. I'll use the lessons that I've learned – take every opportunity that I have – and try to mould my life into everything that I want it to be. Life is a rollercoaster, and we have absolutely no clue what's around the corner – saying that, my experience has more than prepared me for the 'ups and downs' to come. When I do eventually find myself going through a difficult period in my life,

I know that I'll do everything I can to make it better. And if I fail in the attempt, and the rough patch seems like it could take an eternity to end, I'll simply remind myself of what an old friend once said: 'It doesn't matter how long it takes to happen, all that matters is that it will.'

ACKNOWLEDGEMENTS

First I'd like to thank Karen Todner of Kaim Todner Solicitors and Rupert Pardoe of 23 Essex Street Chambers. Together you kindly offered to help me financially while I wrote my draft manuscript and studied towards my degree. I may not have written this book if I hadn't had that initial push. I'd also like to thank my publisher Iain Dale (and Duncan Barkes at LBC for putting me in touch with him). To everyone at Biteback Publishing, I was a student with no writing experience, yet you gave me such a brilliant opportunity. Including Rupert and Karen, thank you all for believing in me. You've helped me turn my life around in a way that I never thought I could. Moreover, I owe a massive acknowledgement to my editor, Victoria Godden, Adonis Pratsides (who kindly agreed to review my draft manuscript and took the time to help me edit it before submission) and Fivos Kalfopoulos (for checking over the Greek translations). Your contributions made a huge difference to the production of this memoir and I'm very grateful for your help.

To all those who protested outside of Westminster Magistrates' Court or stood in the freezing cold and chanted outside of the Greek embassy – words can't really describe how much I thank you. Many people wrote letters to politicians and/or signed my petition. When all failed, many donated money to the campaign (which paid for defence witnesses to fly to Greece). I have no idea how we would have coped if we hadn't had such incredible support. I thank you all very much – you went through this journey with us. I'd also like to express my gratitude to the politicians who acknowledged the flaws in the European Arrest Warrant and supported my case, including Baroness Sarah Ludford (Lib Dem), Gerard Batten (UKIP), Joan Ryan (and her then assistant James Kilmarten, Labour), and most importantly Nick de Bois (Conservative).

I'd like to thank John Jones QC and Edward Fitzgerald QC of the Doughty Street Chambers for representing me in my extradition appeals in London. We were up against a formidable law, yet you both did absolutely everything that you could to fight against the injustice. Unfortunately the EAW was an all-too-powerful rival at the time, which was completely out of our control. I'd like to thank everyone at Linn and Associates, Corker Binning and the AIRE centre; your help to us was very much appreciated. Jago Russell and everyone at Fair Trials International – you made me feel strong when I was at my weakest point. You are an incredible organisation and I thank you for everything that you've done for my family and me. Furthermore, one of my most important acknowledgements is to George Pyromallis, who defended me in my trial in 2011. It was a long and stressful period but the truth came out in the end. Although you didn't like to show it, I know how emotionally attached you became towards our case. Thanks to you, Vanessa Katsara and everyone at your office at the time who fought for me, I have been able to put it all behind me (as best I can) and move on with my life. I'll never forget you.

To all my family and friends, especially those who were at our house almost every day during the extradition appeals (you know who you are), you were amazing throughout this ordeal.

Thank you to Teresa and Leslie Johnson, Georgina Paraskeva, my godfather Eleftherios Panayiotou (Lef) and all of your families for being there for us through thick and thin. Simeos Yiannikaris always drove us to court, Nick Demetriades chanted through a bullhorn in the cold, Nick Paraskeva made a website for us and Andy Spyrou (and several others) went out of their way to give me advice that I'll never forget. These are things that you didn't have to do, but you did, and it means more to me than you'd know. Thank you to the Kouttis family for hosting a very success-ful fund-raising event and Gabriella Bord for everything you did to help. Kristianna Paraskeva, you were such a good friend to me when I was going through hell; and Andrew Demetriou you were too. Of course, I can't forget the 'Bum Squad!': Andrew, Maria Demetriou and Sophia Di Piazza – you guys are the best.

Thank you to my grandparents, Bappou Andrico, Yiayia Nitsa and Yiayia Sofoulla, I love you all very much. I know how dif-ficult this was for you but you all showed remarkable strength. Thank you to my uncle Theo Constantinou, uncle George and auntie Mary Nicolaides – and all of my cousins, especially An-dreas Nicolaides who paid me a surprise visit in Athens when I was at a very low point in my life. On that note, thank you to my relatives from Cyprus who visited us in Greece, especially Louis Pericleous; and everyone who visited me in prison or at the trial; Uncle Spyros and Auntie Niki Spyrou, Uncle Bambos and Auntie Sotoulla Demetriou, Luke Cutajar and Maria Michael. My auntie Avgi Pericleous – I know how passionate you felt about me writing this book; I've dedicated it to Uncle Andreas because I can't even begin to describe how much I appreciate eve-rything you both did for us – he was a very good man. I also owe a huge thank you to Riya, who lived through this experience with me and dealt with a hell of a lot. We were victims of bad timing and circumstances, but even throughout the bad times there were a lot of good. Thank you to her mum Ansuya, who came all the way to Athens with her while I was in prison. I appreciate how supportive you were to her regarding this terrible situation.

We met some incredible people in Greece – thank you to all those who we didn't even know before but who helped us in some way or another. Especially Eugenia Iordanidi (Siozos), Father Malcolm Bradshaw, Christine and Cliff Sakali (and friends), thank you for showing us such kindness. Arnas Pakrosnis, Fivos Kalfopoulos and Vasilis Keritis – we met in the hardest of times in our lives: locked up in prison with our pending court cases always at the back of our minds. You all became good friends to me and I hope I had as much of a positive effect on your lives as you did mine. (I told you guys that I'd write a book when I was out, and I'm a man of my word!) Styliana Vasili, you were my only friend in Athens when I was on bail (and a very good one at that). Auntie Sotira Theodorou, it was amazing seeing you so much and I wish you were in London more often. Thank you for making us feel like we were at home with our family when I wasn't allowed to leave Greece – and I miss your amazing cooking.

To all the witnesses who took the time to fly to Greece and defend my innocence, I can't thank you enough, especially Georgina Clay, Toni Martelli and Christina Christou. Andrew Christophides, Aron Rouse, Alex Kalli, Jason Demetriou and George Georgiou – thank you for being a huge part of the trial. To all my best friends, 'the boys' and the Bournemouth Uni lot (you all know who you are), I couldn't ask for better, more supportive friends.

Lastly, the people who I owe everything to are my family. To my sister Sophie, you are very special to me and I know how much this has affected you. You are a strong person and I want you to know that I'm here for you through thick and thin. Vasos Polycarpou, you are a brother to me and I hope that you can rely on me as much as I do you. To my parents, you brought me into the world, taught me right from wrong, and showed me how to be a good person. You were strong for me throughout, even though I know how easy it could have been to fall apart. Life changed in an instant, then you dropped your lives and we got through it together as a family. Not only have you given me life, but you've saved it. A 'thank you' is nowhere near enough, so I guess the only way for me to show you how grateful I am is to make the most of it. I love you all very much.

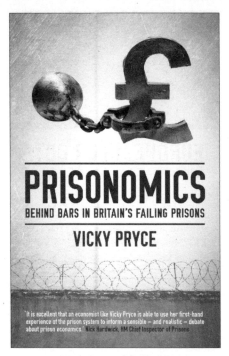